# MILESTONES OF THOUGHT

*Joseph* *Butler*

# THE ANALOGY
# OF RELIGION

*Introduction by*
ERNEST C. MOSSNER
*University of Texas*

FREDERICK UNGAR PUBLISHING CO.
*NEW YORK*

# MILESTONES
# OF THOUGHT
*in the History of Ideas*

General Editor
## F. W. STROTHMANN
*Stanford University*

# CONTENTS

## *PART I*
## OF NATURAL RELIGION

## *PART II*
## OF REVEALED RELIGION

# INTRODUCTION

*by Ernest C. Mossner*

Theology is not always philosophy and is seldom literature. *The Analogy of Religion, Natural and Revealed, to the Constitution and Course of Nature* (1736), one of the most famous of English theological works, is both philosophy and literature. It is philosophy in that the approach to religion is neither dogmatical nor inspirational, but exploratory. Dealing with religion as matter of fact, the author, Joseph Butler, eschews "the high Priori Road," or, as he puts it, "that idle and not very innocent employment of forming imaginary models of a world, and schemes of governing it," and he acknowledges that certainty cannot be achieved. Imperfect human nature must be satisfied with an imperfect kind of information, for "to Us, probability is the very guide of life." What makes the philosophy literature is not that the style is particularly refined and polished but that the author has lived up to his own precept: "Confusion and perplexity in writing is indeed without excuse, because anyone may, if he pleases, know whether he understands and sees through what he is about: and it is unpardonable for a man to lay his thoughts before others, when he is conscious that he himself does not know whereabouts he is, or how the matter before him stands. It is coming abroad in disorder, which he ought to be dissatisfied to find himself in at home."

Joseph Butler (1692-1752) showed an early inclination to philosophy when, as a student of twenty-one, he opened a spirited correspondence with Dr. Samuel Clarke, who as a distinguished Boyle Lecturer had supplied a demonstrative proof of the being of God. The youth, however, remained a confirmed empiricist in the contemporary school of Newton and Locke. At Oxford, which he entered after leaving the Presbyterian for the Anglican Church, Butler found the "frivolous lectures and unintelligible disputations" uncongenial, lamenting that "our people here never had any doubt in their lives concerning a received opinion; so that I cannot mention a difficulty to them." Disappointed with the university, the inquiring mind found a more hospitable atmosphere in the Church. His *Fifteen Sermons Preached at the Rolls Chapel* (1726) established him

vii

as a moral philosopher in the line of Shaftesbury and Hutcheson and, later, of Hume and Adam Smith.

With the success of his first publication, Butler's ecclesiastical career was assured. In 1736 he became Clerk of the Closet to Queen Caroline and published *The Analogy of Religion*. In 1738, after the death of the Queen, he was appointed Bishop of Bristol by George II; two years later, dean of St Paul's; and in 1750, Bishop of Durham. The often repeated story that he refused the Primacy of England in 1747 because he thought it too late for him to support a falling Church has been finally discredited. Butler died as he lived, a good man, a good churchman, and a good philosopher, one who always lived up to his youthful avowal to Clarke: "As I design the search after truth as the business of my life, I shall not be ashamed to learn from any person."

In the *Fifteen Sermons,* particularly in the first three originally entitled "Upon humane nature, or man considered as a moral agent," Butler approaches the subject of morals as matter of fact, "namely, what the particular nature of man is, its several parts, their economy or constitution; from whence it proceeds to determine what course of life it is, which is correspondent to this whole nature." In *The Analogy of Religion* Butler approaches the subject of religion also as a matter of fact. Taking for proved that there is an intelligent Author of Nature and Natural Governor of the world, he addresses himself to the Deists, who believe in Natural Religion, that is, religion as known to man by reason or by evidence of the senses but not by revelation; the Deists tend to be sceptical, therefore, of any revelation, particularly, of course, that of Christianity. Christians, on the contrary, believe in Revelation as well as in Natural Religion. Butler, it is to be observed, makes no attempt to argue with either agnostics or atheists.

Designed to offer a "practical proof," a "proof from fact," the argument of *The Analogy of Religion* seeks to calculate the probabilities of both types of religion by a painstaking search for analogies with the constitution and course of nature. Origen observes that "he who believes the Scripture to have proceeded from Him who is the Author of Nature, may well expect to find the same sort of difficulties in it, as are found in the constitution of Nature." Butler observes further that "he who denies the Scripture to have been from God upon account of these difficulties, may, for the very same reason, deny the world to have been formed by Him"—an argument of weight with Deists, although not, to be sure, with atheists. The difficulties discovered by the mind of man in the known course of nature are analagous, according to Butler, to the difficulties insisted upon by some men in the order of religion, both natural and. revealed, because the same Being is the Author of both. The most recent English Deist that Butler had in mind was Matthew Tindal, the learned Fellow of All Souls, Oxford, whose *Christianity as old as the Creation: Or, the Gospel, a Republication of the Religion of Nature* (1730) was received as "the Deist's Bible." Christian apologists were well aware of the implications of Tindal's subtitle, which rendered Christian Revelation a work of supererogation.

The analogy employed by Butler is, properly speaking, a negative analogy in the sense that it is drawn by way of answering Deistical objections; it is drawn for Natural Religion in Part I of Butler's work and for Revealed Religion in Part II. Without attempting a summary here, it may be said that *The Analogy of Religion* represents a broad attempt to bring the latest knowledge and techniques from science and from philosophy, in fact, from Newton and from Locke, to the problems of religion. To Butler religion is thus always a practical rather than a theoretical matter.

"The greatest name in the Anglican Church" is John Henry Newman's tribute to Butler in the mid-nineteenth century at the height of Butler's reputation. The greatest British philosopher of Butler's own century would not have disagreed. For David Hume on two occasions proved his high respect for the author of the "Sermons upon humane nature" and *The Analogy of Religion*. Upon completion of the manuscript of his *Treatise of Human Nature* in 1737, the youthful Hume sought to obtain Butler's opinion of it. "Endeavouring it shall give as little Offence as possible; before which I could not pretend to put it into the Drs. hands," Hume "castrated" his work by deleting certain "Reasonings concerning Miracles." Although several times unsuccessful in finding Butler at home, Hume did not restore the deletion when he published in 1739; and "Of Miracles," as it was to be entitled, did not see the light until 1748. The *Treatise*, however, names Butler with approbation as among "some late philosophers in England who have begun to put the science of man on a new footing, and have engaged the attention, and excited the curiosity of the public." It is perhaps not so well known that "Cleanthes," the empirically minded, teleologically oriented theologian of Hume's posthumous *Dialogues concerning Natural Religion* (1779), consistently follows the major arguments of *The Analogy of Religion*. There can be little doubt that Hume had in mind

Butler, the only contemporary theologian whom he deemed worthy of a refutation.

Welcomed at the two English universities by the middle of the eighteenth century, Butler's works became fixtures in the curricula until about 1870, one or the other or both, from time to time, being set for examination purposes. Particularly at Oxford were they regarded, as Matthew Arnold observes, as sacrosanct, "with the same absolute faith in the classicality of their matter as in the classicality of Homer's form" that rendered them "so terrible to undergraduates." Arnold might well have repeated the very words of another alert undergraduate concerning the Oxford of an earlier day: "Our people here never had any doubt in their lives concerning a received opinion; so that I cannot mention a difficulty to them." A reaction set in, however, with the arrival of the Age of Evolutionary Theory in the 1860s, and Butler came under severe attack from such figures as Charles Darwin, Thomas Huxley, John Stewart Mill, Mark Pattison, Baden Powell, Goldwin Smith, Leslie Stephen, and John Tyndall. While vigorously defended by the statesman-philosopher, W. E Gladstone, *The Analogy of Religion* ultimately lost its position at the universities as a classic, although still retaining considerable influence; the *Sermons* retained more prestige. The great rationalist Leslie Stephen, nevertheless, expressed a genuine appreciation of Butler toward the close of this period of controversy over his works: "We can but honor him as an honest and brave man—honest enough to admit the existence of doubts, and brave enough not to be paralyzed by their existence."

Though the age of Deism has long since passed and with it the relevance of some aspects of Butler's argument, *The Analogy of Religion* will always appeal to those who approach religious thinking with a passion for matter of fact and a distrust of over-refinement. Not all of Butler's writings may have withstood the passage of time, but there is in them much that is timeless, both as philosophy and as literature. Some of these living thoughts will perhaps have a peculiarly familiar ring to readers who may no longer associate them with Butler:

*Everything is what it is, and not another thing.*

*Things and actions are what they are, and the consequences of them will be what they will be: why then should we desire to be deceived?*

*It is as easy to close the eyes of the mind, as those of the*

*body: and the former is more frequently done with wilful-
ness, and yet not attended to, than the latter.*

*Language is, in its very nature, inadequate, ambiguous,
liable to infinite abuse, even from negligence; and so liable
to it from design, that every man can deceive and betray
by it.*

*I express myself with caution, lest I should be mistaken to
vilify reason; which is indeed the only faculty we have
wherewith to judge concerning anything.*

*All reasonable men know certainly, that there cannot, in
reality, be any such thing as chance; and conclude, that
the things which have this appearance are the result of
general laws, and may be reduced into them.*

*There are as real and the same kind of indications in human
nature, that we were made for society and to do good to
our fellow-creatures; as that we were intended to take care
of our own health and private good.*

*That mankind is a community, that we all stand in a rela-
tion to each other, that there is a public end and interest of
society which each particular is obliged to promote is the
sum of morals.*

*Why might not whole communities and public bodies be
seized with fits of insanity, as well as individuals? Nothing
but this principle, that they are liable to insanity, equally
at least with private persons, can account for the major
part of those transactions of which we read in history.*

*What a wonderful incongruity it is for a man to see the
doubtfulness in which things are involved, and yet be impatient out of action, or vehement in it! To Us, probability
is the very guide of life.*

*As I design the search after truth as the business of my
life, I shall not be ashamed to learn from any person.*

The earnestness of the writer is beyond doubt: it is the
prime characteristic of his style and dictates its precision. The
intrinsic inadequacies of language so much deplored by Butler
may be circumvented in his view only by presenting thoughts
in their full development and in their proper context: "I must
desire the reader not to take any assertion alone by itself,
but to consider the whole of what is said upon it: because this
is necessary, not only in order to judge of the truth of it, but

often, such is the nature of language, to see the very meaning of the assertion." Elegance and ease of style, consequently, are neither aimed at nor are they often realized. Butler's earnestness of mind and his precision of writing do, however, frequently reach a high level of presentation of the "irreducible brute facts" of hardheaded thinking. Such, indeed, is the literary achievement of the above sampling of Butler's "living thoughts."

For these are the courageous and exploratory and, at the same time, cautionary thoughts of a significant English philosopher of the Age of Enlightenment. They remain valuable to all serious thinkers of the mid-twentieth century because, as the Abbé Dubos has observed, "Every nation, has, 'tis true, a particular library of good books written in their own language, but there is besides a common one for all nations—the library of mankind." To that library the philosopher of Anglicanism has made no inconsiderable contribution.

# SELECTED BIBLIOGRAPHY

*The Works of Bishop Butler,* ed. J. H. Bernard. London, 1900. 2 vols. Vol. I: *Sermons, Charges, Fragments, and Correspondence;* Vol. II: *The Analogy of Religion.* The only complete modern edition and the most authoritative text.

Mossner, Ernest C. *Bishop Butler and the Age of Reason: A Study in the History of Thought.* New York, 1936. Fullest modern survey of Butler's historical position.

———"The Enigma of Hume" *Mind,* XLV (1936), 334-49. Historical identification of the "Cleanthes" of Hume's *Dialogues concerning Natural Religion* with Butler.

Norton, William J. *Bishop Butler, Moralist and Divine.* New Brunswick, 1940. Fullest modern exposition of Butler's ethics and metaphysics.

# INTRODUCTION BY THE AUTHOR

PROBABLE evidence is essentially distinguished from demonstrative by this, that it admits of degrees; and of all variety of them, from the highest moral certainty, to the very lowest presumption. We cannot indeed say a thing is probably true upon one very slight presumption for it; because, as there may be probabilities on both sides of a question, there may be some against it; and though there be not, yet a slight presumption does not beget that degree of conviction which is implied in saying a thing is probably true. But that the slightest possible presumption is of the nature of a probability, appears from hence; that such low presumption often repeated, will amount even to moral certainty. Thus a man's having observed the ebb and flow of the tide to-day, affords some sort of presumption, though the lowest imaginable, that it may happen again to-morrow; but the observation of this event for so many days, and months, and ages together, as it has been observed by mankind, gives us a full assurance that it will.

That which chiefly constitutes Probability is expressed in the word Likely, *i. e.*, like some truth, or true event (*verisimile*); like it, in itself, in its evidence, in some more or fewer of its circumstances [1]. For when we determine a thing to be probably true, suppose that an event has or will come to pass, it is from the mind's remarking in it a likeness to some other event, which we have observed has come to pass. And this observation forms, in numberless daily instances, a presumption, opinion, or full conviction, that such event has or will come to pass; according as the observation is, that the like event has sometimes, most commonly, or always, so far as our observation reaches, come to pass at like distances of time, or place,

---

[1] He observes, with reference to this subject, "Though the common experience of the ordinary course of things have justly a mighty influence on the minds of men, to make them give or refuse credit to anything proposed to their belief, yet there is *one case* wherein the strangeness of the fact lessens not the assent to a fair testimony given of it. For where such supernatural events are suitable to ends aimed at by Him who has the power to change the course of nature, then, under such circumstances, *they may be fitter to procure belief, by how much the more they are beyond or contrary to ordinary observation.* This is the proper case with miracles, which, well attested, do not only find credit themselves, but give it also to other truths which need such confirmation."—*Ed.*

or upon like occasions. Hence arises the belief, that a child, if it lives twenty years, will grow up to the stature and strength of a man; that food will contribute to the preservation of its life, and the want of it for such a number of days be its certain destruction. So likewise the rule and measure of our hopes and fears concerning the success of our pursuits; our expectations that others will act so and so in such circumstances; and our judgment that such actions proceed from such principles; all these rely upon our having observed the like to what we hope, fear, expect, judge; I say, upon our having observed the like, either with respect to others or ourselves. And thus, whereas the prince [1] who had always lived in a warm climate, naturally concluded in the way of analogy, that there was no such thing as water's becoming hard, because he had always observed it to be fluid and yielding; we, on the contrary, from analogy conclude, that there is no presumption at all against this [2]; that it is supposable there may be frost in England any given day in January next; probable that there will on some day of the month; and that there is a moral certainty, *i. e.*, ground for an expectation without any doubt of it, in some part or other of the winter.

Probable evidence, in its very nature, affords but an imperfect kind of information; and is to be considered as relative only to beings of limited capacities. For nothing which is the possible object of knowledge, whether past, present, or future, can be probable to an infinite Intelligence; since it cannot but be discerned absolutely as it is in itself—certainly true, or certainly false. But to us, probability is the very guide of life.

From these things it follows, that in questions of difficulty, or such as are thought so, where more satisfactory evidence cannot be had, or is not seen; if the result of examination be, that there appears upon the whole, any the lowest presumption on one side, and none on the other, or greater presumption on one side, though in the lowest degree greater; this determines the question, even

---

[1] The story is thus told by Mr. Locke in the "Chapter of Probability:"— "A Dutch ambassador, entertaining the King of Siam with the particularities of Holland, which he was inquisitive after, amongst other things told him, that the water in his country would sometimes be so hard in cold weather that men walked upon it, and that it would bear an elephant, if he were there. To which the king replied, ' Hitherto I have believed the strange things you have told me, because I looked upon you as a sober fair man; but now I am sure you lie.' "—*Ed.*

[2] But it has been well observed by Dr. Leland, that experience may assure us *that facts or events are possible, but not that the contrary is impossible*. The greatest uniformity and frequency of experience cannot prove the *certainty* of an event, nor even afford the least *probability* that it would *never* happen otherwise. For aught we know, there may be occasions on which it would fail, and secret causes in the frame of things which sometimes may counteract those by which it is produced.—*Ed.*

in matters of speculation; and in matters of practice, will lay us under an absolute and formal obligation, in point of prudence and of interest, to act upon that presumption or low probability, though it be so low as to leave the mind in very great doubt which is the truth. For surely a man is as really bound in prudence to do what upon the whole appears, according to the best of his judgment, to be for his happiness, as what he certainly knows to be so. Nay further, in questions of great consequence, a reasonable man will think it concerns him to remark lower probabilities and presumptions than these; such as amount to no more than showing one side of a question to be as supposable and credible as the other: nay, such as but amount to much less even than this. For numberless instances might be mentioned respecting the common pursuits of life, where a man would be thought, in a literal sense, distracted, who would not act, and with great application too, not only upon an even chance, but upon much less, and where the probability or chance was greatly against his succeeding [1].

It is not my design to inquire further into the nature, the foundation, and measure of probability; or whence it proceeds that *likeness* [2] should beget that presumption, opinion, and full conviction, which the human mind is formed to receive from it, and which it does necessarily produce in every one; or to guard against the errors to which reasoning from analogy is liable. This belongs to the subject of Logic, and is a part of that subject which has not yet been thoroughly considered. Indeed I shall not take upon me to say, how far the extent, compass, and force, of analogical reasoning, can be reduced to general heads and rules, and the whole be formed into a system. But though so little in this way has been attempted by those who have treated of our intellectual powers, and the exercise of them; this does not hinder but that we may be, as we unquestionably are, assured, that analogy is of weight, in various degrees, towards determining our judgment and our practice. Nor does it in anywise cease to be of weight in those cases, because persons, either given to dispute, or who require things to be stated with greater exactness than our faculties appear to admit of in practical matters, may find other cases in

---

[1] See Part II. chap. vi.

[2] Likeness, that is, of ratios or relations, λόγων ὁμοιότης (Archbishop Whately's "Rhetoric"). In every analogical argument there must be two ratios, and, of course, two terms in each ratio. The ratios must be distinct, but all the four terms need not; one term may be repeated in each ratio, and so three distinct terms are sufficient. One ratio being better known than another, serves to explain it. Thus in Origen's and Butler's analogical arguments, one term is repeated in each ratio, and one ratio explains the other: the ratio of the Author of nature to difficulties in nature is like the ratio of the Author of nature to difficulties in Scripture; and again, the ratio of God to the present experienced dispensation is like the ratio of God to the future revealed dispensation.—(*W.*)

which it is not easy to say whether it be, or be not, of any weight; or instances of seeming analogies, which are really of none. It is enough to the present purpose to observe, that this general way of arguing is evidently natural, just, and conclusive. For there is no man can make a question but that the sun will rise to-morrow [1], and be seen, where it is seen at all, in the figure of a circle, and not in that of a square.

Hence, namely from analogical reasoning, Origen [2] has with singular sagacity observed, that *he who believes the Scripture to have proceeded from him who is the Author of Nature, may well expect to find the same sort of difficulties in it as are found in the constitution of Nature.* And in a like way of reflection it may be added, that he who denies the Scripture to have been from God upon account of these difficulties, may, for the very same reason, deny the world to have been formed by him. On the other hand, if there be an analogy or likeness between that system of things and dispensation of Providence, which Revelation informs us of, and that system of things and dispensation of Providence which Experience together with Reason informs us of, *i. e.*, the known course of Nature ; this is a presumption that they have both the same author and cause; at least so far as to answer objections against the former's being from God, drawn from anything which is analogical or similar to what is in the latter, which is acknowledged to be from him; for an Author of Nature is here supposed.

Forming our notions of the constitution and government of the world upon reasoning, without foundation for the principles which we assume, whether from the attributes of God, or anything else, is building a world upon hypothesis, like Des Cartes. Forming our notions upon reasoning from principles which are certain, but applied to cases to which we have no ground to apply them

---

[1] A man brought into being at maturity, and placed in a desert island, would abandon himself to despair when he first saw the sun set and the night come on; for he could have no expectation that ever the day would be renewed. But he is transported with joy when he again beholds the glorious orb appearing in the east, and the heavens and the earth illuminated as before. He again views the declining sun with apprehension, yet not without hope; the second night is less dismal than the first, but still very uncomfortable, owing to the weakness of the probability produced by one favourable instance. As the instances grow more numerous, the probability becomes stronger and stronger; yet it may be questioned whether a man in these circumstances would ever arrive at so high a degree of moral certainty in this matter as we experience, who know not only that the sun has risen every day since we began to exist, but also that the same phenomenon has happened regularly for more than five thousand years, without failing in a single instance.—*Beattie on Truth.* (*Ed.*)

[2] Χρὴ μέν τοι γὲ τὸν ἅπαξ παραδιξάμινον τοῦ κτίσαντος τὸν κόσμον εἶναι ταύτας τὰς γραφὰς πιπιῖσθαι, ὅτι ὅσα πιρὶ τῆς κτίσιως ἀπαντᾷ τοῖς ζητοῦσι τὸν πιρὶ αὐτῆς λόγον, ταῦτα καὶ πιρὶ τῶν γραφῶν.—Philocal. p. 23. Ed. Cant.

(like those who explain the structure of the human body and the nature of diseases and medicines from mere mathematics without sufficient *data*), is an error much akin to the former; since what is assumed in order to make the reasoning applicable, is Hypothesis. But it must be allowed just, to join abstract reasonings with the observation of facts, and argue from such facts as are known to others that are like them; from that part of the divine government over intelligent creatures which comes under our view, to that larger and more general government over them which is beyond it; and from what is present to collect what is likely, credible, or not incredible, will be hereafter.

This method, then, of concluding and determining being practical, and what, if we will act at all, we cannot but act upon in the common pursuits of life; being evidently conclusive, in various degrees, proportionable to the degree and exactness of the whole analogy or likeness; and having so great authority for its introduction into the subject of religion, even revealed religion; my design is to apply it to that subject in general, both natural and revealed: taking for proved, that there is an intelligent Author of Nature, and *natural* Governor of the world. For as there is no presumption against this prior to the proof of it, so it has been often proved with accumulated evidence; from this argument of analogy and final causes, from abstract reasonings, from the most ancient tradition and testimony, and from the general consent of mankind. Nor does it appear, so far as I can find, to be denied by the generality of those who profess themselves dissatisfied with the evidence of religion.

As there are some who, instead of thus attending to what is in fact the constitution of Nature, form their notions of God's government upon hypothesis, so there are others who indulge themselves in vain and idle speculations how the world might possibly have been framed otherwise than it is; and upon supposition that things might, in imagining that they should, have been disposed and carried on after a better model than what appears in the present disposition and conduct of them. Suppose now a person of such a turn of mind to go on with his reveries till he had at length fixed upon some particular plan of Nature as appearing to him the best. One shall scarce be thought guilty of detraction against human understanding, if one should say, even beforehand, that the plan which this speculative person would fix upon, though he were the wisest of the sons of men, probably would not be the very best, even according to his own notions of *best;* whether he thought that to be so which afforded occasions and motives for the exercise of the greatest virtue, or which was productive of the greatest happiness, or that these two were necessarily connected, and run up into one and the same plan. However, it may not be amiss, once for all, to see what would be the amount of these emendations and imaginary improvements upon the system of Nature, or how far they would mislead us. And it seems there could be no stopping till we came to some such conclusions as these : that all creatures should at first be made as perfect and as happy as they were capable of ever being; that nothing, to be sure, of hazard or danger should be put upon them to do—some indolent persons would perhaps think nothing at all—or, certainly, that effectual care should be taken that they should, whether necessarily or not, yet eventually and in fact, always do what was right and most conducive to happiness, which would be thought easy for infinite power to effect, either by not giving them any principles which would endanger their going wrong, or by laying the right motive of action in every instance before their minds continually in so strong a manner as would never fail of inducing them to act conformably to it : and that the whole method of government by punishments should be rejected as absurd ; as an awkward roundabout method of carrying things on ; nay, as contrary to a principal purpose for which it would be supposed creatures were made, namely, happiness.

Now, without considering what is to be said in particular to the several parts of this train of folly and extravagance, what has been above intimated is a full direct general answer to it, namely, that we may see beforehand that we have not faculties for this kind of speculation. For though it be admitted that, from the first principles of our nature, we unavoidably judge or determine some ends to be absolutely in themselves preferable to others, and that the ends now mentioned, or if they run up into one, that this one is absolutely the best, and consequently that we must conclude the ultimate end designed in the constitution of Nature and conduct of Providence is the most virtue and happiness possible ; yet we are far from being able to judge what particular disposition of things would be most friendly and assistant to virtue ; or what means might be absolutely necessary to produce the most happiness in a system of such extent as our own world may be, taking in all that is past and to come, though we should suppose it detached from the whole of things. Indeed we are so far from being able to judge of this, that we are not judges what may be the necessary means of raising and conducting one person to the highest perfection and happiness of his nature. Nay, even in the little affairs of the present life, we find men of different educations and ranks are not competent judges of the conduct of each other. Our whole nature leads us to ascribe all moral perfection to God, and to deny all imperfection of him. And this will for ever be a practical proof of his moral character, to such as will consider what a practical proof is ; because it is the voice of God speaking in us. And from hence we conclude, that virtue must be the happiness, and vice the misery, of every creature ; and that regularity and order and right cannot but

prevail finally in a universe under his government. But we are
in no sort judges what are the necessary means of accomplishing
this end.

Let us then, instead of that idle and not very innocent employment of forming imaginary models of a world, and schemes of
governing it, turn our thoughts to what we experience to be the
conduct of Nature with respect to intelligent creatures; which
may be resolved into general laws or rules of administration, in
the same way as many of the laws of Nature respecting inanimate matter may be collected from experiments. And let us
compare the known constitution and course of things with what
is said to be the moral system of Nature, the acknowledged dispensations of Providence, or that government which we find ourselves under, with what religion teaches us to believe and expect,
and see whether they are not analogous and of a piece. And
upon such a comparison it will, I think, be found that they are
very much so; that both may be traced up to the same general
laws, and resolved into the same principles of divine conduct.

The analogy here proposed to be considered is of pretty large
extent, and consists of several parts; in some more, in others less
exact. In some few instances perhaps it may amount to a real
practical proof; in others not so. Yet in these it is a confirmation
of what is proved otherwise. It will undeniably show, what too
many want to have shown them, that the system of Religion, both
natural and revealed, considered only as a system, and prior to
the proof of it, is not a subject of ridicule, unless that of Nature
be so too. And it will afford an answer to almost all objections
against the system both of natural and revealed Religion; though
not perhaps an answer in so great a degree, yet in a very considerable degree an answer to the objections against the evidence of it;
for objections against a proof, and objections against what is said
to be proved, the reader will observe are different things.

Now the divine government of the world, implied in the notion
of religion in general and of Christianity, contains in it—that
mankind is appointed to live in a future state[1]; that there every
one shall be rewarded or punished[2]; rewarded or punished respectively for all that behaviour here, which we comprehend under
the words virtuous or vicious, morally good or evil[3]; that our present life is a probation, a state of trial[4], and of discipline[5], for
that future one; notwithstanding the objections, which men may
fancy they have, from notions of Necessity, against there being
any such moral plan as this at all[6]; and whatever objections may
appear to lie against the wisdom and goodness of it, as it stands
so imperfectly made known to us at present[7]; that this world
being in a state of apostasy and wickedness, and consequently of
ruin, and the sense both of their condition and duty being greatly

[1] Ch. i.     [2] Ch. ii.     [3] Ch. iii.     [4] Ch. iv.     [5] Ch. v.     [6] Ch. vi.
[7] Ch. vii.

corrupted amongst men, this gave occasion for an additional
dispensation of Providence of the utmost importance[1]; proved
by miracles[2]; but containing in it many things appearing to us
strange, and not to have been expected[3]; a dispensation of Providence, which is a scheme or system of things[4]; carried on by the
mediation of a divine person, the Messiah, in order to the recovery
of the world[5]; yet not revealed to all men, nor proved with the
strongest possible evidence to all those to whom it is revealed;
but only to such a part of mankind, and with such particular
evidence, as the wisdom of God thought fit[6]. The design then
of the following Treatise[7] will be to show that the several parts
principally objected against in this moral and Christian dispensation, including its scheme, its publication, and the proof which
God has afforded us of its truth; that the particular parts principally objected against in this whole dispensation, are analogous to
what is experienced in the constitution and course of Nature, or
Providence; that the chief objections themselves which are
alleged against the former, are no other than what may be alleged
with like justness against the latter, where they are found in fact
to be inconclusive; and that this argument from analogy is in
general unanswerable, and undoubtedly of weight on the side of
religion[8], notwithstanding the objections which may seem to lie
against it, and the real ground which there may be for difference
of opinion, as to the particular degree of weight which is to be
laid upon it. This is a general account of what may be looked
for in the following Treatise. And I shall begin it with that which
is the foundation of all our hopes and of all our fears—all our
hopes and fears, which are of any consideration—I mean a Future
Life.

---

[1] Part II. ch. i.       [2] Ch. ii.        [3] Ch. iii.        [4] Ch. iv.        [5] Ch. v.
[6] Ch. vi. vii.
    [7] I know no author who has made a more just and happy use of analogical
reasoning than Bishop Butler, in his "Analogy of Religion." In that excellent
work, the author does not ground any of the truths of religion upon analogy
as their proper evidence. He only makes use of analogy to answer objections
against them. When objections are made against the truths of religion, which
may be made with equal strength against *what we know to be true* in the
course of nature, such objections can have no weight.—*Dr. Reid.*
    [8] Ch. viii.

# PART I

## OF NATURAL RELIGION

# CHAPTER I.

## OF A FUTURE LIFE.

STRANGE difficulties have been raised by some concerning personal identity, or the sameness of living agents, implied in the notion of our existing now and hereafter, or in any two successive moments; which, whoever thinks it worth while, may see considered in the first Dissertation at the end of this Treatise. But without regard to any of them here, let us consider what the analogy of nature, and the several changes which we have undergone, and those which we know we may undergo without being destroyed, suggest, as to the effect which death may, or may not, have upon us; and whether it be not from thence probable, that we may survive this change, and exist in a future state of life and perception.

I. From our being born into the present world in the helpless imperfect state of infancy, and having arrived from thence to mature age, we find it to be a general law of nature in our own species, that the same creatures, the same individuals, should exist in degrees of life and perception, with capacities of action, of enjoyment and suffering, in one period of their being, greatly different from those appointed them in another period of it. And in other creatures the same law holds. For the difference of their capacities and states of life at their birth (to go no higher) and in maturity: the change of worms into flies, and the vast enlargement of their locomotive powers by such change; and birds and in sects bursting the shell of their habitation, and by this means entering into a new world, furnished with new accommodations for them, and finding a new sphere of action assigned them; these are instances of this general law of nature. Thus all the various and wonderful transformations of animals are to be taken into consideration here. But the states of life in which we ourselves existed formerly in the womb and in our infancy, are almost as different from our present in mature age, as it is possible to conceive any two states or degrees of life can be. Therefore that we are to exist hereafter, in a state as different (suppose) from our present, as this is from our former, is but according to the analogy of nature; according to a natural order or appointment, of the very same kind with what we have already experienced.

II. We know we are endued with capacities of action, of happiness and misery; for we are conscious of acting, of enjoying pleasure and suffering pain. Now that we have these powers and capacities before death, is a presumption that we shall retain them through and after death; indeed a probability of it abundantly sufficient to act upon, unless there be some positive reason to think that death is the destruction of those living powers: because there is in every case a probability, that all things will continue as we experience they are, in all respects, except those in which we have some reason to think they will be altered. This is that *kind*[1] of presumption or probability from analogy, expressed in the very word *continuance*, which seems our only natural reason for believing the course of the world will continue to-morrow, as it has done so far as our experience or knowledge of history can carry us back. Nay, it seems our only reason for believing, that any one substance now existing will continue to exist a moment longer; the self-existent substance only excepted. Thus, if men were assured that the unknown event, death, was not the destruction of our faculties of perception and of action, there would be no apprehension that any other power or event, unconnected with this of death, would destroy these faculties just at the instant of each creature's death; and therefore no

[1] I say *kind* of presumption or probability; for I do not mean to affirm that there is the same *degree* of conviction, that our living powers will continue after death, as there is that our substances will.

doubt but that they would remain after it; which shows the
high probability that our living powers will continue after
death, unless there be some ground to think that death is
their destruction [1]. For, if it would be in a manner certain
that we should survive death, provided it were certain that
death would not be our destruction, it must be highly probable we shall survive it, if there be no ground to think
death will be our destruction.

Now, though I think it must be acknowledged, that prior
to the natural and moral proofs of a future life commonly
insisted upon, there would arise a general confused suspicion, that in the great shock and alteration which we shall
undergo by death, we, *i. e.*, our living powers, might be
wholly destroyed ; yet even prior to those proofs, there is
really no particular distinct ground or reason for this apprehension at all, so far as I can find. If there be, it must
arise either from *the reason of the thing*, or from *the analogy
of nature*.

But we cannot argue from *the reason of the thing*, that
death is the destruction of living agents, because we know
not at all what death is in itself; but only some of its
effects, such as the dissolution of flesh, skin, and bones.
And these effects do in no wise appear to imply the destruction of a living agent. And besides, as we are greatly in
the dark, upon what the exercise of our living powers depends, so we are wholly ignorant what the powers themselves depend upon ; the powers themselves as distinguished, not only from their actual exercise, but also from
the present capacity of exercising them, and as opposed to
their destruction ; for sleep, or however a swoon, shows us,
not only that these powers exist when they are not exercised,
as the passive power of motion does in inanimate matter ;

[1] *Destruction of living powers* is a manner of expression unavoidably
ambiguous; and may signify either *the destruction of a living being, so as
that the same living being shall be incapable of ever perceiving or acting
again at all ; or the destruction of those means and instruments by which it
is capable of its present life, of its present state of perception and of action.*
It is here used in the former sense. When it is used in the latter, the epithet
*present* is added. The loss of a man's eye is a destruction of living powers
in the latter sense. But we have no reason to think the destruction of living
powers, in the former sense, to be possible. We have no more reason to
think a being endued with living powers, ever loses them during its whole
existence, than to believe that a stone ever acquires them.

but shows also that they exist when there is no present capacity of exercising them; or that the capacities of exercising them for the present, as well as the actual exercise of them, may be suspended, and yet the powers themselves remain undestroyed. Since then we know not at all upon what the existence of our living powers depends, this shows further, there can no probability be collected from the reason of the thing, that death will be their destruction; because their existence may depend upon somewhat in no degree affected by death; upon somewhat quite out of the reach of this king of terrors. So that there is nothing more certain, than that *the reason of the thing* shows us no connection between death and the destruction of living agents. Nor can we find anything throughout the whole *analogy of nature*, to afford us even the slightest presumption, that animals ever lose their living powers; much less if it were possible that they lose them by death; for we have no faculties wherewith to trace any beyond or through it, so as to see what becomes of them. This event removes them from our view. It destroys the *sensible* proof, which we had before their death, of their being possessed of living powers, but does not appear to afford the least reason to believe that they are, then, or by that event, deprived of them.

And our knowing that they were possessed of these powers, up to the very period to which we have faculties capable of tracing them, is itself a probability of their retaining them beyond it. And this is confirmed, and a sensible credibility is given to it, by observing the very great and astonishing changes which we have experienced; so great, that our existence in another state of life, of perception and of action, will be but according to a method of providential conduct, the like to which has been already exercised even with regard to ourselves; according to a course of nature, the like to which we have already gone through.

However, as one cannot but be greatly sensible, how difficult it is to silence imagination enough to make the voice of reason even distinctly heard in this case; as we are accustomed, from our youth up, to indulge that forward, delusive faculty [1]; ever obtruding beyond its sphere; of

[1] There is no subject on which doubts and difficulties may not be started by ingenious and disputatious men; and, therefore, from the number of their

some assistance indeed to apprehension, but the author of
all error: as we plainly lose ourselves in gross and crude
conceptions of things, taking for granted that we are acquainted with what indeed we are wholly ignorant of: it
may be proper to consider the imaginary presumptions, that
death will be our destruction arising from these kinds of
early and lasting prejudices; and to show how little they
can really amount to, even though we cannot wholly divest
ourselves of them. And,

I. All presumption of death's being the destruction of
living beings must go upon supposition that they are compounded and so discerptible [1]. But since consciousness is
a single and indivisible power, it should seem that the subject
in which it resides must be so too. For were the motion of
any particle of matter absolutely one and indivisible, so as
that it should imply a contradiction to suppose part of this
motion to exist, and part not to exist, *i. e.*, part of this matter
to move and part to be at rest, then its power of motion
would be indivisible; and so also would the subject in which
the power inheres, namely, the particle of matter: for if
this could be divided into two, one part might be moved
and the other at rest, which is contrary to the supposition [2].
In like manner it has been argued [3], and, for anything appearing to the contrary, justly, that since the perception or

objections, and the length of the controversy to which they give occasion, we
cannot in any case conclude that the original evidence is weak, or even that
it is not obvious and striking. Were we to presume that every principle is
dubious against which spurious objections may be contrived, we should be
quickly led into universal scepticism. The two ways in which the ingenuity
of speculative men has been most commonly employed, are dogmatical assertions of doubtful opinions, *and subtle cavils against certain truths.—Gerard's
Dissertations*, ii. 4. (*Ed.*)

[1] There are three distinct questions relating to a future life here considered. Whether death be the destruction of living agents; if not, whether
it be the destruction of their *present* powers of reflection, as it certainly is
the destruction of their present powers of sensation; and, if not, whether it be
the suspension, or discontinuance of the exercise, of these present reflecting
powers. Now, if there be no reason to believe the last, there will be, if that
were possible, less for the next, and less still for the first.—*Ed.*

[2] The above argument may be thus stated: "If we could be divided, each
separate part of us would have the power of consciousness in itself; and
there would follow separate consciousnesses, which is contrary to our
hypothesis. We, therefore, the living beings that we call ourselves, are
indivisible."—(*D.*)

[3] See Dr. Clarke's Letter to Mr. Dodwell, and the defences of it.

consciousness, which we have of our own existence, is indivisible, so as that it is a contradiction to suppose one part of it should be here and the other there [1], the perceptive power, or the power of consciousness, is indivisible too, and consequently the subject in which it resides, *i. e.*, the conscious Being. Now upon supposition that the living agent which each man calls himself, is thus a single being, there is at least no more difficulty in conceiving than in conceiving it to be a compound, and of which there is the proof now mentioned; it follows, that our organized bodies are no more ourselves, or part of ourselves, than any other matter around us. And it is as easy to conceive how matter, which is no part of ourselves, may be appropriated to us in the manner which our present bodies are, as how we can receive impressions from, and have power over, any matter. It is as easy to conceive that we may exist out of bodies as in them; that we might have animated bodies of any other organs and senses wholly different from these now given us, and that we may hereafter animate these same or new bodies variously modified and organized, as to conceive how we can animate such bodies as our present. And, lastly, the dissolution of all these several organized bodies, supposing ourselves to have successively animated them, would have no more conceivable tendency to destroy the living beings ourselves, or deprive us of living faculties—the faculties of perception and of action—than the dissolution of any foreign matter, which we are capable of receiving impressions from, and making use of, for the common occasions of life [2].

II. The simplicity and absolute oneness of a living agent

[1] That it is highly unreasonable and absurd to suppose the soul made up of innumerable consciousnesses, as matter is necessarily made up of innumerable parts; and, on the contrary, that it is highly reasonable to believe the *seat of thought* to be a simple substance, such as cannot naturally be divided and crumbled into pieces, as all matter is naturally subject to be,— must of necessity be confessed. Consequently, the soul will not be liable to be dissolved at the dissolution of the body, and therefore it will naturally be immortal. All this seems to follow, at least, with the highest degree of probability, from the single consideration of the soul being endued with sense, thought, or consciousness.—*Clarke's Evidences*. (*Ed.*)

[2] To avoid the fallacy which all modes of expression would occasion which involve particular theories in them, Butler is often obliged to employ a circuitous, and apparently awkward style, in stating his arguments. . . . Thus in his chapter, "On a Future Life," he does not speak of the soul as

cannot indeed, from the nature of the thing, be properly
proved by experimental observations. But as these *fall in*
with the supposition of its unity, so they plainly lead us to
*conclude* certainly, that our gross organized bodies, with
which we perceive the objects of sense, and with which we
act, are no part of ourselves; and therefore show us, that
we have no reason to believe their destruction to be ours,
even without determining whether our living substances be
material or immaterial. For we see by experience, that men
may lose their limbs, their organs of sense, and even the
greatest part of these bodies, and yet remain the same living
agents. And persons can trace up the existence of themselves to a time, when the bulk of their bodies was extremely small, in comparison of what it is in mature age;
and we cannot but think that they might then have lost a
considerable part of that small body, and yet have remained
the same living agents; as they may now lose great part of
their present body and remain so. And it is certain, that
the bodies of all animals are in a constant flux, from that
never-ceasing attrition, which there is in every part of them.
Now things of this kind unavoidably teach us to distinguish
between these living agents ourselves and large quantities
of matter, in which we are very nearly interested, since
these may be alienated, and actually are in a daily course of
succession, and changing their owners; whilst we are
assured that each living agent remains one and the same
permanent being [1]. And this general observation leads us
on to the following ones.

*First.* That we have no way of determining by experience,
what is the certain bulk of the living being each man calls
himself; and yet, till it be determined that it is larger in
bulk than the solid elementary particles of matter, which

an immaterial or naturally immortal principle, since his object is to employ
such arguments as would be conclusive, whatever theory of the soul be maintained; appealing simply to such facts as are signs of its posthumous
existence, whatever may be its nature. Hence his use of such expressions
as "faculties of perception and action," "living powers," "living agents,"
"the living being each man calls himself," &c., which, to be justly estimated,
must be regarded as exclusions of any particular theory concerning the soul;
so as to leave the question of a future life, as there entered into, purely a
question of fact.—*Preface to Hampden's Essay on the Philosophical
Evidences of Christianity.* (*Ed.*)

[1] See Dissertation I.

there is no ground to think any natural power can dissolve, there is no sort of reason to think death to be the dissolution of it, of the living being, even though it should not be absolutely indiscerptible.

*Secondly.* From our being so nearly related to and interested in certain systems of matter, suppose our flesh and bones, and afterwards ceasing to be at all related to them, the living agents ourselves remaining all this while undestroyed notwithstanding such alienation, and consequently these systems of matter not being ourselves; it follows further, that we have no ground to conclude any other, suppose *internal systems* of matter, to be the living agents ourselves; because we can have no ground to conclude this, but from our relation to and interest in such other systems of matter; and therefore we can have no reason to conclude what befalls those systems of matter at death to be the destruction of the living agents. We have already several times over lost a great part or perhaps the whole of our body, according to certain common established laws of nature; yet we remain the same living agents: when we shall lose as great a part, or the whole, by another common established law of nature, death, why may we not also remain the same? That the alienation has been gradual in one case, and in the other will be more at once, does not prove anything to the contrary. We have passed undestroyed through those many and great revolutions of matter, so peculiarly appropriated to us ourselves; why should we imagine death will be so fatal to us? Nor can it be objected, that what is thus alienated or lost, is no part of our original solid body, but only adventitious matter; because we may lose entire limbs, which must have contained many solid parts and vessels of the original body; or if this be not admitted, we have no proof that any of these solid parts are dissolved or alienated by death. Though, by the way, we are very nearly related to that extraneous or adventitious matter, whilst it continues united to, and distending the several parts of our solid body. But after all, the relation a person bears to those parts of his body, to which he is the most nearly related; what does it appear to amount to but this, that the living agent, and those parts of the body mutually affect each other? And the same thing, the same thing in kind though not in degree, may be said of *all foreign* matter, which gives us ideas, and which we have any power over. From these observations the whole ground of the imagination is removed, that the dissolution of any matter is the destruction of a living agent, from the interest he once had in such matter.

*Thirdly.* If we consider our body somewhat more distinctly, as made up of organs and instruments of perception and of motion, it will bring us to the same conclusion. Thus the common optical experiments show, and even the observation how sight is assisted by glasses shows, that we see with our eyes in the same sense as we see with glasses. Nor is there any reason to believe that we see with them in any other sense ; any other, I mean, which would lead us to think the eye itself a percipient. The like is to be said of hearing; and our feeling distant solid matter by means of somewhat in our hand seems an instance of the like kind, as to the subject we are considering. All these are instances of foreign matter, or such as is no part of our body being instrumental in preparing objects for, and conveying them to, the perceiving power, in a manner similar or like to the manner in which our organs of sense prepare and convey them. Both are in a like way instruments of our receiving such ideas from external objects, as the Author of Nature appointed those external objects to be the occasions of exciting in us. However, glasses are evidently instances of this ; namely, of matter which is no part of our body preparing objects for, and conveying them towards the perceiving power, in like manner as our bodily organs do. And if we see with our eyes only in the same manner as we do with glasses, the like may justly be concluded, from analogy, of all other senses. It is not intended by anything here said, to affirm that the whole apparatus of vision, or of perception by any other of our senses, can be traced through all its steps, quite up to the living power of seeing or perceiving ; but that so far as it can be traced by experimental observations, so far it appears that our organs of sense prepare and convey on objects, in order to their being perceived in like manner as foreign matter does, without affording any shadow of appearance that they themselves perceive. And that we have no reason to think our organs of sense percipients is confirmed by instances of persons losing some of them, the living beings themselves, their former occupiers, remaining unimpaired. It is confirmed also by the experience of dreams; by which we find we are at present possessed of a latent, and what would otherwise be an unimagined unknown power of perceiving sensible objects, in as strong and lively a manner without our external organs of sense as with them.

So also with regard to our power of moving, or directing motion by will and choice; upon the destruction of a limb, this active power remains, as it evidently seems, unlessened; so as that the living being who has suffered this loss, would be capable of moving as before, if it had another limb to move with. It can walk by the help of an artificial leg; just as it can make use of a pole or a lever, to reach towards itself and to move things, beyond the length and the power of its natural arm; and this last it does in the same manner as it reaches and moves, with its natural arm, things nearer and of less weight. Nor is there so much as any appearance of our limbs being endued with a power of moving or directing themselves; though they are adapted, like the several parts of a machine, to be the instruments of motion to each other, and some parts of the same limb to be instruments of motion to other parts of it.

Thus a man determines, that he will look at such an object through a microscope; or being lame, suppose, that he will walk to such a place with a staff a week hence. His eyes and his feet no more determine in these cases, than the microscope and the staff. Nor is there any ground to think they any more put the determination in practice; or that his eyes are the seers or his feet the movers, in any other sense than as the microscope and the staff are. Upon the whole then, our organs of sense and our limbs are certainly instruments, which the living persons ourselves make use of to perceive and move with: there is not any probability, that they are any more; nor, consequently, that we have any other kind of relation to them, than what we have to any other foreign matter formed into instruments of perception and motion, suppose into a microscope or a staff (I say any other kind of relation, for I am not speaking of the degree of it); nor consequently is there any probability, that the alienation or dissolution of these instruments is the destruction of the perceiving and moving agent[1].

[1] Butler's caution, in treating this subject, is a striking contrast to the boldness of those philosophers who have concluded, with all the confidence of demonstration, that what is not compounded nor made up of parts cannot

And thus our finding, that the dissolution of matter in which living beings were most nearly interested, is not their dissolution; and that the destruction of several of the organs and instruments of perception and of motion belonging to them, is not their destruction; shows demonstratively, that there is no ground to think that the dissolution of any other matter, or destruction of any other organs and instruments, will be the dissolution or destruction of living agents, from the like kind of relation. And we have no reason to think we stand in any other kind of relation to anything which we find dissolved by death[1].

be dissolved; (Butler says, " which *there is no ground* to think *any natural power can dissolve;*") and, therefore, that the human soul is *essentially* and *necessarily* immortal. " Et cum simplex natura animi esset, neque haberet in se quidquam admetum dispar sui atque dissimile, non posse eum dividi; quod si non possit, non posse interire." " But this argument," says Dugald Stewart, " I am afraid, supposing it were logical, proves too much; for it concludes as strongly against the possibility of the soul's being *created* as *dissolved;* and, accordingly, we find that almost all the ancient philosophers who believed in a future state maintained also the doctrine of the soul's pre-existence. Nay, some of them seem to have considered the latter point as still better established than the former. In the Phædon of Plato, in which Socrates is introduced as stating to his friends, immediately before his execution, the proofs of a future state, Cebes, who is one of the speakers in the dialogue, admits that he has been successful in establishing the doctrine of the soul's pre-existence, but insists on further proofs of the possibility of its surviving the body. Although our knowledge of the nature of man may not be sufficient to afford us any positive argument on the subject, yet if it can be shown that the dissolution of the body does not *necessarily infer* the extinction of the soul; and still more, if it can be shown that the presumption is in favour of the contrary supposition; the moral proof of a future retribution will meet with a more easy reception, when the doctrine is freed from the metaphysical difficulties which it has been apprehended to involve. It is in this moderate form that the argument from the light of nature is stated by Butler; and the considerations he mentions prove fully, not only that *no presumption* against a future state can be collected from the dissolution of the body, but that the contrary supposition is more agreeable to the analogy of nature." Surely this is contrary to what Dugald Stewart has stated, " that the more common fact is, that the body and mind seem to decay together;" for this common fact must be considered as a presumption against a future state, which is collected from the dissolution of the body. It is a *valid* presumption, although it may be overbalanced by greater probabilities on the other particular theory concerning the soul; so as to leave the question of a future life, as there entered into, purely a question of fact.—*Preface to Hampden's Essay on the Philosophical Evidence of Christianity. (Ed.)*

[1] The sum of the argument is this. It is found by experience that the dissolution of systems of matter with which we are connected is not the destruction of ourselves, as living beings. And, therefore, it admits of

But it is said these observations are equally applicable to brutes; and it is thought an insuperable difficulty, that they should be immortal, and by consequence capable of ever-lasting happiness. Now this manner of expression is both invidious and weak; but the thing intended by it is really no difficulty at all, either in the way of natural or moral consideration. For 1st, Suppose the invidious thing, designed in such a manner of expression, were really implied, as it is not in the least, in the natural immortality of brutes: namely, that they must arrive at great attainments, and become rational and moral agents; even this would be no difficulty: since we know not what latent powers and capacities they may be endued with. There was once, prior to experience, as great presumption against human creatures as there is against the brute creatures, arriving at that degree of understanding, which we have in mature age. For we can trace up our own existence to the same original with theirs. And we find it to be a general law of nature, that creatures endued with capacities of virtue and religion should be placed in a condition of being, in which they are altogether without the use of them, for a considerable length of their duration, as in infancy and childhood. And great part of the human species go out of the present world, before they come to the exercise of these capacities in any degree at all. But then, 2ndly, the natural immortality of brutes does not in the least imply, that they are endued with any latent capacities of a rational or moral nature. And the economy of the universe might require, that there should be living creatures without any capacities of this kind. And all difficulties as to the manner how they are to be disposed of are so apparently and wholly founded in our ignorance, that it is wonderful they should be insisted upon by any, but such as are weak enough to think they are acquainted with the whole system of things. There is then absolutely nothing at all in this objection, which is so rhetorically urged, against the greatest part of the natural proofs or presumptions of the immortality of human minds; I say the greatest part; for it is less applicable to the following observation, which is more peculiar to mankind:

III. That as it is evident our *present* powers and capacities

demonstrative proof that it is in no degree probable that any other system of matter, standing to us in a like relation, could by its dissolution affect us more fatally than these.—(*D.*)

Of a Future Life 23

of *reason, memory,* and *affection,* do not depend upon our gross body in the manner in which perception *by our organs of sense* does; so they do not appear to depend upon it at all in any such manner, as to give ground to think, that the dissolution of this body will be the destruction of these our *present* powers of *reflection,* as it will of our powers of *sensation;* or to give ground to conclude, even that it will be so much as a suspension of the former.

Human creatures exist at present in two states of life and perception, greatly different from each other; each of which has its own peculiar laws and its own peculiar enjoyments and sufferings. When any of our senses are affected or appetites gratified with the objects of them, we may be said to exist or live in a state of sensation. When none of our senses are affected or appetites gratified, and yet we perceive, and reason, and act, we may be said to exist or live in a state of reflection. Now it is by no means certain, that anything which is dissolved by death is any way necessary to the living being in this its state of reflection, after ideas are gained. For, though, from our present constitution and condition of being, our external organs of sense are necessary for conveying in ideas to our reflecting powers, as carriages, and levers, and scaffolds are in architecture; yet when these ideas are brought in, we are capable of reflecting in the most intense degree, and of enjoying the greatest pleasure, and feeling the greatest pain, by means of that reflection, without any assistance from our senses; and without any at all, which we know of, from that body which will be dissolved by death. It does not appear then, that the relation of this gross body to the reflecting being is, in any degree, necessary to thinking; to our intellectual enjoyments or sufferings; nor, consequently, that the dissolution or alienation of the former by death, will be the destruction of those present powers, which render us capable of this state of reflection. Further, there are instances of mortal diseases, which do not at all affect our present intellectual powers; and this affords a presumption, that those diseases will not destroy these present powers. Indeed, from the observations made above[1], it appears, that there is no presumption, from their mutually affecting each

[1] Pp. 85—90.

other, that the dissolution of the body is the destruction of
the living agent. And by the same reasoning, it must appear too, that there is no presumption, from their mutually
affecting each other, that the dissolution of the body is the
destruction of our present reflecting powers; but instances
of their not affecting each other, afford a presumption of
the contrary. Instances of mortal diseases not impairing our
present reflecting powers, evidently turn our thoughts even
from imagining such diseases to be the destruction of them.
Several things, indeed, greatly affect all our living powers,
and at length suspend the exercise of them; as for instance
drowsiness, increasing till it ends in sound sleep; and from
hence we might have imagined it would destroy them, till
we found by experience the weakness of this way of judging.
But in the diseases now mentioned, there is not so much as
this shadow of probability, to lead us to any such conclusion,
as to the reflecting powers which we have at present. For
in those diseases, persons the moment before death appear
to be in the highest vigour of life. They discover apprehension, memory, reason, all entire; with the utmost force
of affection; sense of a character, of shame and honour;
and the highest mental enjoyments and sufferings, even to
the last gasp: and these surely prove even greater vigour of
life than bodily strength does [1]. Now what pretence is there
for thinking, that a progressive disease when arrived to such
a degree, I mean that degree which is mortal, will destroy
those powers, which were not impaired, which were not
affected by it, during its whole progress quite up to that degree? And if death by diseases of this kind is not the
destruction of our present reflecting powers, it will scarce
be thought that death by any other means is.

It is obvious that this general observation may be carried
on further; and there appears so little connection between
our bodily powers of sensation, and our present powers of
reflection, that there is no reason to conclude that death,
which destroys the former, does so much as suspend the
exercise of the latter, or interrupt our *continuing* to exist in
the like state of reflection which we do now. For suspension of reason, memory, and the affections which they excite,

[1] Just as there is no presumption, from the body and the living being
mutually affecting one another, that the destruction of the one is the destruction of the other.—(*W.*)

is no part of the idea of death, nor is implied in our notion of it. And our daily experiencing these powers to be exercised, without any assistance, that we know of, from those bodies which will be dissolved by death; and our finding often that the exercise of them is so lively to the last; these things afford a sensible apprehension, that death may not, perhaps, be so much as a discontinuance of the exercise of these powers, nor of the enjoyments and sufferings which it implies[1]. So that our posthumous life, whatever there may be in it additional to our present, yet may not be entirely beginning anew, but going on. Death may, in some sort and in some respects, answer to our birth; which is not a suspension of the faculties which we had before it, or a total change of the state of life in which we existed when in the womb, but a continuation of both, with such and such great alterations.

Nay, for ought we know of ourselves, of our present life and of death, death may immediately, in the natural course of things, put us into a higher and more enlarged state of life, as our birth does[2]; a state in which our capacities, and sphere of perception and of action, may be much greater than at present. For as our relation to our external organs of sense renders us capable of existing in our present state of sensation, so it may be the only natural hindrance to our existing, immediately, and of course, in a higher state of reflection. The truth is, reason does not at all show us in what state death naturally leaves us. But were we sure that it would suspend all our perceptive and active powers; yet the suspension of a power and the destruction of it, are effects so totally different in kind, as we experience from

[1] There are three distinct questions, relating to a future life, here considered: Whether death be the destruction of living agents; if not, Whether it be the destruction of their *present* powers of reflection, as it certainly is the destruction of their present powers of sensation; and if not, Whether it be the suspension, or discontinuance of the exercise of these present reflecting powers. Now, if there be no reason to believe the last, there will be, if that were possible, less for the next, and less still for the first.—*Ed.*

[2] This, according to Strabo, was the opinion of the Brachmans, νομίζειν μὲν γὰρ δὴ τὸν μὲν ἐνθάδε βίον, ὡς ἂν ἀκμὴν κυομένων εἶναι· τὸν δὲ θάνατον, γένεσιν εἰς τὸν ὄντως βίον, καὶ τὸν εὐδαίμονα τοῖς φιλοσοφήσασι. Lib. xv. p. 1039, Ed. Amst. 1707. To which opinion perhaps Antoninus may allude in these words, ὡς νῦν περιμένεις, πότε ἔμβρυον ἐκ τῆς γαστρὸς τῆς γυναικός σου ἐξέλθη, οὕτως ἐκδέχεσθαι, τὴν ὥραν ἐν ᾗ τὸ ψυχάριόν σου τοῦ ἐλύτρου τούτου ἐκπεσεῖται. Lib. ix. c. 3.

sleep and a swoon, that we cannot in any wise argue from one to the other; or conclude even to the lowest degree of probability, that the same kind of force which is sufficient to suspend our faculties, though it be increased ever so much, will be sufficient to destroy them.

These observations together may be sufficient to show how little presumption there is, that death is the destruction of human creatures. However, there is the shadow of an analogy [1], which may lead us to imagine it is the supposed likeness which is observed between the decay of vegetables and of living creatures. And this likeness is, indeed, sufficient to afford the poets very apt allusions to the flowers of the field, in their pictures of the frailty of our present life. But in reason, the analogy is so far from holding, that there appears no ground even for the comparison, as to the present question, because one of the two subjects compared is wholly void of that which is the principal and chief thing in the other, the power of perception and of action, and which is the only thing we are inquiring about the continuance of. So that the destruction of a vegetable is an event not similar or analogous to the destruction of a living agent [2].

But if, as was above intimated, leaving off the delusive custom of substituting imagination in the room of experience, we would confine ourselves to what we do know and understand; if we would argue only from that [3], and from

---

[1] St. Paul, indeed, as our blessed Lord had already done (St. John xii. 24), in a popular and unsystematic way, does answer objections against the resurrection, by analogy from the works of nature. (1 Cor. xv. 36.) "The seed dies; it is only the germ or bud that springs up: the body of the seed first feeds this bud, and then turns to corruption." It is particularly to be noted that St. Paul is not speaking of the *identity* of the raised bodies.—See Whitby *in loco.* (*Ed.*)

[2] It is insisted on that there is nothing in the doctrine of a future state to take it out of the class of *natural* truths, or of those truths which make a part of *natural* religion; since by " natural " we are not to understand merely " what we see at present," but as implying that which is stated, fixed, and settled. Therefore that there should be another life, and that a social one, that its blessings should be exactly proportioned to our virtues, and that all its blessings should flow more directly from God Himself than is the case here,—all of this may be both true and *natural.*—(*D.*)

[3] It is thus that Herodotus, for example, is continually arguing. (See Book ii., ch. 33, ὡς ἐγὼ συμβάλλομαι, τοῖσι ἐμφανέσι τὰ μὴ γιγνωσκόμενα τεκμαιρόμενος.)—*Ed.*

that form our expectations, it would appear at first sight, that as no probability of living beings ever ceasing to be so can be concluded from the reason of the thing, so none can be collected from the analogy of nature, because we cannot trace any living beings beyond death. But as we are conscious that we are endued with capacities of perception and of action, and are living persons; what we are to go upon is, that we shall continue so till we foresee some accident or event, which will endanger those capacities, or be likely to destroy us, which death does in nowise appear to be.

And thus, when we go out of this world, we may pass into new scenes, and a new state of life and action, just as naturally as we came into the present. And this new state may naturally be a social one. And the advantages of it, advantages of every kind, may naturally be bestowed, according to some fixed general laws of wisdom, upon every one in proportion to the degrees of his virtue. And though the advantages of that future natural state should not be bestowed, as those of the present in some measure are, by the will of the society, but entirely by his more immediate action, upon whom the whole frame of nature depends; yet this distribution may be just as natural, as their being distributed here by the instrumentality of men. And, indeed, though one were to allow any confused undetermined sense, which people please to put upon the word *natural*, it would be a shortness of thought scarce credible, to imagine that no system or course of things can be so, but only what we see at present[1]: especially whilst the probability of a future life, or the natural immortality of the soul, is admitted upon the evidence of reason; because this is really both admitting and denying at once a state of being different from the present to be natural. But the only distinct meaning of that word is, *stated*, *fixed*, or *settled;* since what is natural as much requires and presupposes an intelligent agent to render it so, *i. e.*, to effect it continually, or at stated times, as what is supernatural or miraculous does to effect it for once. And from hence it must follow, that persons' notion of what is natural will be enlarged in proportion to their greater knowledge of the works of God, and the dispensations of his Providence. Nor is there any absurdity in supposing that

[1] See Part II. chap. ii. and Part II. chap. iv.

there may be beings in the universe, whose capacities, and knowledge, and views, may be so extensive, as that the whole Christian dispensation may to them appear natural, *i. e.*, analogous or conformable to God's dealings with other parts of his creation ; as natural as the visible known course of things appears to us. For there seems scarce any other possible sense to be put upon the word, but that only in which it is here used ; similar, stated, or uniform.

This credibility of a future life, which has been here insisted upon, how little soever it may satisfy our curiosity, seems to answer all the purposes of religion in like manner as a demonstrative proof would. Indeed a proof, even a demonstrative one, of a future life, would not be a proof of religion. For that we are to live hereafter is just as reconcilable with the scheme of atheism, and as well to be accounted for by it, as that we are now alive is ; and therefore nothing can be more absurd than to argue from that scheme, that there can be no future state. But as religion implies a future state, any presumption against such a state is a presumption against religion. And the foregoing observations remove all presumptions of that sort, and prove, to a very considerable degree of probability, one fundamental doctrine of religion, which, if believed, would greatly open and dispose the mind seriously to attend to the general evidence of the whole.

## CHAPTER II.

### OF THE GOVERNMENT OF GOD BY REWARDS AND PUNISHMENTS; AND PARTICULARLY OF THE LATTER.

THAT which makes the question concerning a future life to be of so great importance to us, is our capacity of happiness and misery. And that which makes the consideration of it to be of so great importance to us, is the supposition of our happiness and misery hereafter depending upon our actions here. Without this, indeed, curiosity could not but sometimes bring a subject, in which we may be so highly interested, to our thoughts, especially upon the mortality of others, or the near prospect of our own. But reasonable men would not take any further thought about hereafter, than what should happen thus occasionally to rise in their

minds, if it were certain that our future interest no way depended upon our present behaviour [1]; whereas, on the contrary, if there be ground, either from analogy or anything
else, to think it does, then there is reason also for the most
active thought and solicitude, to secure that interest, to behave so as that we may escape that misery, and obtain that
happiness in another life, which we not only suppose ourselves capable of, but which we apprehend also is put in
our own power.    And whether there be ground for this last
apprehension certainly would deserve to be most seriously
considered, were there no other proof of a future life and
interest than that presumptive one, which the foregoing
observations amount to [2].

Now in the present state, all which we enjoy, and a great
part of what we suffer, *is put in our own power.*  For pleasure
and pain are the consequences of our actions, and we are
endued by the Author of our nature with capacities of foreseeing these consequences.   We find by experience he does
not so much as preserve our lives, exclusively of our own care
and attention, to provide ourselves with, and to make use of,
that sustenance, by which he has appointed our lives shall
be preserved, and without which he has appointed they shall
not be preserved at all.   And in general we foresee that the
external things, which are the objects of our various passions,
can neither be obtained nor enjoyed, without exerting ourselves in such and such manners ; but by thus exerting
ourselves we obtain and enjoy these objects, in which our
natural good consists, or by this means God gives us the
possession and enjoyment of them.   I know not that we
have any one kind or degree of enjoyment, but by the means
of our own actions.   And by prudence and care we may, for
the most part, pass our days in tolerable ease and quiet; or,

[1] Butler means to assert, in conformity with the principle laid down in the
introduction as to the necessity of our balancing chances in cases of uncertainty, and taking what, upon the whole, appears to be the safer course, that
unless we could be quite sure that our future happiness does *not* depend upon
our conduct here, we are bound, as reasonable beings, to act as if it did so
depend, and to endeavour by a good life to secure an interest in eternity.—*Ed.*

[2] While, on the one hand, more than casual thought about a future state
would be unreasonable, if it could be proved that there is no connection
between our conduct and our happiness there, on the other, there is cause for
the most active thought concerning our behaviour in this world, if it can be
shown to be probable, in ever so slight a degree, that such is the case.—(*D.*)

on the contrary, we may, by rashness, ungoverned passion, wilfulness, or even by negligence, make ourselves as miserable as ever we please. And many do please to make themselves extremely miserable, *i. e.*, to do what they know beforehand will render them so. They follow those ways, the fruit of which they know, by instruction, example, experience, will be disgrace, and poverty, and sickness, and untimely death. This every one observes to be the general course of things, though it is to be allowed, we cannot find by experience that all our sufferings are owing to our own follies.

Why the Author of Nature does not give his creatures promiscuously such and such perceptions without regard to their behaviour, why he does not make them happy without the instrumentality of their own actions, and prevent their bringing any sufferings upon themselves, is another matter. Perhaps there may be some impossibilities in the nature of things which we are unacquainted with[1]. Or less happiness, it may be, would upon the whole be produced by such a method of conduct than is by the present[2]. Or, perhaps, divine goodness, with which, if I mistake not, we make very free in our speculations, may not be a bare single disposition to produce happiness, but a disposition to make the good, the faithful, the honest man happy. Perhaps an infinitely perfect Mind may be pleased with seeing his creatures behave suitably to the nature which he has given them, to the relations which he has placed them in to each other, and to that which they stand in to himself; that relation to himself, which, during their existence, is even necessary, and which is the most important one of all : perhaps, I say, an infinitely perfect Mind may be pleased with this moral piety of moral agents in and for itself, as well as upon account of its being essentially conducive to the happiness of his creation. Or the whole end, for which God made, and

---

[1] Part I. chap. vii.

[2] As in the physical world, much that appears rough and rugged, when viewed closely, becomes smooth and level at a more distant glance, or viewed in a more comprehensive light, just so partial evil may be, and probably is, in some way or other, subservient to universal good. It will be observed that Butler is very fond of this argument, which is nearly identical with that which he so often alleges as the ground of his conclusions, viz., the ignorance of man as to the things around him, when viewed as a whole. Here "we see in part." (1 Cor. xiii. 9.)—*Ed.*

thus governs the world, may be utterly beyond the reach of our faculties; there may be somewhat in it as impossible for us to have any conception of as for a blind man to have a conception of colours. But however this be, it is certain matter of universal experience that the general method of Divine administration is forewarning us, or giving us capacities to foresee, with more or less clearness, that if we act so and so, we shall have such enjoyments, if so and so, such sufferings, and giving us those enjoyments, and making us feel those sufferings, in consequence of our actions.

"But all this is to be ascribed to the general course of nature." True. This is the very thing which I am observing. It is to be ascribed to the general course of nature; *i. e.*, not surely to the words or ideas *course of nature*, but to him who appointed it and put things into it, or to a course of operation from its uniformity or constancy called natural [1], and which necessarily implies an operating agent. For when men find themselves necessitated to confess an Author of Nature, or that God is the natural governor of the world, they must not deny this again, because his government is uniform; they must not deny that he does things at all, because he does them constantly, because the effects of his acting are permanent, whether his acting be so or not, though there is no reason to think it is not [2]. In short every man in everything he does, naturally acts upon the forethought and apprehension of avoiding evil or obtaining good; and if the natural course of things be the appointment of God, and our natural faculties of knowledge and experience are given us by him, then the good and bad consequences which follow our actions are his appointment, and our foresight of those consequences is a warning given us by him how we are to act [3].

[1] Pages 97, 98.

[2] God being admitted as the Author of nature, we can prove demonstratively that these results are to be ascribed to his agency. For the particular is contained in the universal; and if the *whole* course of nature be from God, then this one *particular* course of things, namely, the consequences of our actions, must be from God also.—(*D.*)

[3] If the "*general* course of nature" be God's appointment, and *all* our natural faculties of knowledge his gift, then are these consequences his appointment, and our foresight of them his gift; for the particular, in either case, comes under the universal; and this foresight, moreover, was intended for a warning as to action, and for an inducement thereto.—(*W.*)

"Is the pleasure, then, naturally accompanying every particular gratification of passion, intended to put us upon gratifying ourselves in every such particular instance, and as a reward to us for so doing?" No, certainly. Nor is it to be said that our eyes were naturally intended to give us the sight of each particular object to which they do or can extend, objects which are destructive of them, or which for any other reason it may become us to turn our eyes from. Yet there is no doubt but that our eyes were intended for us to see with. So neither is there any doubt, but that the foreseen pleasures and pains belonging to the passions were intended in general to induce mankind to act in such and such manners.

Now from this general observation, obvious to every one, that God has given us to understand he has appointed satisfaction and delight to be the consequence of our acting in one manner, and pain and uneasiness of our acting in another, and of our not acting at all; and that we find the consequences, which we were beforehand informed of, uniformly to follow, we may learn that we are at present actually under his government in the strictest and most proper sense, in such a sense as that he rewards and punishes us for our actions [1]. An Author of Nature being supposed, it is not so much a deduction of reason as a matter of experience, that we are thus under his government; under his government in the same sense as we are under the government of civil magistrates. Because the annexing pleasure to some actions and pain to others, in our power to do or forbear, and giving notice of this appointment beforehand to those whom it concerns, is the proper formal notion of government. Whether the pleasure or pain which thus follows upon our behaviour be owing to the Author of Nature's acting upon us every moment which we feel it, or to his having at once contrived and executed his own part in the plan of the world, makes no alteration as to the matter before us. For if civil magistrates could make the sanctions of their laws take place without interposing at all, after they had passed them, with-

[1] From the experienced fact that happiness and misery are appointed by God to depend upon our own conduct in a certain uniform and foreseen order of consequences, we proceed to argue that we are at present actually under God's government, in that most strict and proper sense which implies rewards and punishments for our conduct.—(W.)

out a trial, and the formalities of an execution; if they were able to make their laws execute themselves, or every offender to execute them upon himself, we should be just in the same sense under their government then as we are now, but in a much higher degree and more perfect manner Vain is the ridicule with which one foresees some persons will divert themselves upon finding lesser pains considered as instances of divine punishment. There is no possibility of answering or evading the general thing here intended, without denying all final causes. For final causes being admitted, the pleasures and pains now mentioned must be admitted, too, as instances of them. And if they are, if God annexes delight to some actions and uneasiness to others, with an apparent design to induce us to act so and so, then he not only dispenses happiness and misery, but also rewards and punishes actions. If, for example, the pain which we feel, upon doing what tends to the destruction of our bodies, suppose upon too near approaches to fire, or upon wounding ourselves, be appointed by the Author of Nature to prevent our doing what thus tends to our destruction; this is altogether as much an instance of his punishing our actions, and consequently of our being under his government, as declaring by a voice from heaven, that if we acted so, he would inflict such pain upon us, and inflicting it, whether it be greater or less.

Thus we find, that the true notion or conception of the Author of Nature is that of a master or governor, prior to the consideration of his moral attributes. The fact of our case, which we find by experience, is, that he actually exercises dominion or government over us at present by rewarding and punishing us for our actions, in as strict and proper a sense of these words, and even in the same sense, as children, servants, subjects, are rewarded and punished by those who govern them[1].

And thus the whole analogy of Nature, the whole present course of things, most fully shows that there is nothing in-

[1] The sum of the argument is to this effect:—In this natural course of things we find the true conception of its Author, prior to any consideration of his moral attributes, to be the less a *governor*; that, as a fact, his government over us is being now carried on by means of rewards and punishments; and that, therefore, it is in no sort incredible that he will show himself in the same character and carry on a similar government in a future state of things.—(*D.*)

credible in the general doctrine of religion, that God will reward and punish men for their actions hereafter; nothing incredible, I mean, arising out of the notion of rewarding and punishing. For the whole course of nature is a present instance of his exercising that government over us, which implies in it rewarding and punishing [1].

But, as divine punishment is what men chiefly object against, and are most unwilling to allow, it may be proper to mention some circumstances in the natural course of punishments at present, which are analogous to what religion teaches us concerning a future state of punishment; indeed, so analogous, that as they add a further credibility to it, so they cannot but raise a most serious apprehension of it in those who will attend to them.

It has been now observed, that such and such miseries naturally follow such and such actions of imprudence and wilfulness, as well as actions more commonly and more distinctly considered as vicious; and that these consequences, when they may be foreseen, are properly natural punishments annexed to such actions. For the general thing here insisted upon is, not that we see a great deal of misery in the world, but a great deal which men bring upon themselves by their own behaviour, which they might have foreseen and avoided. Now the circumstances of these natural punishments, particularly deserving our attention, are such as these: —that oftentimes they follow, or are inflicted in consequence of, actions which procure many present advantages, and are accompanied with much present pleasure; for instance, sickness and untimely death are the consequence of intemperance, though accompanied with the highest mirth and jollity; that these punishments are often much greater than the advantages or pleasures obtained by the actions, of which they are the punishments or consequences; that though we may imagine a constitution of nature, in which these natural punishments, which are, in fact, to follow, would follow immediately upon such actions being done, or very soon after; we find, on the contrary, in our world, that they are often

---

[1] The eternity of Divine punishments is one of those doctrines which are most extensively assailed in the present day. The eternity of punishments and of rewards, however, must stand or fall together; and when the former comes to be denied, it will not be long before the latter is disputed also.—*Ed.*

delayed a great while, sometimes even till long after the actions occasioning them are forgot; so that the constitution of nature is such, that delay of punishment is no sort nor degree of presumption of final impunity; that after such delay these natural punishments or miseries often come, not by degrees, but suddenly, with violence, and at once; however, the chief misery often does; that as certainty of such distant misery following such actions is never afforded persons; so, perhaps, during the actions, they have seldom a distinct full expectation of its following[1]; and many times the case is only thus—that they see in general, or may see, the credibility, that intemperance, suppose, will bring after it diseases, civil crimes, civil punishments; when yet the real probability often is, that they shall escape; but things notwithstanding take their destined course, and the misery inevitably follows at its appointed time, in very many of these cases. Thus, also, though youth may be alleged as an excuse for rashness and folly, as being naturally thoughtless, and not clearly foreseeing all the consequences of being untractable and profligate, this does not hinder, but that these consequences follow, and are grievously felt throughout the whole course of mature life. Habits contracted even in that age are often utter ruin; and men's success in the world, not only in the common sense of worldly success, but their real happiness and misery, depends, in a great degree, and in various ways, upon the manner in which they pass their youth, which consequences they for the most part neglect to consider, and perhaps seldom can properly be said to believe, beforehand. It requires also to be mentioned, that in numberless cases the natural course of things affords us opportunities for procuring advantages to ourselves at certain times, which we cannot procure when we will, nor ever recall the opportunities if we have neglected them. Indeed the general course of nature is an example of this. If during the opportunity of youth, persons are indocile and self-willed, they inevitably suffer in their future life for want of those acquirements, which they neglected the natural season of attaining. If the husbandman lets his seedtime pass without sowing, the whole year is lost to him beyond recovery. In like manner, though after men have been guilty of folly and extravagance *up to a certain degree*, it is often in

[1] See Part II. chap vi.

their power, for instance, to retrieve their affairs, to recover
their health and character, at least in good measure; yet
real reformation is in many cases of no avail at all towards
preventing the miseries, poverty, sickness, infamy, naturally
annexed to folly and extravagance *exceeding that degree*.
There is a certain bound to imprudence and misbehaviour,
which, being transgressed, there remains no place for repentance in the natural course of things.    It is further very
much to be remarked, that neglects from inconsiderateness,
want of attention[1], not looking about us to see what we
have to do, are often attended with consequences altogether
as dreadful as any active misbehaviour, from the most extravagant passion.   And, lastly, civil government being natural,
the punishments of it are so too; and some of these punishments are capital, as the effects of a dissolute course of pleasure are often mortal.   So that many natural punishments
are final[2] to him who incurs them, if considered only in his
temporal capacity; and seem inflicted by natural appointment, either to remove the offender out of the way of being
further mischievous, or as an example, though frequently a
disregarded one, to those who are left behind.

These things are not what we call accidental, or to be
met with only now and then; but they are things of every
day's experience: they proceed from general laws, very gene

[1] Part II. chap. vi.

[2] The general consideration of a future state of panishment, most evidently
belongs to the subject of natural Religion.   But if any of these reflections
should be thought to relate more peculiarly to this doctrine, as taught in
Scripture, the reader is desired to observe, that Gentile writers, both moralists
and poets, speak of the future punishment of the wicked, both as to the
duration and degree of it, in a like manner of expression and of description,
as the Scripture does.   So that all which can positively be asserted to be
matter of mere Revelation, with regard to this doctrine, seems to be, that
the great distinction between the righteous and the wicked, shall be made at
the end of this world; that each shall *then* receive according to his deserts.
Reason did, as it well might, conclude that it should, finally and upon the
whole, be well with the righteous, and ill with the wicked; but it could not
be determined upon any principles of reason, whether human creatures might
not have been appointed to pass through other states of life and being, before
that distributive justice should finally and effectually take place.   Revelation
teaches us, that the next state of things after the present is appointed for
the execution of this justice; that it shall be no longer delayed; but *the
mystery of God*, the great mystery of his suffering vice and confusion to prevail, *shall then be finished;* and he will *take to him his great power, and will
reign* by rendering to every one according to his works.

ral ones, by which God governs the world in the natural course of his providence. And they are so analogous to what Religion teaches us concerning the future punishment of the wicked, so much of a piece with it, that both would naturally be expressed in the very same words, and manner of description. In the book of *Proverbs*[1], for instance, Wisdom is introduced as frequenting the most public places of resort, and as rejected when she offers herself as the natural appointed guide of human life. *How long*, speaking to those who are passing through it, *how long, ye simple ones, will ye love folly, and the scorners delight in their scorning, and fools hate knowledge? Turn ye at my reproof. Behold, I will pour out my spirit upon you, I will make known my words unto you.* But upon being neglected, *Because I have called, and ye refused, I have stretched out my hand, and no man regarded; but ye have set at nought all my counsel, and would none of my reproof: I also will laugh at your calamity, I will mock when your fear cometh; when your fear cometh as desolation, and your destruction cometh as a whirlwind; when distress and anguish cometh upon you. Then shall they call upon me, but I will not answer; they shall seek me early, but they shall not find me.* This passage every one sees is poetical, and some parts of it are highly figurative; but their meaning is obvious. And the thing intended is expressed more literally in the following words: *For that they hated knowledge, and did not choose the fear of the Lord—therefore shall they eat of the fruit of their own way, and be filled with their own devices. For the security of the simple shall slay them, and the prosperity of fools shall destroy them.* And the whole passage is so equally applicable to what we experience in the present world concerning the consequences of men's actions, and to what Religion teaches us is to be expected in another, that it may be questioned which of the two was principally intended.

Indeed, when one has been recollecting the proper proofs of a future state of rewards and punishments, nothing methinks can give one so sensible an apprehension of the latter, or representation of it to the mind; as observing, that after the many disregarded checks, admonitions, and warnings, which people meet with in the ways of vice and folly and extravagance; warnings from their very nature; from the examples of others; from the lesser inconveniences

[1] Chap. i.

which they bring upon themselves; from the instructions of
wise and virtuous men : after these have been long despised,
scorned, ridiculed; after the chief bad consequences, temporal consequences, of their follies have been delayed for a
great while; at length they break in irresistibly like an
armed force; repentance is too late to relieve, and can serve
only to aggravate their distress, the case has become despe-
rate, and poverty and sickness, remorse and anguish, infamy and death, the effects of their own doings, overwhelm
them beyond possibility of remedy or escape.  This is an
account of what is in fact the general constitution of
nature [1].

It is not in any sort meant that, according to what appears at present of the natural course of things, men are
always uniformly punished in proportion to their misbehaviour; but that there are very many instances of misbehaviour punished in the several ways now mentioned, and
very dreadful instances too, sufficient to show what the laws
of the universe may admit; and, if thoroughly considered,
sufficient fully to answer all objections against the credibility of a future state of punishments, from any imaginations, that the frailty of our nature and external temptations almost annihilate the guilt of human vices, as well as
objections of another sort, from necessity [2], from suppositions
that the will of an infinite Being cannot be contradicted, or
that he must be incapable of offence and provocation [3].

Reflections of this kind are not without their terrors to
serious persons, the most free from enthusiasm, and of the
greatest strength of mind; but it is fit things be stated and
considered as they really are.  And there is, in the present
age, a certain fearlessness with regard to what may be hereafter under the government of God, which nothing but an
universally acknowledged demonstration on the side of

---

[1] Hence may be deduced experimental answers to many popular objections and excuses; as, that God is *too merciful* to inflict eternal punishment;
that we were *sincere* in our intentions; that we *did not know* it was a sin
which we were committing, &c.  Our misery, like our neglect, is self-
induced.—(*H.*)

[2] That is, as is more fully explained in chap. vi., the supposition that men
are compelled by necessity to sin : a doctrine which, by destroying the doctrine
of free will, overthrows all notions of moral responsibility, saps the founda-
tions of morality and virtue, and destroys God's attribute of justice.

[3] See Chap. iv. and vi.

atheism can justify, and which makes it quite necessary that men be reminded, and if possible, made to feel, that there is no sort of ground for being thus presumptuous, even upon the most sceptical principles. For, may it not be said of any person upon his being born into the world, he may behave so as to be of no service to it, but by being made an example of the woful effects of vice and folly? That he may, as any one may, if he will, incur an infamous execution from the hands of civil justice; or in some other course of extravagance shorten his days; or bring upon himself infamy and diseases worse than death? So that it had been better for him, even with regard to the present world, that he had never been born. And is there any pretence of reason, for people to think themselves secure, and talk as if they had certain proof that, let them act as licentiously as they will, there can be nothing analogous to this, with regard to a future and more general interest, under the providence and government of the same God?

## CHAPTER III[1].

### OF THE MORAL GOVERNMENT OF GOD.

As the manifold appearances of design and of final causes, in the constitution of the world, prove it to be the work of an intelligent Mind; so the particular final causes of pleasure and pain distributed amongst his creatures prove that they are under his government; what may be called his natural government of creatures endued with sense and reason. This, however, implies somewhat more than seems usually attended to, when we speak of God's natural government of the world. It implies government of the very same kind with that which a master exercises over his servants, or a civil magistrate over his subjects. These latter instances of final causes as really prove an intelligent *Governor* of the world, in the sense now mentioned, and before[2] distinctly

---

[1] The subject is thus introduced. From the particular final causes of happiness and misery, it has been argued in the last chapter that we are actually under God's government, under what may be called his *natural* government. But the *moral* character of this government has not been, as yet, directly determined. As then, in the last chapter, the fact of God's *natural* government was proved, so in this is the fact of his *moral* government established.—(*W.*)

[2] Chap. ii.

treated of, as any other instances of final causes prove an intelligent *Maker* of it.

But this alone does not appear, at first sight, to determine anything certainly, concerning the moral character of the Author of Nature, considered in this relation of governor; does not ascertain his government to be moral, or prove that he is the righteous judge of the world. Moral government consists not barely in rewarding and punishing men for their actions, which the most tyrannical person may do, but in rewarding the righteous, and punishing the wicked—in rendering to men according to their actions, considered as good or evil. And the perfection of moral government consists in doing this, with regard to all intelligent creatures, in an exact proportion to their personal merits or demerits.

Some men seem to think the only character of the Author of Nature to be that of simple absolute benevolence[1]. This, considered as a principle of action and infinite in degree, is a disposition to produce the greatest possible happiness, without regard to persons' behaviour, otherwise than as such regard would produce higher degrees of it. And supposing this to be the only character of God, veracity and justice in him would be nothing but benevolence conducted by wisdom. Now, surely this ought not to be asserted, unless it can be proved, for we should speak with cautious reverence upon such a subject. And whether it can be proved or no, is not the thing here to be inquired into; but whether in the constitution and conduct of the world, a righteous government be not discernibly planned out, which necessarily implies a righteous governor. There may possibly be in the creation beings, to whom the Author of Nature manifests himself under this most amiable of all characters, this of infinite absolute benevolence, for it is the most amiable, supposing it not, as perhaps it is not, incompatible with justice; but he manifests himself to us under the character

---

[1] This objection may be examined by tracing it into its consequences. Simple absolute benevolence implies a disregard of moral character; but truth and justice imply a regard of moral character; it would follow, then, that these two qualities could not exist in the same subject. But may there not be a point above our sight in which both simple benevolence and simple justice meet together? There may be beings towards whom God shows simple benevolence; nay, in the sense explained a little below, he *may* exercise simple and absolute benevolence even towards us.—*Ed.*

of a righteous governor.  He may, consistently with this
be simply and absolutely benevolent in the sense now explained; but he is (for he has given us a proof in the constitution and conduct of the world that he is) a governor over
servants, as he rewards and punishes us for our actions.
And in the constitution and conduct of it he may also have
given, besides the reason of the thing, and the natural presages of conscience, clear and distinct intimations that his
government is righteous or moral; clear to such as think
the nature of it deserving their attention; and yet not to
every careless person who casts a transient reflection upon
the subject[1].

But it is particularly to be observed, that the divine government, which we experience ourselves under in the
present state, taken alone, is allowed not to be the perfection of moral government[2].  And yet this by no means
hinders, but that there may be somewhat, be it more or
less, truly moral in it.  A righteous government may plainly
appear to be carried on to some degree; enough to give us
the apprehension that it shall be completed, or carried on to
that degree of perfection which religion teaches us it shall :
but which cannot appear, till much more of the divine administration be seen, than can in the present life.  And the
design of this chapter is to inquire how far this is the case:
how far, over and above the moral nature[3] which God has
given us, and our natural notion of him as righteous governor of those his creatures, to whom he has given this
nature[4]; I say how far besides this, the principles and be-

---

[1] The objections against religion, from the evidence of it not being universal, nor so strong as might possibly have been, may be urged against
natural religion, as well as against revealed.  And therefore the consideration of them belongs to the first part of this Treatise, as well as the second.
But as these objections are chiefly urged against revealed religion, I choose
to consider them in the second part.  And the answer to them there, Chap.
vi., as urged against Christianity, being almost equally applicable to them as
urged against the Religion of Nature, to avoid repetition, the reader is referred to that chapter.

[2] This expression is, perhaps, liable to be misunderstood.  It does not, of
course, mean to assert that there is any error or defect in God's moral government, but only that, owing to the partial view which alone we can obtain
on earth of a system so great and comprehensive, it seems to us, as it were,
imperfect and unfinished.—*Ed.*

[3] Dissertation II.

[4] Chap. vi.

ginnings of a moral government over the world may be discerned, notwithstanding and amidst all the confusion and disorder of it.

Now one might mention here[1], what has been often urged with great force, that, in general, less uneasiness and more satisfaction, are the natural consequences[2] of a virtuous than of a vicious course of life, in the present state, as an instance of a moral government established in nature; an instance of it collected from experience and present matter of fact. But it must be owned a thing of difficulty to weigh and balance pleasures and uneasinesses, each amongst themselves, and also against each other, so as to make an estimate with any exactness, of the overplus of happiness on the side of virtue. And it is not impossible, that, amidst the infinite disorders of the world, there may be exceptions to the happiness of virtue; even with regard to those persons whose course of life from their youth up has been blameless; and more with regard to those who have gone on for some time in the ways of vice, and have afterwards reformed. For suppose an instance of the latter case; a person with his passions inflamed, his natural faculty of self-government impaired by habits of indulgence, and with all his vices about him, like so many harpies, craving for their accustomed gratification : who can say how long it might be before such a person would find more satisfaction in the reasonableness and present good consequences of virtue, than difficulties and self-denial in the restraints of it? Experience also shows, that men can, to a great degree, get over their sense of shame, so as that by professing themselves to be without principle, and avowing even direct villany, they can support themselves against the infamy of it. But as the ill actions of any one will probably be more talked of, and oftener thrown in his way, upon his reformation; so the infamy of them will be much more felt, after the natural sense of virtue and of honour is recovered. Uneasinesses of this kind ought indeed to be put to the account of former vices; yet it will be said they are in part

---

[1] The popular argument to the effect that more satisfaction, on the whole, results from virtue than from vice, is here examined; and Butler rejects it as not accurate enough for this treatise. It is difficult to strike an accurate balance in such matters.—(D.)

[2] See Lord Shaftesbury's Inquiry concerning Virtue, Part II.

the consequences of reformation. Still I am far from allowing it doubtful, whether virtue, upon the whole, be happier than vice in the present world. But if it were, yet the beginnings of a righteous administration may, beyond all question, be found in nature, if we will attentively inquire after them. And,

I. In whatever manner the notion of God's moral government over the world might be treated, if it did not appear, whether he were in a proper sense our governor at all; yet when it is certain matter of experience, that he does manifest himself to us under the character of a governor in the sense explained[1]; it must deserve to be considered, whether there be not reason to apprehend, that he may be a righteous or moral governor. Since it appears to be fact, that God does govern mankind by the method of rewards and punishments, according to some settled rules of distribution; it is surely a question to be asked, what presumption is there against his finally rewarding and punishing them according to this particular rule, namely, as they act reasonably or unreasonably, virtuously or viciously? since rendering men happy or miserable by this rule certainly falls in, much more falls in, with our natural apprehensions and sense of things, than doing so by any other rule whatever; since rewarding and punishing actions by any other rule would appear much harder to be accounted for, by minds formed as he has formed ours. Be the evidence of religion then more or less clear, the expectation which it raises in us, that the righteous shall, upon the whole, be happy, and the wicked miserable, cannot however possibly be considered as absurd or chimerical; because it is no more than an expectation, that a method of government already begun shall be carried on, the method of rewarding and punishing actions; and shall be carried on by a particular rule, which unavoidably appears to us at first sight more natural than any other, the rule which we call distributive justice. Nor,

II. Ought it to be entirely passed over, that tranquillity, satisfaction, and external advantages, being the natural consequences of prudent management of ourselves, and our affairs; and rashness, profligate negligence, and wilful folly, bringing after them many inconveniences and sufferings; these afford instances of a right constitution of na-

[1] Chap. ii.

ture[1]: as the correction of children, for their own sakes,
and by way of example, when they run into danger or hurt
themselves, is a part of right education. And thus, that
God governs the world by general fixed laws, that he has
endued us with capacities of reflecting upon this constitution of things, and foreseeing the good and bad consequences of our behaviour, plainly implies some sort of
moral government; since from such a constitution of things
it cannot but follow, that prudence and imprudence, which
are of the nature of virtue and vice[2], must be, as they are,
respectively rewarded and punished[3].

III. From the natural course of things, vicious actions
are, to a great degree, actually punished as mischievous to
society; and besides punishment actually inflicted upon this
account, there is also the fear and apprehension of it in
those persons, whose crimes have rendered them obnoxious
to it in case of a discovery; this state of fear being itself
often a very considerable punishment. The natural fear
and apprehension of it, too, which restrains from such
crimes, is a declaration of nature against them. It is necessary to the very being of society, that vices, destructive of it,
should be punished *as being so;* the vices of falsehood, injustice, cruelty: which punishment therefore is as natural as
society; and so is an instance of a kind of moral government, naturally established, and actually taking place. And,
since the certain natural course of things is the conduct of
Providence or the government of God, though carried on by
the instrumentality of men; the observation here made
amounts to this, that mankind find themselves placed by
him in such circumstances, as that they are unavoidably
accountable for their behaviour, and are often punished,
and sometimes rewarded, under his government, in the
view of their being mischievous, or eminently beneficial to
society.

If it be objected that good actions, and such as are benefi-

---

[1] It is observed, by way of illustration, that the moral education of
children includes, as one of its subordinate parts, the punishing of them if
they run into danger or hurt themselves through carelessness.—(*D.*)

[2] See Dissertation II.

[3] The argument may be stated in a different form: "A moral constitution
of things being supposed to exist in the world, we should expect the consequences of prudence and imprudence above-mentioned to be found there; and
they are found among us."—(*D.*)

cial to society, are often punished, as in the case of persecu-
tion and in other cases, and that ill and mischievous actions are often rewarded, it may be answered distinctly:
first, that this is in no sort necessary, and consequently not
natural, in the sense in which it is necessary, and therefore
natural, that ill or mischievous actions should be punished;
and in the next place, that good actions are never punished,
considered as beneficial to society, nor ill actions rewarded,
under the view of their being hurtful to it.   So that it
stands good, without anything on the side of vice to be set
over against it, that the Author of Nature has as truly directed that vicious actions, considered as mischievous to
society, should be punished, and put mankind under a necessity of thus punishing them, as he has directed and
necessitated us to preserve our lives by food.

IV. In the natural course of things virtue *as such* is actually rewarded, and vice *as such* punished[1]; which seems to
afford an instance or example, not only of government, but
of moral government begun and established, moral in the
strictest sense, though not in that perfection of degree which
religion teaches us to expect.   In order to see this more
clearly, we must distinguish between actions themselves,
and that quality ascribed to them which we call virtuous
or vicious.   The gratification itself of every natural passion
must be attended with delight; and acquisitions of fortune,
however made, are acquisitions of the means or materials of
enjoyment.   An action, then, by which any natural passion
is gratified or fortune acquired, procures delight or advantage,
abstracted from all consideration of the morality of such
action.   Consequently, the pleasure or advantage in this
case is gained by the action itself, not by the morality, the
virtuousness or viciousness of it, though it be, perhaps, virtuous or vicious.   Thus, to say such an action or course of
behaviour procured such pleasure or advantage, or brought
on such inconvenience and pain, is quite a different thing
from saying that such good or bad effect was owing to the
virtue or vice of such action or behaviour.   In one case, an
action abstracted from all moral consideration produced its
effect; in the other case, for it will appear that there are
such cases, the morality of the action under a moral con-

[1] In other words, virtue is rewarded for its virtuousness, and vice punished
for its viciousness.—*Ed.*

sideration, *i. e.*, the virtuousness or viciousness of it, produced the effect. Now I say virtue as such, naturally procures considerable advantages to the virtuous, and vice as such naturally occasions great inconvenience, and even misery to the vicious, in very many instances. The immediate effects of virtue and vice upon the mind and temper are to be mentioned as instances of it. Vice as such is naturally attended with some sort of uneasiness, and, not uncommonly, with great disturbance and apprehension. That inward feeling[1] which, respecting lesser matters and in familiar speech, we call being vexed with oneself, and in matters of importance, and in more serious language, remorse, is an uneasiness naturally arising from an action of a man's own, reflected upon by himself as wrong, unreasonable, faulty, *i. e.*, vicious in greater or less degree; and this manifestly is a different feeling from that uneasiness which arises from a sense of mere loss or harm. What is more common than to hear a man lamenting an accident or event, and adding—— but, however, he has the satisfaction that he cannot blame himself for it; or, on the contrary, that he has the uneasiness of being sensible it was his own doing? Thus, also, the disturbance and fear which often follow upon a man's having done an injury arise from a sense of his being blameworthy, otherwise there would in many cases be no ground of disturbance, nor any reason to fear resentment or shame. On the other hand, inward security and peace, and a mind open to the several gratifications of life, are the natural attendants of innocence and virtue. To which must be added, the complacency, satisfaction, and even joy of heart, which accompany the exercise, the real exercise, of gratitude, friendship, benevolence.

And here, I think, ought to be mentioned the fears of future punishment, and peaceful hopes of a better life, in those who fully believe or have any serious apprehension of religion; because these hopes and fears are present uneasiness and satisfaction to the mind, and cannot be got

---

[1] That we have an approving and disapproving faculty of this kind, is evident from our own experience—from the words right and wrong, odious and amiable, base and worthy, with many others of like signification in all languages, applied to actions and characters—from the many written systems of morals which suppose it—from our natural sense of gratitude, which implies a distinction between merely being the instrument of good and intending it, &c.—(*H.*) See *Butler on the Nature of Virtue,* Dis. ii. 2.

rid of by great part of the world, even by men who have thought most thoroughly upon that subject of religion. And no one can say how considerable this uneasiness and satisfaction may be, or what upon the whole it may amount to.

In the next place comes in the consideration, that all honest and good men are disposed to befriend honest good men as such, and to discountenance the vicious as such, and do so in some degree, indeed in a considerable degree; from which favour and discouragement cannot but arise considerable advantage and inconvenience. And though the generality of the world have little regard to the morality of their own actions, and may be supposed to have less to that of others, when they themselves are not concerned; yet let any one be known to be a man of virtue, somehow or other he will be favoured, and good offices will be done him, from regard to his character, without remote views, occasionally, and in some low degree, I think, by the generality of the world, as it happens to come in their way. Public honours, too, and advantages are the natural consequences, are sometimes at least the consequences, in fact, of virtuous actions, of eminent justice, fidelity, charity, love to our country, considered in the view of being virtuous. And sometimes even death itself, often infamy and external inconveniences, are the public consequences of vice as vice. For instance, the sense which mankind have of tyranny, injustice, oppression, additional to the mere feeling or fear of misery, has doubtless been instrumental in bringing about revolutions, which make a figure even in the history of the world. For it is plain, men resent injuries as implying faultiness, and retaliate, not merely under the notion of having received harm, but of having received wrong; and they have this resentment in behalf of others, as well as of themselves. So likewise even the generality are, in some degree, grateful, and disposed to return good offices, not merely because such a one has been the occasion of good to them, but under the view that such good offices implied kind intention and good desert in the doer. To all this may be added two or three particular things, which many persons will think frivolous; but to me nothing appears so which at all comes in towards determining a question of such importance, as whether there be or be not a moral institution of government, in the strictest sense moral *visibly* established and begun in nature. The particular things are these: that in domestic government, which is doubtless natural, children and others also are very generally punished for falsehood and injustice, and ill-behaviour as such, and rewarded for the contrary; which are instances where veracity and justice and right behaviour *as such* are *naturally* enforced by rewards and punishments, whether more or less considerable in degree: that, though civil government be supposed to take cognizance of actions in no other view than as prejudicial to society, without respect to the immorality of them, yet as such actions are immoral, so the sense which men have of the immorality of them very greatly contributes in different ways to bring offenders to justice: and that entire absence of all crime and guilt in the moral sense, when plainly appearing, will almost of course procure, and circumstances of aggravated guilt prevent, a remission of the penalties annexed to civil crimes, in many cases, though by no means in all.

Upon the whole, then, besides the good and bad effects of virtue and vice upon men's own minds, the course of the world does in some measure turn upon the approbation and disapprobation of them as such, in others. The sense of well and ill doing[1], the presages of conscience, the love of good characters and dislike of bad ones, honour, shame, resentment, gratitude; all these considered in themselves, and in their effects, do afford manifest real instances of virtue as such naturally favoured, and of vice as such discountenanced, more or less, in the daily course of human life, in every age, in every relation, in every general circumstance of it. That God has given us a moral nature[2] may most justly be urged as a proof of our being under his moral government; but that he has placed us in a condition which gives this nature, as one may speak, scope to operate, and in which it does unavoidably operate; *i.e.*, influence mankind to act, so as thus to favour and reward virtue, and

[1] The existence of a principle within our breasts, which approves good actions and disapproves bad ones, is admirably drawn out and vindicated, in opposition to the views of such philosophers as Hobbes and Shaftesbury, by Bishop Butler in his preface to the Sermons, and also in Sermons i. ii. and iii. —*Ed.*

[2] See Dissertation II.

discountenance and punish vice; this is not the same, but a further additional proof of his moral government; for it is an instance of it. The first is a proof that he will finally favour and support virtue effectually; the second is an example of his favouring and supporting it at present in some degree[1].

If a more distinct inquiry be made, whence it arises, that virtue as such is often rewarded, and vice as such is punished, and this rule never inverted, it will be found to proceed, in part, immediately from the moral nature itself, which God has given us; and also in part, from his having given us, together with this nature, so great a power over each other's happiness and misery. For, *first*, it is certain that peace and delight, in some degree and upon some occasions, is the necessary and present effect of virtuous practice; an effect arising immediately from that constitution of our nature. We are so made, that well-doing as such gives us satisfaction, at least, in some instances; ill-doing as such, in none. And, *secondly*, from our moral nature, joined with God's having put our happiness and misery in many respects in each other's power, it cannot but be, that vice as such, some kinds and instances of it at least, will be infamous, and men will be disposed to punish it as in itself detestable; and the villain will by no means be able always to avoid feeling that infamy, any more than he will be able to escape this further punishment, which mankind will be disposed to inflict upon him, under the notion of his deserving it. But there can be nothing on the side of vice to answer this; because there is nothing in the human mind contradictory, as the logicians speak, to virtue. For virtue consists in a regard to what is right and reasonable, as being so; in a regard to veracity, justice, charity, in themselves; and there is surely no such thing as a like natural regard to falsehood, injustice, cruelty. If it be thought that there are instances of an approbation of vice, as such in itself, and for its own sake (though it does not appear to me that there is

---

[1] The conclusion to be drawn from the foregoing instances of virtue being rewarded as *such*, and vice punished as *such*, in the natural course of things throughout human life, in its various relations, is this: our moral nature is one proof of God's moral government, and these instances are another; the first is a proof of a future and perfect, the second are examples of a present, though a modified, moral government.—(*W.*)

any such thing at all; but supposing there be), it is evidently
monstrous[1]; as much so as the most acknowledged perversion of any passion whatever.    Such instances of perversion
then being left out as merely imaginary, or, however, un-
natural; it must follow, from the frame of our nature, and
from our condition in the respects now described, that
vice cannot at all be, and virtue cannot but be favoured as
such by others, upon some occasions, and happy in itself, in
some degree. For what is here insisted upon, is not the degree in which virtue and vice are thus distinguished, but only
the thing itself, that they are so in some degree; though
the whole good and bad effect of virtue and vice as such, is
not inconsiderable in degree.    But that they must be thus
distinguished, in some degree, is in a manner necessary: it
is matter of fact of daily experience, even in the greatest
confusion of human affairs.

It is not pretended but that, in the natural course of
things, happiness and misery appear to be distributed by
other rules, than only the personal merit and demerit of
characters.    They may sometimes be distributed by way of
mere discipline.    There may be the wisest and best reasons
why the world should be governed by general laws, from
whence such promiscuous distribution perhaps must follow;
and also why our happiness and misery should be put in
each other's power, in the degree which they are.    And
these things, as in general they contribute to the rewarding
virtue and punishing vice, as such, so they often contribute also, not to the inversion of this, which is impossible;
but to the rendering persons prosperous, though wicked;
afflicted, though righteous; and, which is worse, to the
*rewarding some actions*, though vicious, and *punishing other
actions*, though virtuous.    But all this cannot drown the
voice of Nature in the conduct of Providence, plainly declaring itself for virtue, by way of distinction from vice, and
preference to it.    For our being so constituted as that virtue
and vice are thus naturally favoured and discountenanced,
rewarded and punished. respectively as such, is an intuitive
proof of the intent of Nature that it should be so; other

---

[1] By "monstrous," Butler means contrary to the ordinary course of natural
experience; and, therefore, as exceptional cases, not to be taken into account
in a philosophical disquisition. For it is an admitted principle, οὐδεμία τέχνη
τὰ καθ' ἕκαστα σκοπεῖ.—*Ed.*

wise the constitution of our mind, from which it thus immediately and directly proceeds, would be absurd. But it cannot be said, because virtuous actions are sometimes punished, and vicious actions rewarded, that Nature intended it. For, though this great disorder is brought about, as all actions are done, by means of some natural passion; yet *this may be*, as it undoubtedly is, brought about by the perversion of such passion, implanted in us for other, and those very good purposes. And indeed these other and good purposes, even of every passion, may be clearly seen [1].

We have then a declaration, in some degree of present effect, from Him who is supreme in Nature, which side he is of, or what part he takes; a declaration for virtue, and against vice. So far therefore as a man is true to virtue, to veracity and justice, to equity and charity, and the right of the case, in whatever he is concerned; so far he is on the side of the divine administration, and co-operates with it; and from hence, to such a man, arises naturally a secret satisfaction and sense of security, and implicit hope of somewhat further. And,

V. This hope is confirmed by the necessary tendencies of virtue, which, though not of present effect, yet are at present discernible in nature, and so afford an instance of somewhat moral in the essential constitution of it. There is, in the nature of things, a tendency in virtue and vice to produce the good and bad effects now mentioned, in a greater degree than they do in fact produce them. For instance, good and bad men would be much more rewarded and punished as such, were it not, that justice is often artificially eluded, that characters are not known, and many, who would thus favour virtue and discourage vice, are hindered from doing so by accidental causes. These tendencies of virtue and vice are obvious with regard to *individuals*. But it may require more particularly to be considered, that power in a *society*, by being under the

---

[1] The distinctions between virtue and vice, above mentioned, flow from our natural constitution; but this constitution must be absurd, unless it have some final cause; therefore this intention of Nature is denoted and implied by it. But on the other hand, the irregular distribution of rewards and punishments does not prove a similar intention of Nature; for they flow from no essential principle of our nature; therefore the natural passions which procure them *may be* in a state of perversion, which evidently and undoubtedly they are.—(*D.*)

direction of virtue, naturally increases, and has a necessary tendency to prevail over opposite power, not under the direction of it; in like manner, as power, by being under the direction of reason, increases, and has a tendency to prevail over brute force. There are several brute creatures of equal, and several of superior strength, to that of men; and possibly the sum of the whole strength of brutes may be greater than that of mankind: but reason gives us the advantage and superiority over them; and thus man is the acknowledged governing animal upon the earth. Nor is this superiority considered by any as accidental; but as what reason has a tendency, in the nature of the thing, to obtain. And yet perhaps difficulties may be raised about the meaning, as well as the truth, of the assertion, that virtue has the like tendency.

To obviate these difficulties, let us see more distinctly, how the case stands with regard to reason, which is so readily acknowledged to have this advantageous tendency. Suppose then two or three men, of the best and most improved understanding, in a desolate open plain, attacked by ten times the number of beasts of prey: would their reason secure them the victory in this unequal combat? Power then, though joined with reason, and under its direction, cannot be expected to prevail over opposite power, though merely brutal, unless the one bears some proportion to the other. Again: put the imaginary case, that rational and irrational creatures were of like external shape and manner: it is certain, before there were opportunities for the first to distinguish each other, to separate from their adversaries, and to form a union among themselves, they might be upon a level, or in several respects upon great disadvantage; though united they might be vastly superior; since union is of such efficacy, that ten men united, might be able to accomplish what ten thousand of the same natural strength and understanding wholly ununited could not. In this case, then, brute force might more than maintain its ground against reason, for want of union among the rational creatures. Or suppose a number of men to land upon an island inhabited only by wild beasts; a number of men who, by the regulations of civil government, the inventions of art, and the experience of some years, could they be preserved so long, would be really sufficient to subdue the wild beasts, and to preserve themselves in security from them; yet a conjuncture of accidents might give such advantage to the irrational animals as that they might at once overpower, and even extirpate, the whole species of rational ones. Length of time then, proper scope and opportunities, for reason to exert itself, may be absolutely necessary to its prevailing over brute force. Further still: there are many instances of brutes succeeding in attempts, which they could not have undertaken, had not their irrational nature rendered them incapable of foreseeing the danger of such attempts, or the fury of passion hindered their attending to it; and there are instances of reason and real prudence preventing men's undertaking what, it hath appeared afterwards, they might have succeeded in by a lucky rashness. And in certain conjunctures, ignorance and folly, weakness and discord, may have their advantages. So that rational animals have not necessarily the superiority over irrational ones; but, how improbable soever it may be, it is evidently possible, that in some globes the latter may be superior. And were the former wholly at variance and disunited, by false self-interest and envy, by treachery and injustice, and consequent rage and malice against each other, whilst the latter were firmly united among themselves by instinct; this might greatly contribute to the introducing such an inverted order of things. For every one would consider it as inverted: since reason has, in the nature of it, a tendency to prevail over brute force; notwithstanding the possibility it may not prevail, and the necessity, which there is, of many concurring circumstances to render it prevalent.

Now I say, virtue in a society has a like tendency to procure superiority and additional power, whether this power be considered as the means of security from opposite power, or of obtaining other advantages. And it has this tendency, by rendering public good an object and end to every member of the society, by putting every one upon consideration and diligence, recollection and self-government, both in order to see what is the most effectual method, and also in order to perform their proper part, for obtaining and preserving it; by uniting a society within itself, and so increasing its strength; and, which is particularly to be mentioned, uniting it by means of veracity and justice. For as these last are principal bonds of union, so benevolence, or public spirit, undirected, unrestrained by them, is, nobody knows what.

And suppose the invisible world and the invisible dispensations of Providence to be in any sort analogous to what appears, or that both together make up one uniform scheme, the two parts of which, the part which we see, and that which is beyond our observation, are analogous to each other, then there must be a like natural tendency in the derived power throughout the universe, under the direction of virtue, to prevail in general over that which is not under its direction, as there is in reason, derived reason in the universe, to prevail over brute force[1]. But then, in order to the prevalence of virtue, or that it may actually produce what it has a tendency to produce, the like concurrences are necessary as are to the prevalence of reason. There must be some proportion between the natural power or force which is, and that which is not, under the direction of virtue; there must be sufficient length of time; for the complete success of virtue, as of reason, cannot, from the nature of the thing, be otherwise than gradual; there must be, as one may speak, a fair field of trial, a stage large and extensive enough, proper occasions and opportunities for the virtuous to join together, to exert themselves against lawless force, and to reap the fruit of their united labours. Now indeed it is to be hoped, that the disproportion between the good and bad, even here on earth, is not so great but that the former have natural power sufficient to their prevailing to a considerable degree, if circumstances would permit this power to be united. For, much less, very much less, power under the direction of virtue, would prevail over much greater not under the direction of it. However, good men over the face of the earth cannot unite, as for other reasons, so because they cannot be sufficiently ascertained of each other's characters. And the known course of human things, the scene we are now passing through, particularly the shortness of life, denies to virtue its full scope in several other respects. The natural ten-

---

[1] From two hypothetical, but easily conceivable, cases, in which the tendency of virtue to prevail is developed and its hindrances removed, we may see more clearly the *natural* character of this tendency, and at the same time the merely *accidental* character of these hindrances.—(*W.*)

dency which we have been considering, though real, is
*hindered* from being carried into effect in the present state;
but these hindrances may be removed in a future one.
Virtue, to borrow the Christian allusion, is militant here,
and various untoward accidents contribute to its being often
overborne; but it may combat with greater advantage hereafter, and prevail completely, and enjoy its consequent
rewards, in some future states. Neglected as it is, perhaps
unknown, perhaps despised and oppressed here, there may
be scenes in eternity, lasting enough, and in every other
way adapted to afford it a sufficient sphere of action, and a
sufficient sphere for the natural consequences of it to follow
in fact. If the soul be naturally immortal, and this state
be a progress towards a future one, as childhood is towards
mature age, good men may naturally unite, not only
amongst themselves, but also with other orders of virtuous
creatures, in that future state. For virtue, from the very
nature of it, is a principle and bond of union, in some
degree, amongst all who are endued with it, and known to
each other, so as that by it, a good man cannot but recommend himself to the favour and protection of all virtuous
beings throughout the whole universe who can be acquainted with his character and can any way interpose in
his behalf in any part of his duration. And one might
add, that suppose all this advantageous tendency of virtue
to become effect amongst one or more orders of creatures
in any distant scenes and periods, and to be seen by any
orders of vicious creatures throughout the universal kingdom
of God, this happy effect of virtue would have a tendency,
by way of example, and possibly in other ways, to amend
those of them who are capable of amendment, and being
recovered to a just sense of virtue. If our notions of the
plan of Providence were enlarged in any sort proportionable to what late discoveries have enlarged our views with
respect to the material world, representations of this kind
would not appear absurd or extravagant. However, they are
not to be taken as intended for a literal delineation of what
is in fact the particular scheme of the universe, which
cannot be known without revelation; for suppositions are
not to be looked on as true because not incredible; but they
are mentioned to show that our finding virtue to be hindered from procuring to itself such superiority and advan-

tages, is no objection against its having, in the essential
nature of the thing, a tendency to procure them. And the
suppositions now mentioned do plainly show this, for they
show, that these hindrances are so far from being necessary, that we ourselves can easily conceive how they may be
removed in future states, and full scope be granted to
virtue. And all these advantageous tendencies of it are to
be considered as declarations of God in its favour. This,
however, is taking a pretty large compass, though it is
certain, that, as the material world appears to be, in a
manner, boundless and immense, there must be *some*
scheme of Providence vast in proportion to it.

But let us return to the earth our habitation; and we
shall see this happy tendency of virtue, by imagining an
instance not so vast and remote; by supposing a kingdom
or society of men upon it, perfectly virtuous, for a succession of many ages; to which, if you please, may be given
a situation advantageous for universal monarchy[1]. In such
a state, there would be no such thing as faction; but men
of the greatest capacity would of course, all along, have
the chief direction of affairs willingly yielded to them; and
they would share it among themselves without envy. Each
of these would have the part assigned him, to which his
genius was peculiarly adapted; and others, who had not
any distinguished genius, would be safe, and think themselves very happy, by being under the protection and
guidance of those who had. Public determinations would
really be the result of the united wisdom of the
community; and they would faithfully be executed, by
the united strength of it. Some would in a higher way
contribute, but all would in some way contribute, to the
public prosperity; and in it, each would enjoy the fruits of
his own virtue. And as injustice, whether by fraud or
force, would be unknown among themselves, so they would
be sufficiently secured from it in their neighbours. For
cunning and false self-interest, confederacies in injustice,

[1] The truth which supplies the basis of Butler's argument is supported
by exhibiting to our minds the scheme in its developed state, wherein the
impediments of virtue are supposed to have been removed, and the effect of
its tendencies completed; in this manner causing us to observe how readily
our minds apprehend its propriety; in other words, how easily and entirely it
coincides with the conceptions of that reason which God has given us.—(*D.*)

ever slight, and accompanied with faction and intestine
treachery; these on one hand would be found mere childish
folly and weakness, when set in opposition against wisdom,
public spirit, union inviolable, and fidelity on the other;
allowing both a sufficient length of years to try their force.
Add the general influence, which such a kingdom would
have over the face of the earth, by way of example particularly, and the reverence which would be paid it.   It would
plainly be superior to all others, and the world must gradually
come under its empire; not by means of lawless violence,
but partly by what must be allowed to be just conquest,
and partly by other kingdoms submitting themselves voluntarily to it, throughout a course of ages, and claiming its
protection, one after another, in successive exigencies.   The
head of it would be an universal monarch, in another sense
than any mortal has yet been; and the eastern style
would be literally applicable to him, *that all people, nations,
and languages should serve him.*   And though indeed our
knowledge of human nature, and the whole history of mankind, show the impossibility, without some miraculous
interposition, that a number of men here on earth should
unite in one society or government, in the fear of God and
universal practice of virtue, and that such a government
should continue so united for a succession of ages; yet
admitting or supposing this, the effect would be as now
drawn out.   And thus, for instance, the wonderful power
and prosperity promised to the Jewish nation in the Scripture would be in a great measure the consequence of what
is predicted of them, that the *people should be all righteous,
and inherit the land for ever*[1]; were we to understand the
latter phrase of a long continuance, only sufficient to
give things time to work.   The predictions of this kind, for
there are many of them, cannot come to pass, in the
present known course of nature; but suppose them come
to pass, and then the dominion and pre-eminence promised
must naturally follow, to a very considerable degree.

Consider now the general system of religion: that the
government of the world is uniform, and one, and moral;
that virtue and right shall finally have the advantage, and
prevail over fraud and lawless force, over the deceits as well
as the violence of wickedness, under the conduct of one

[1] Isa. lx. 21.

supreme governor; and from the observations above made, it will appear, that God has, by our reason, given us to see a peculiar connection in the several parts of this scheme. and a tendency towards the completion of it, arising out of the very nature of virtue : which tendency is to be considered as somewhat moral in the essential constitution of things. If any one should think all this to be of little importance, I desire him to consider, what he would think if vice had essentially and in its nature these advantageous tendencies, or if virtue had essentially the direct contrary ones.

But it may be objected, that notwithstanding all these natural effects and these natural tendencies of virtue, yet things may be now going on throughout the universe, and may go on hereafter, in the same mixed way as here at present upon earth : virtue sometimes prosperous, sometimes depressed; vice sometimes punished, sometimes successful. The answer to which is, that it is not the purpose of this chapter, nor of this treatise, properly to prove God's perfect moral government over the world, or the truth of Religion; but to observe what there is in the constitution and course of nature to confirm the proper proof of it, supposed to be known; and that the weight of the foregoing observations to this purpose may be thus distinctly proved. Pleasure and pain are indeed to a certain degree, say to a very high degree, distributed amongst us without any apparent regard to the merit or demerit of characters. And were there nothing else concerning this matter discernible in the constitution and course of nature, there would be no ground from the constitution and course of nature to hope or to fear, that men would be rewarded or punished hereafter according to their deserts; which, however, it is to be remarked, implies, that even then there would be no ground from appearances to think, that vice upon the whole would have the advantage, rather than that virtue would. And thus the proof of a future state of retribution would rest upon the usual known arguments for it, which are I think plainly unanswerable; and would be so, though there were no additional confirmation of them from the things above insisted on. But these things are a very strong confirmation of them. For,

*First.* They show that the Author of Nature is not indifferent to virtue and vice. They amount to a declaration, from him, determinate, and not to be evaded, in favour of one, and against the other; such a declaration, as there is nothing to be set over against or answer, on the part of vice. So that were a man, laying aside the proper proof of Religion, to determine from the course of nature only, whether it were most probable, that the righteous or the wicked would have the advantage in a future life, there can be no doubt but that he would determine the probability to be, that the former would. The course of nature then, in the view of it now given, furnishes us with a real practical proof of the obligations of Religion.

*Secondly.* When, conformably to what Religion teaches us, God shall reward and punish virtue and vice as such, so as that every one shall, upon the whole, have his deserts; this distributive justice will not be a thing different in *kind*, but only in *degree*, from what we experience in his present government. It will be that in *effect* toward which we now see a *tendency*. It will be no more than the *completion* of that moral government, the *principles and beginning* of which have been shown, beyond all dispute, discernible in the present constitution and course of nature. And from hence it follows,

*Thirdly.* That, as under the natural government of God, our experience of those kinds and degrees of happiness and misery, which we do experience at present, gives just ground to hope for, and to fear, higher degrees and other kinds of both in a future state, supposing a future state admitted: so under his moral government our experience, that virtue and vice are, in the manners above mentioned, actually rewarded and punished at present, in a certain degree, gives just ground to hope and to fear, that they *may* be rewarded and punished in a higher degree hereafter. It is acknowledged indeed that this alone is not sufficient ground to think, that they *actually will be* rewarded and punished in a higher degree, rather than in a lower; but then,

*Lastly.* There is sufficient ground to think so, from the good and bad tendencies of virtue and vice. For these tendencies are essential, and founded in the nature of things; whereas the hindrances to their becoming effect are, in numberless cases, not necessary, but artificial only.

Now it may be much more strongly argued, that these tendencies, as well as the actual rewards and punishments, of
virtue and vice, which arise directly out of the nature of
things, will remain hereafter, than that the accidental
hindrances of them will. And if these hindrances do not
remain, those rewards and punishments cannot but be
carried on much farther towards the perfection of moral
government; i. e., the tendencies of virtue and vice will
become effect: but when, or where, or in what particular
way, cannot be known at all but by revelation.

Upon the whole, there is a kind of moral government
implied in God's natural government[1]; virtue and vice are
naturally rewarded and punished as beneficial and mischievous to society[2], and rewarded and punished directly
as virtue and vice[3]. The notion, then, of a moral scheme
of government is not fictitious, but natural; for it is suggested to our thoughts by the constitution and course of
nature; and the execution of this scheme is actually begun
in the instances here mentioned; and these things are to
be considered as a declaration of the Author of Nature, for
virtue, and against vice; they give a credibility to the supposition of their being rewarded and punished hereafter,
and also ground to hope and to fear that they may be rewarded and punished in higher degrees than they are here[4],
and as all this is confirmed, so the argument for religion
from the constitution and course of nature is carried on
farther, by observing that there are natural tendencies, and,
in innumerable cases, only artificial hindrances, to this
moral scheme's being carried on much farther towards perfection than it is at present[5]. The notion, then, of a moral
scheme of government, much more perfect than what is
seen, is not a fictitious, but a natural notion; for it is suggested to our thoughts by the essential tendencies of virtue
and vice; and these tendencies are to be considered as intimations, as implicit promises and threatenings from the
Author of Nature of much greater rewards and punishments

[1] P. 113.              [2] P. 114.              [3] P. 115, &c.
[4] Butler concludes, not only that "the notion of a moral scheme of government is not fictitious but natural," but also that "the notion of a moral
scheme far more perfect than what we see realized here is not fictitious, but
*natural;* that is, it is in strict accordance with the constitution and course of
nature, as it presents itself to our sight."—*Ed.*
[5] P. 121, &c.

to follow virtue and vice than do at present; and indeed every *natural* tendency which is to continue, but which is hindered from becoming effect by only *accidental* causes, affords a presumption that such tendency will some time or other become effect, a presumption in degree proportionable to the length of the duration through which such tendency will continue; and from these things together arises a real presumption that the moral scheme of government established in nature shall be carried on much farther towards perfection hereafter, and, I think, a presumption that it will be absolutely completed. But from these things, joined with the moral nature which God has given us, considered as given us by him, arises a practical proof [1] that it will be completed; a proof from fact; and therefore a distinct one from that which is deduced from the eternal and unalterable relations, the fitness and unfitness of actions [2].

## CHAPTER IV [3].

### OF A STATE OF PROBATION, AS IMPLYING TRIAL, DIFFICULTIES, AND DANGER.

THE general doctrine of religion, that our present life is a state of probation for a future one, comprehends under it several particular things distinct from each other. But the first and most common meaning of it seems to be, that our future interest is now depending, and depending upon our-

[1] See this proof drawn out briefly, Chap. vi.—*Ed.*

[2] Throughout the present work, Butler has considered only the *moral* difference, by which virtue and vice, as such, are approved and disapproved. Dr. S. Clarke has demonstrated, in his sermons at Boyle's lecture, that there are *essential differences* in the qualities of human actions established in nature; and that this *natural* difference of things, prior to and independent of all will, creates a natural *fitness* in the agent to act agreeably to it. It is obvious that the introduction of this principle would materially confirm Bishop Butler's argument.—(*H.*)

[3] Though religious probation means, generally, the same thing as God's moral government (for both imply temptations, whence arise those difficulties and dangers which belong to probation, and without which there could be no possibility of vice nor ground for rewards and punishments in moral government), yet there is this difference, that the word "*probation*" expresses, more distinctly than the words "*moral government*," a state of trial; *i. e.*, of difficulties and dangers through temptations. Probation then, in this sense, may require to be more particularly considered.—(*W.*)

selves; that we have scope and opportunities here for that good and bad behaviour which God will reward and punish hereafter, together with temptations to one, as well as inducements of reason to the other; and this is in a great measure the same with saying that we are under the moral government of God, and to give an account of our actions to him, for the notion of a future account and general righteous judgment implies some sort of temptations to what is wrong; otherwise there would be no moral possibility of doing wrong, nor ground for judgment or discrimination; but there is this difference, that the word *probation* is more distinctly and particularly expressive of allurements to wrong, or difficulties in adhering uniformly to what is right, and of the danger of miscarrying by such temptations, than the words *moral government*. A state of probation then, as thus particularly implying in it trial, difficulties, and danger, may require to be considered distinctly by itself.

And as the moral government of God, which religion teaches us, implies that we are in a state of trial with regard to a future world; so also his natural government over us implies that we are in a state of trial in the like sense with regard to the present world. Natural government by rewards and punishments as much implies natural trial, as moral government does moral trial. The natural government of God here meant [1] consists in his annexing pleasure to some actions, and pain to others, which are in our power to do or forbear, and in giving us notice of such appointment beforehand. This necessarily implies that he has made our happiness and misery, or our interest, to depend in part upon ourselves; and so far as men have temptations to any course of action which will probably occasion them greater temporal inconvenience and uneasiness than satisfaction, so far their temporal interest is in danger from themselves, or they are in a state of trial with respect to it. Now people often blame others, and even themselves, for their misconduct in their temporal concerns; and we find many are greatly wanting to themselves, and miss of that natural happiness which they might have obtained in the present life: perhaps every one does in some degree. But many run themselves into great inconvenience, and into

[1] Chap. ii.

extreme distress and misery; not through incapacity of knowing better and doing better for themselves, which would be nothing to the present purpose, but through their own fault. And these things necessarily imply temptation and danger of miscarrying in a greater or less degree with respect to our worldly interest or happiness. Every one too, without having religion in his thoughts, speaks of the hazards which young people run upon their setting out in the world; hazards from other causes than merely their ignorance and unavoidable accidents; and some courses of vice, at least, being contrary to men's worldly interest or good, temptations to these must at the same time be temptations to forego our present and our future interest. Thus in our natural or temporal capacity, we are in a state of trial, *i. e.*, of difficulty and danger, analogous, or like to our moral and religious trial.

This will more distinctly appear to any one who thinks it worth while more distinctly to consider what it is which constitutes our trial in both capacities, and to observe how mankind behave under it[1].

And that which constitutes this our trial, in both these capacities, must be somewhat either in our external circumstances, or in our nature. For, on the one hand, persons may be betrayed into wrong behaviour upon surprise, or overcome upon any other very singular and extraordinary external occasions, who would otherwise have preserved their character of prudence and of virtue : in which cases every one, in speaking of the wrong behaviour of these persons, would impute it to such particular external circumstances. And on the other hand, men who have contracted habits of vice and folly of any kind, or have some particular passions in excess, will seek opportunities, and, as it were, go out of their way to gratify themselves in these respects, at the expense of their wisdom and their virtue; led to it, as every one would say, not by external temptations, but by such habits and passions. And the account of this last case is, that particular passions are no more coincident with prudence, or that reasonable self-love the end of which is our worldly interest, than they are with the principle of virtue and religion, but often draw contrary ways to one,

[1] Here some particulars are noted relative to this subject, and illustrating alike the nature of our natural and moral temptations.—(*D.*)

as well as to the other; and so such particular passions ar as much temptations to act imprudently with regard to our worldly interest as to act viciously [1]. However, as when we say men are misled by external circumstances of temptation, it cannot but be understood that there is somewhat within themselves to render those circumstances temptations, or to render them susceptible of impressions from them; so when we say they are misled by passions, it is always supposed that there are occasions, circumstances, and objects exciting these passions, and affording means for gratifying them. And therefore, temptations from within and from without coincide and mutually imply each other. Now the several external objects of the appetites, passions, and affections being present to the senses, or offering themselves to the mind, and so exciting emotions suitable to their nature, not only in cases where they can be gratified consistently with innocence and prudence, but also in cases where they cannot, and yet can be gratified imprudently and viciously: this as really puts them in danger of voluntarily foregoing their present interest or good as their future, and as really renders self-denial necessary to secure one as the other; *i. e.*, we are in a like state of trial with respect to both, by the very same passions, excited by the very same means. Thus mankind having a temporal interest depending upon themselves, and a prudent course of behaviour being necessary to secure it, passions inordinately excited, whether by means of example or by any other external circumstance, towards such objects, at such times or in such degrees as that they cannot be gratified consistently with worldly prudence, are temptations—dangerous, and too often successful, temptations—to forego a greater temporal good for a less; *i. e.*, to forego what is, upon the whole, our temporal interest for the sake of a present gratification. This is a description of our state of trial in our temporal capacity. Substitute now the word *future* for *temporal*, and *virtue* for *prudence* [2]; and it will be just as proper

[1] See Sermons preached at the *Rolls*, 1726, 2nd edit. p. 205, &c.   Pref. p. 25, &c.   Serm. p. 21, &c.

[2] Parables are founded on analogical reasoning. See, in this case, the Scripture parable of the Ten Virgins, but more especially that of the Unjust Steward. "The lord commended the unjust steward, because he had done wisely : for the children of this world are in their generation wiser than the children of light." (St. Luke xvi. 8.)—*Ed.*

a description of our state of trial in our religious capacity, so analogous are they to each other.

If, from consideration of this our like state of trial in both capacities, we go on to observe farther how mankind behave under it, we shall find there are some who have so little sense of it that they scarce look beyond the passing day; they are so taken up with present gratifications as to have, in a manner, no feeling of consequences, no regard to their future ease or fortune in this life, any more than to their happiness in another. Some appear to be blinded and deceived by inordinate passion, in their worldly concerns as much as in Religion. Others are not deceived, but, as it were, forcibly carried away by the like passions against their better judgment, and feeble resolutions too, of acting better. And there are men, and truly they are not a few, who shamelessly avow, not their interest, but their mere will and pleasure, to be their law of life, and who, in open defiance of everything that is reasonable, will go on in a course of vicious extravagance, foreseeing, with no remorse and little fear, that it will be their temporal ruin; and some of them under the apprehension of the consequences of wickedness in another state. And to speak in the most moderate way, human creatures are not only continually liable to go wrong voluntarily, but we see likewise that they often actually do so with respect to their temporal interests, as well as with respect to Religion.

Thus our difficulties and dangers, or our trials in our temporal and our religious capacity, as they proceed from the same causes and have the same effect upon men's behaviour, are evidently analogous and of the same kind.

It may be added, that as the difficulties and dangers of miscarrying in our religious state of trial are greatly increased, and one is ready to think in a manner wholly *made* by the ill behaviour of others, by a wrong education, wrong in a moral sense, sometimes positively vicious; by general bad example; by the dishonest artifices which are got into business of all kinds, and in very many parts of the world, by religion's being corrupted into superstitions which indulge men in their vices; so, in like manner, the difficulties of conducting ourselves prudently in respect to our present interest, and our danger of being led aside from pursuing it, are greatly increased by a foolish education; and, after we come to mature age, by the extravagance and carelessness of others whom we have intercourse with, and by mistaken notions, very generally prevalent and taken up from common opinion, concerning temporal happiness and wherein it consists. And persons, by their own negligence and folly in their temporal affairs, no less than by a course of vice, bring themselves into new difficulties, and, by habits of indulgence, become less qualified to go through them; and one irregularity after another embarrasses things to such a degree that they know not whereabout they are, and often makes the path of conduct so intricate and perplexed that it is difficult to trace it out—difficult even to determine what is the prudent or the moral part. Thus, for instance, wrong behaviour in one stage of life, youth—wrong, I mean, considering ourselves only in our temporal capacity, without taking in religion—this, in several ways, increases the difficulties of right behaviour in mature age; *i. e.*, puts us into a more disadvantageous state of trial in our temporal capacity.

We are an inferior part of the creation of God[1]. There are natural appearances of our being in a state of degradation[2]. And we certainly are in a condition which *does not seem* by any means the most advantageous we could imagine or desire, either in our natural or moral capacity, for securing either our present or future interest. However, this condition, low and careful and uncertain as it is, does not afford any just ground of complaint[3]. For, as men may manage their temporal affairs with prudence, and so pass their days here on earth in tolerable ease and satisfaction, by a mode-

---

[1] Part II., chap. v.

[2] We are not hence to infer that Bishop Butler was a believer in those doctrines which represent the whole human race, in consequence of the fall, as having wholly lost *all* traces of original righteousness. Were such the case, he could not have argued, as he has done in his sermons, on the natural supremacy of conscience even in fallen human nature. He knew that although at the fall the *image* of God was lost by men, the *likeness* still remained.—*Ed.*

[3] Two possible complaints and objections are here answered by implication: first, that a state of religious probation is improbable, because it implies difficulties from temptation, and because our fallen state makes the chance of success to be against us; and, secondly, that a state of probation implies danger of failure and hazard, and that it is improbable that any hazard should be imposed upon us by an omniscient Being, who knows our danger of falling.—(*W.*)

rate degree of care; so likewise with regard to religion, there is no more required than what they are well able to do, and what they must be greatly wanting to themselves if they neglect.  And for persons to have that put upon them which they are well able to go through, and no more, we naturally consider as an equitable thing, supposing it done by proper authority.  Nor have we any more reason to complain of it, with regard to the Author of Nature, than of his not having given us other advantages belonging to other orders of creatures.

But the thing here insisted upon is that the state of trial which Religion teaches us we are in is rendered credible by its being throughout uniform and of a piece with the general conduct of Providence towards us, in all other respects within the compass of our knowledge.  Indeed if mankind, considered in their natural capacity as inhabitants of this world only, found themselves from their birth to their death in a settled state of security and happiness, without any solicitude or thought of their own, or if they were in no danger of being brought into inconveniences and distress by carelessness, or the folly of passion, through bad example, the treachery of others, or the deceitful appearances of things; were this our natural condition, then it might seem strange and be some presumption against the truth of Religion that it represents our future and more general interest, as not secure of course, but as depending upon our behaviour, and requiring recollection and self-government to obtain it.  For it might be alleged, " What you say is our condition in one respect, is not in anywise of a sort with what we find, by experience, our condition is in another.  Our whole present interest is secured to our hands without any solicitude of ours, and why should not our future interest, if we have any such, be so too?"  But since, on the contrary, thought and consideration, the voluntary denying ourselves many things which we desire, and a course of behaviour, far from being always agreeable to us, are absolutely necessary to our acting even a common decent and common prudent part, so as to pass with any satisfaction through the present world, and be received upon any tolerable good terms in it; since this is the case, all presumption against self-denial and attention being necessary to secure our higher interest, is removed.  Had we not experience, it might, perhaps speciously, be urged that it is improbable anything of hazard and danger should be put upon us by an infinite Being, when everything which is hazard and danger in our manner of conception, and will end in error, confusion, and misery, is now already certain in his fore-knowledge. And indeed, why anything of hazard and danger should be put upon such frail creatures as we are, may well be thought a difficulty in speculation, and cannot but be so till we know the whole, or, however, much more of the case. But still the consti- tution of nature is as it is. Our happiness and misery are trusted to our conduct, and made to depend upon it. Somewhat, and, in many circumstances, a great deal too, is put upon us, either to do, or to suffer, as we choose. And all the various miseries of life, which people bring upon themselves by negligence and folly, and might have avoided by proper care, are instances of this, which miseries are beforehand just as contingent and undetermined as their conduct, and left to be determined by it.

These observations are an answer to the objections against the credibility of a state of trial, as implying temptations, and real danger of miscarrying with regard to our general interest, under the moral government of God; and they show, that, if we are at all to be considered in such a capacity and as having such an interest, the general analogy of Providence must lead us to apprehend ourselves in danger of miscarrying, in different degrees, as to this interest, by our neglecting to act the proper part belonging to us in that capacity. For we have a present interest under the government of God, which we experience here upon earth. And this interest, as it is not forced upon us, so neither is it offered to our acceptance, but to our acquisi- tion; in such sort, as that we are in danger of missing it, by means of temptations to neglect or act contrary to it, and without attention and self-denial must and do miss of it. It is then perfectly credible that this may be our case with respect to that chief and final good which Religion proposes to us.

# CHAPTER V.

## OF A STATE OF PROBATION, AS INTENDED FOR MORAL DISCIPLINE AND IMPROVEMENT.

FROM the consideration of our being in a probation-state of so much difficulty and hazard, naturally arises the question, how we came to be placed in it [1]? But such a general inquiry as this would be found involved in insuperable difficulties. For though some of these difficulties would be lessened by observing that all wickedness is voluntary, as is implied in its very notion, and that many of the miseries of life have apparent good effects, yet when we consider other circumstances belonging to both, and what must be the consequence of the former in a life to come, it cannot but be acknowledged plain folly and presumption to pretend to give an account of the whole reasons of this matter; the whole reasons of our being allotted a condition out of which so much wickedness and misery, so circumstanced, would in fact arise. Whether it be not beyond our faculties, not only to find out, but even to understand, the whole account of this, or, though we should be supposed capable of understanding it, yet, whether it would be of service or prejudice to us to be informed of it, is impossible to say. But as our present condition can in no wise be shown inconsistent with the perfect moral government of God, so Religion teaches us we were placed in it that we might qualify ourselves, by the practice of virtue, for another state which is to follow it. And this, though but a partial answer, a very partial one indeed, to the inquiry now mentioned, yet is a more satisfactory answer to another, which is of real, and of the utmost importance to us to have answered: the inquiry, What is our business here? The known end, then, why we are placed in a state of so much affliction, hazard, and difficulty, is, our improvement in

---

[1] From the matter of the foregoing chapter, two questions naturally arise: first, how we came to be placed in it? second, what is the end designed by God in placing us where He has placed us? The former question is set aside as involved in endless difficulties; the latter can be more distinctly answered from Revelation.—*Ed.*

virtue and piety, as the requisite qualification for a future
state of security and happiness[1].

Now the beginning of life, considered as an education for
mature age in the present world, appears plainly, at first
sight, analogous to this our trial for a future one, the
former being in our temporal capacity what the latter is in
our religious capacity. But some observations common to
both of them, and a more distinct consideration of each,
will more distinctly show the extent and force of the
analogy between them; and the credibility which arises
from hence, as well as from the nature of the thing, that
the present life was intended to be a state of discipline for
a future one.

I. Every species of creatures is, we see, designed for a
particular way of life, to which the nature, the capacities,
temper, and qualifications of each species, are as necessary
as their external circumstances. Both come into the notion
of such state or particular way of life, and are constituent
parts of it. Change a man's capacities or character to the
degree in which it is conceivable they may be changed, and
he would be altogether incapable of a human course of life,
and human happiness; as incapable as if, his nature continuing unchanged, he were placed in a world where he had
no sphere of action, nor any objects to answer his appetites,
passions, and affections of any sort. One thing is set over
against another, as an ancient writer expresses it. Our
nature corresponds to our external condition[2]. Without this
correspondence there would be no possibility of any such
thing as human life and human happiness, which life and
happiness are, therefore, a *result* from our nature and condition jointly; meaning by human life, not living in the
literal sense, but the whole complex notion commonly
understood by those words. So that, without determining
what will be the employment and happiness, the particular

[1] A probation state having been considered and established in the last
chapter, as implying *trial, i. e.,* difficulties and dangers, is here considered in
this other sense as implying *moral discipline and improvement.*—(*W.*)

[2] Bishop Butler, in his sermons, has clearly shown the peculiar correspondence between the inward frame of man and the external conditions and
circumstances of life; that the several passions and affections of the heart,
compared with those circumstances, are certain instances of final causes; for
example, anger leads us to the immediate resistance of injury, and compassion prompts us to relieve the distressed.—(*H.*)

life, of good men hereafter, there must be some determinate capacities, some necessary character and qualifications, without which persons cannot but be utterly incapable of it; in like manner, as there must be some, without which men would be incapable of their present state of life. Now,

II. The constitution of human creatures, and indeed of all creatures which come under our notice, is such, as that they are capable of naturally becoming qualified for states of life for which they were once wholly unqualified. In imagination we may indeed conceive of creatures, as incapable of having any of their faculties naturally enlarged. or as being unable naturally to acquire any new qualifications; but the faculties of every species known to us are made for enlargement, for acquirements of experience and habits. We find ourselves in particular endued with capacities, not only of perceiving ideas, and of knowledge or perceiving truth, but also of storing up our ideas and knowledge by memory. We are capable, not only of acting, and of having different momentary impressions made upon us, but of getting a new facility in any kind of action, and of settled alterations in our temper or character. The power of the two last is the power of habits. But neither the perception of ideas, nor knowledge of any sort, are habits, though absolutely necessary to the forming of them. However, apprehension, reason, memory, which are the capacities of acquiring knowledge, are greatly improved by exercise. Whether the word habit is applicable to all these improvements, and in particular how far the powers of memory and of habits may be powers of the same nature, I shall not inquire. But that perceptions come into our minds readily and of course, by means of their having been there before, seems a thing of the same sort as readiness in any particular kind of action, proceeding from being accustomed to it. And aptness to recollect practical observations of service in our conduct, is plainly habit in many cases. There are habits of perception and habits of action. An instance of the former is our constant and even involuntary readiness, in correcting the impressions of our sight concerning magnitudes and distances, so as to substitute judgment in the room of sensation imperceptibly to ourselves And it seems as if all other associations of ideas not natu

rally connected might be called passive habits; as properly
as our readiness in understanding languages upon sight,
or hearing of words. And our readiness in speaking and
writing them is an instance of the latter, of active habits.
For distinctness, we may consider habits as belonging to
the body or the mind, and the latter will be explained by
the former. Under the former are comprehended all bodily
activities or motions, whether graceful or unbecoming,
which are owing to use; under the latter, general habits of
life and conduct, such as those of obedience and submission
to authority, or to any particular person; those of veracity,
justice, and charity; those of attention, industry, self-
government, envy, revenge. And habits of this latter kind
seem produced by repeated acts, as well as the former. And
in like manner as habits belonging to the body are produced by external acts, so habits of the mind are produced
by the exertion of inward practical principles, i. e., by carrying them into act, or acting upon them; the principles of
obedience, of veracity, justice, and charity. Nor can those
habits be formed by any external course of action, otherwise than as it proceeds from these principles; because it
is only these inward principles exerted, which are strictly
acts of obedience, of veracity, of justice, and of charity.
So likewise habits of attention, industry, self-government,
are in the same manner acquired by exercise; and habits
of envy and revenge by indulgence, whether in outward act,
or in thought and intention, i. e., inward act, for such intention is an act. Resolutions also to do well are properly
acts. And endeavouring to enforce upon our own minds a
practical sense of virtue, or to beget in others that practical
sense of it which a man really has himself, is a virtuous
act. All these, therefore, may and will contribute towards
forming good habits. But going over the theory of virtue
in one's thoughts, talking well, and drawing fine pictures of
it,—this is so far from necessarily or certainly conducing to
form a habit of it, in him who thus employs himself, that it
may harden the mind in a contrary course, and render it
gradually more insensible, i. e., form a habit of insensibility
to all moral considerations. For from our very faculty of
habits, passive impressions, by being repeated, grow weaker[1].

---

[1] Passive impressions are weakened by being repeated, as is evidenced
by the result of familiarity with danger, with the sight of distress, or with

Thoughts, by often passing through the mind, are felt less sensibly; being accustomed to danger begets intrepidity, *i. e.*, lessens fear; to distress, lessens the passion of pity; to instances of others' mortality, lessens the sensible apprehension of our own. And from these two observations together—that practical habits are formed and strengthened by repeated acts, and that passive impressions grow weaker by being repeated upon us—it must follow that active habits may be gradually forming and strengthening by a course of acting upon such and such motives and excitements, whilst these motives and excitements themselves are, by proportionable degrees, growing less sensible; *i. e.*, are continually less and less sensibly felt, even as the active habits strengthen. And experience confirms this; for active principles, at the very time that they are less lively in perception than they were, are found to be, somehow, wrought more thoroughly into the temper and character, and become more effectual in influencing our practice. The three things just mentioned may afford instances of it. Perception of danger is a natural excitement of passive fear and active caution, and by being inured to danger habits of the latter are gradually wrought, at the same time that the former gradually lessens. Perception of distress in others is a natural excitement, passively to pity, and actively to relieve it: but let a man set himself to attend to, inquire out, and relieve distressed persons, and he cannot but grow less and less sensibly affected with the various miseries of life with which he must become acquainted; when yet, at the same time, benevolence, considered not as a passion, but as a practical principle of action, will strengthen; and whilst he passively compassionates the distressed less, he will acquire a greater aptitude actively to assist and befriend them. So also at the same time that the daily instances of men's dying around us give us daily a less sensible passive feeling or appre-

instances of mortality. Then, since practical habits are formed and strengthened by the repetition of acts, and the passive impressions which excite to those acts are weakened by repetition of them, it follows, that active habits are being strengthened in proportion as the excitements to action are less sensibly felt; or, if we reverse the statement, that passive impressions are less perceived as the active habits which have arisen out of them, gain strength.—(*D.*)

hension of our own mortality, such instances greatly con
tribute to the strengthening a practical regard to it in
serious men, *i. e.*, to forming a habit of acting with a constant
view to it.  And this seems again further to show that
passive impressions made upon our minds by admonition,
experience, example, though they may have a remote
efficacy, and a very great one, towards forming active
habits, yet can have this efficacy no otherwise than by inducing us to such a course of action; and that it is not
being affected so and so, but acting, which forms those
habits ; only it must be always remembered, that real endeavours to enforce good impressions upon ourselves are a
species of virtuous action.  Nor do we know how far it is
possible, in the nature of things, that effects should be
wrought in us at once, equivalent to habits, *i. e.*, what is
wrought by use and exercise.  However, the thing insisted
upon is, not what may be possible, but what is in fact the
appointment of nature, which is, that active habits are to
be formed by exercise.  Their progress may be so gradual
as to be imperceptible in its steps; it may be hard to
explain the faculty by which we are capable of habits,
throughout its several parts, and to trace it up to its original, so as to distinguish it from all others in our mind;
and it seems as if contrary effects were to be ascribed to it.
But the thing in general, that our nature is formed to yield,
in some such manner as this, to use and exercise, is matter
of certain experience.

Thus by accustoming ourselves to any course of action,
we get an aptness to go on, a facility, readiness, and often
pleasure, in it.  The inclinations which rendered us averse
to it grow weaker; the difficulties in it, not only the imaginary but the real ones, lessen; the reasons for it offer
themselves of course to our thoughts upon all occasions;
and the least glimpse of them is sufficient to make us go
on in a course of action to which we have been accustomed.
And practical principles appear to grow stronger, absolutely
in themselves, by exercise, as well as relatively, with regard
to contrary principles; which, by being accustomed to
submit, do so habitually, and of course.  And thus a new
character, in several respects, may be formed, and many
habitudes of life, not given by nature, but which nature
directs us to acquire.

III. Indeed we may be assured, that we should never have had these capacities of improving by experience, acquired knowledge, and habits, had they not been necessary, and intended to be made use of[1]. And accordingly we find them so necessary, and so much intended, that without them we should be utterly incapable of that which was the end for which we were made, considered in our temporal capacity only—the employments and satisfactions of our mature state of life.

Nature does in nowise qualify us wholly, much less at once, for this mature state of life. Even maturity of understanding and bodily strength are not only arrived to gradually, but are also very much owing to the continued exercise of our powers of body and mind from infancy. But if we suppose a person brought into the world with both these in maturity, as far as this is conceivable, he would plainly at first be as unqualified for the human life of mature age as an idiot. He would be in a manner distracted with astonishment, and apprehension, and curiosity, and suspense ; nor can one guess how long it would be before he would be familiarized to himself and the objects about him enough even to set himself to anything[2].

---

[1] We not only have a particular kind of life designed for us as human beings, and the faculty of improving our qualifications by habits, but we are made capable of the one only through means of the other. We are not fitted for the end of our creation as inhabitants of this world, prior to our acquisition of knowledge, experience, and habits. For first, as a matter of fact, it is only by degrees that we gain our qualifications for mature life; and secondly, if any one were suddenly ushered into mature life, with full powers, but without experience, he would be altogether unfit for the practical business of life.—*Ed.*

[2] The supposition that for perfect vision there is required, not merely the natural power of the organ, but also experience, is common to Locke with Bishop Butler, and has been confirmed by Cheselden's operation for cataract on a child born blind. It appears that this child, though he obtained the power of sight, could not estimate the size or distance of those objects which he had before discriminated by touch—everything seemed large and touching his eyes—so that he spent a year in learning to see like others; in acquiring (to apply Butler's words) "the perceptive habit of correcting, with constant and even involuntary readiness, the impressions of sight concerning magnitudes and distances, so as to substitute judgment in the room of sensation imperceptibly to ourselves." . . . The connection of the miraculous cure of the blind man by degrees (St. Mark viii. 22, &c.) with this subject, has been before remarked. By the first imposition of our Lord's hands, the natural power of the organ was given, but not the habit of

It may be questioned, too, whether the natural information
of his sight and hearing would be of any manner of use at
all to him in acting, before experience. And it seems that
men would be strangely headstrong and self-willed, and
disposed to exert themselves with an impetuosity which
would render society insupportable, and the living in it
impracticable, were it not for some acquired moderation and
self-government, some aptitude and readiness in restraining
themselves, and concealing their sense of things. Want of
everything of this kind which is learnt would render a man
as uncapable of society as want of language would; or as
his natural ignorance of any of the particular employments
of life would render him uncapable of providing himself
with the common conveniences, or supplying the necessary
wants of it. In these respects, and probably in many more
of which we have no particular notion, mankind is left by
nature an unformed, unfinished creature, utterly deficient
and unqualified, before the acquirement of knowledge, experience, and habits, for that mature state of life, which was
the end of his creation, considering him as related only to
this world.

But then, as nature has endued us with a power of supplying those deficiencies, by acquired knowledge, experience, and habits, so likewise we are placed in a condition,
in infancy, childhood, and youth, fitted for it; fitted for our
acquiring those qualifications of all sorts, which we stand
in need of in mature age. Hence children, from their very
birth, are daily growing acquainted with the objects about
them, with the scene in which they are placed, and to have
a future part; and learning somewhat or other, necessary
to the performance of it. The subordinations, to which
they are accustomed in domestic life, teach them self-
government in common behaviour abroad, and prepare
them for subjection and obedience to civil authority. What
passes before their eyes, and daily happens to them, gives
them experience, caution against treachery and deceit,
together with numberless little rules of action and conduct,

discrimination; men were only by their walking distinguished from trees—
in size the objects seemed trees, in motion, men. By the second imposition
of our Lord's hands, the perceptive habit, usually acquired by experience,
was added, and the vision made perfect; he was restored, and saw every
man clearly.—(*W.*)

which we could not live without, and which are learnt so insensibly and so perfectly, as to be mistaken perhaps for instinct, though they are the effect of long experience and exercise; as much so as language, or knowledge in particular business, or the qualifications and behaviour belonging to the several ranks and professions. Thus the beginning of our days is adapted to be, and is, a state of education in the theory and practice of mature life. We are much assisted in it by example, instruction, and the care of others; but a great deal is left to ourselves to do. And of this, as part is done easily and of course, so part requires diligence and care, the voluntary foregoing many things which we desire, and setting ourselves to what we should have no inclination to, but for the necessity or expedience of it. For that labour and industry, which the station of so many absolutely requires, they would be greatly unqualified for in maturity, as those in other stations would be for any other sorts of application, if both were not accustomed to them in their youth. And according as persons behave themselves in the general education which all go through, and in the particular ones adapted to particular employments, their character is formed and made appear; they recommend themselves more or less; and are capable of, and placed in, different stations in the society of mankind.

The former part of life, then, is to be considered as an important opportunity which nature puts into our hands, and which, when lost, is not to be recovered. And our being placed in a state of discipline throughout this life, for another world is a providential disposition of things, exactly of the same kind as our being placed in a state of discipline during childhood for mature age. Our condition in both respects is uniform and of a piece, and comprehended under one and the same general law of nature.

And if we were not able at all to discern how or in what way the present life could be our preparation for another, this would be no objection against the credibility of its being so. For we do not discern how food and sleep contribute to the growth of the body, nor could have any thought that they would, before we had experience. Nor do children at all think, on the one hand, that the sports and exercises, to which they are so much addicted, contri-

bute to their health and growth, nor, on the other, of the
necessity which there is for their being restrained in them;
nor are they capable of understanding the use of many
parts of discipline, which nevertheless they must be made
to go through, in order to qualify them for the business of
mature age. Were we not able, then, to discover in what
respects the present life could form us for a future one, yet
nothing would be more supposable than that it might, in
some respects or other, from the general analogy of Providence. And this, for aught I see, might reasonably be said
even though we should not take in the consideration of
God's moral government over the world. But,

IV. Take in this consideration, and consequently, that
the character of virtue and piety is a necessary qualification
for the future state[1], and then we may distinctly see how,
and in what respects, the present life may be a preparation
for it; since we *want, and are capable of, improvement in that
character, by moral and religious habits; and the present life is
fit to be a state of discipline for such improvement;* in like
manner as we have already observed how, and in what
respects, infancy, childhood, and youth are a necessary
preparation, and a natural state of discipline, for mature
age.

Nothing which we at present see would lead us to the
thought of a solitary unactive state hereafter; but, if we
judge at all from the analogy of nature, we must suppose,
according to the Scripture account of it, that it will be a
community[2]. And there is no shadow of anything unreasonable in conceiving, though there be no analogy for
it, that this community will be, as the Scripture represents
it, under the more immediate, or, if such an expression
may be used, the more sensible government, of God. Nor

[1] There must be some qualifications necessary for a future state; and these
must be moral, since the state itself is so. And we have reason to believe
that the moral virtues requisite in a community will be among them; for
analogy, no less than Holy Scripture, suggests a social and active, rather than
a solitary and inactive, state.—(*D.*)

[2] That the future state will be an active community, we judge from the
analogy of nature; that it will be under the more sensible moral government
of God, is the reasonable representation of Scripture; and from these things
we infer that the future state will be an *active moral* community, affording
scope and occasion for the exercise of virtues, and for that general moral
improvement in character which results from their exercise here.—(*W.*)

is our ignorance what will be the employments of this happy community, nor our consequent ignorance what particular scope or occasion there will be for the exercise of veracity, justice, and charity, amongst the members of it with regard to each other, any proof that there will be no sphere of exercise for those virtues. Much less, if that were possible, is our ignorance any proof that there will be no occasion for that frame of mind or character which is formed by the daily practice of those particular virtues here, and which is a result from it. This, at least, must be owned in general, that, as the government established in the universe is moral, the character of virtue and piety must, in some way or other, be the condition of our happiness or the qualification for it.

Now from what is above observed, concerning our natural power of habits, it is easy to see that we are *capable* of moral improvement by discipline. And how greatly we *want* it need not be proved to any one who is acquainted with the great wickedness of mankind, or even with those imperfections which the best are conscious of. But it is not perhaps distinctly attended to by every one, that the occasion which human creatures have for discipline, to improve in them this character of virtue and piety, is to be traced up higher than to excess in the passions, by indulgence and habits of vice. Mankind, and perhaps all finite creatures, from the very constitution of their nature, before habits of virtue, are deficient and in danger of deviating from what is right, and therefore stand in need of virtuous habits for a security against this danger. For, together with the general principle of moral understanding, we have in our inward frame various affections towards particular external objects. These affections are naturally, and of right, subject to the government of the moral principle, as to the occasions upon which they may be gratified; as to the times, degrees, and manner, in which the objects of them may be pursued; but then the principle of virtue can neither excite them, nor prevent their being excited. On the contrary, they are naturally felt when the objects of them are present to the mind, not only before all consideration whether they can be obtained by lawful means, but after it is found they cannot. For the natural objects of affection continue so; the necessaries, conveniences, and

pleasures of life, remain naturally desirable, though they
cannot be obtained innocently; nay, though they cannot
possibly be obtained at all. And when the objects of any
affection whatever cannot be obtained without unlawful
means, but may be obtained by them, such affection, though
its being excited, and its continuing some time in the mind,
be as innocent as it is natural and necessary, yet cannot but
be conceived to have a tendency to incline persons to ven-
ture upon such unlawful means, and, therefore, must be
conceived as putting them in some danger of it.    Now
what is the general security against this danger, against
their actually deviating from right? As the danger is, so
also must the security be, from within—from the practical
principle of virtue[1]. And the strengthening or improving
this principle, considered as practical or as a principle of
action, will lessen the danger or increase the security
against it. And this moral principle is capable of improvement by proper discipline and exercise, by recollecting the
practical impressions which example and experience have
made upon us; and, instead of following humour and mere
inclination, by continually attending to the equity and right
of the case in whatever we are engaged, be it in greater or
less matters; and accustoming ourselves always to act upon
it, as being itself the just and natural motive of action;
and as this moral course of behaviour must necessarily,
under the divine government, be our final interest. *Thus
the principle of virtue, improved into a habit, of which improvement we are thus capable, will plainly be, in proportion to the*

[1] It may be thought, that a sense of interest would as effectually restrain
creatures from doing wrong. But if by a *sense of interest* is meant a speculative conviction or belief, that such and such indulgence would occasion
them greater uneasiness, upon the whole, than satisfaction, it is contrary to
present experience to say that this sense of interest is sufficient to restrain
them from thus indulging themselves. And if by a *sense of interest* is
meant a practical regard to what is upon the whole our happiness, this is
not only coincident with the principle of virtue or moral rectitude, but is a
part of the idea itself. And it is evident this reasonable self-love wants to
be improved, as really as any principle in our nature. For we daily see it
overmatched, not only by the more boisterous passions, but by curiosity,
shame, love of imitation—by anything, even indolence : especially if the interest, the temporal interest, suppose, which is the end of such self-love, be
at a distance.    So greatly are profligate men mistaken when they affirm they
are wholly governed by interestedness and self-love, and so little cause is
there for moralists to disclaim this principle.    (See p. 134.)

*strength of it, a security against the danger which finite creatures are in, from the very nature of propension or particular affections.* This way of putting the matter supposes particular affections to remain in a future state, which it is scarce possible to avoid supposing. And if they do, we clearly see that acquired habits of virtue and self-government may be necessary for the regulation of them; however, though we were not distinctly to take in this supposition, but to speak only in general, the thing really comes to the same. For habits of virtue thus acquired by discipline are improvement in virtue; and improvement in virtue must be advancement in happiness, if the government of the universe be moral.

From these things we may observe—and it will further show this our natural and original need of being improved by discipline—how it comes to pass that creatures made upright fall, and that those who preserve their uprightness. by so doing raise themselves to a more secure state of virtue[1]. To say that the former is accounted for by the nature of liberty, is to say no more than that an event's actually happening is accounted for by a mere possibility of its happening. But it seems distinctly conceivable from the very nature of particular affections or propensions. For suppose creatures intended for such a particular state of life for which such propensions were necessary; suppose them endued with such propensions, together with moral understanding, as well including a practical sense of virtue as a speculative perception of it, and that all these several principles, both natural and moral, forming an inward constitution of mind, were in the most exact proportion possible, *i. e.,* in a proportion the most exactly adapted to their intended state of life,—such creatures would be made upright or finitely perfect. Now particular propensions, from their very nature, must be felt, the objects of them being present, though they cannot be gratified at all, or not with the allowance of the moral principle. But if they can be gratified without its allowance or by contradicting it, then they must be conceived to have some tendency, in how

---

[1] We may sum up what follows in this way :—(1.) That an additional security may be needed even by creatures formed in uprightness, and that habits of virtue may be the natural supply of this defect. (2.) That it may be fit and requisite that creatures capable of and requiring virtuous habits should be placed in circumstances especially fitted to their formation.—(*D.*)

low a degree soever, yet some tendency, to induce persons
to such forbidden gratification. This tendency in some
one particular propension may be increased by the greater
frequency of occasions naturally exciting it, than of occasions exciting others. The least voluntary indulgence in
forbidden circumstances, though but in thought, will
increase this wrong tendency, and may increase it further,
till, peculiar conjunctures perhaps conspiring, it becomes
effect, and danger of deviating from right ends in actual
deviation from it, a danger necessarily arising from the very
nature of propension, and which therefore could not have
been prevented, though it might have been escaped, or got
innocently through. The case would be as if we were to
suppose a straight path marked out for a person in which
such a degree of attention would keep him steady; but if
he would not attend in this degree, any one of a thousand
objects catching his eye might lead him out of it.
Now it is impossible to say how much even [1] the first full
overt act of irregularity might disorder the inward constitu
tion, unsettle the adjustments, and alter the proportions
which formed it, and in which the uprightness of its make
consisted; but repetition of irregularities would produce
habits. And thus the constitution would be spoiled, and
creatures made upright become corrupt and depraved in
their settled character proportionably to their repeated
irregularities in occasional acts. But, on the contrary, these
creatures might have improved and raised themselves to a
higher and more secure state of virtue by the contrary
behaviour; by steadily following the moral principle supposed to be one part of their nature, and thus withstanding
that unavoidable danger of defection which necessarily
arose from propension, the other part of it. For by thus
preserving their integrity for some time their danger would
lessen, since propensions, by being inured to submit,
would do it more easily and of course; and their security
against this lessening danger would increase, since the
moral principle would gain additional strength by exercise;
both which things are implied in the notion of virtuous
habits. Thus then vicious indulgence is not only criminal

---

[1] This observation may serve as an answer to the common objection, that
the consequences of a single crime in our first parents are represented in
Holy Scripture as excessive.—(H.)

in itself, but also depraves the inward constitution and character. And virtuous self-government is not only right in itself, but also improves the inward constitution or character, and may improve it to such a degree, that though we should suppose it impossible for particular affections to be absolutely coincident with the moral principle, and consequently should allow that such creatures as have been above supposed would for ever remain defectible, yet their danger of actually deviating from right may be almost infinitely lessened, and they fully fortified against what remains of it, if that may be called danger against which there is an adequate effectual security. But still this their higher perfection may continue to consist in habits of virtue formed in a state of discipline, and this their more complete security remain to proceed from them. And thus it is plainly conceivable, that creatures without blemish, as they came out of the hands of God, may be in danger of going wrong; and so may stand in need of the security of virtuous habits, additional to the moral principle wrought into their natures by him. That which is the ground of their danger, or their want of security, may be considered as a deficiency in them, to which virtuous habits are the natural supply. And as they are naturally capable of being raised and improved by discipline, it may be a thing fit and requisite, that they should be placed in circumstances with an eye to it; in circumstances peculiarly fitted to be to them a state of discipline for their improvement in virtue.

But how much more strongly must this hold with respect to those who have corrupted their natures, are fallen from their original rectitude, and whose passions are become excessive by repeated violations of their inward constitution! Upright creatures[1] may want to be improved; depraved creatures want to be renewed. Education and discipline, which may be in all degrees and sorts of gentleness and of severity, are expedient for those; but must be absolutely necessary for these. For these, discipline of the severer sort too, and in the higher degrees of it, must be necessary,

---

[1] By upright creatures we mean those possessed of an upright constitution, and by such a constitution is meant a constitution in which the moral principle and the particular affections are in the exactest possible proportion with reference to the intended state of life: creatures so constituted would be upright or finitely perfect.—(W.)

in order to wear out vicious habits; to recover their primitive strength of self-government, which indulgence must have weakened; to repair, as well as raise into a habit, the moral principle, in order to their arriving at a secure state of virtuous happiness.

Now, whoever will consider the thing may clearly see, that the present world is *peculiarly fit* to be a state of discipline for this purpose, to such as will set themselves to mend and improve. For, the various temptations with which we are surrounded; our experience of the deceits of wickedness; having been in many instances led wrong ourselves; the great viciousness of the world; the infinite disorders consequent upon it; our being made acquainted with pain and sorrow, either from our own feeling of it, or from the sight of it in others: these things, though some of them may indeed produce wrong effects upon our minds, yet, when duly reflected upon, have, all of them, a direct tendency to bring us to a settled moderation and reasonableness of temper; the contrary both to thoughtless levity, and also to that unrestrained self-will and violent bent to follow present inclination which may be observed in undisciplined minds [1]. Such experience as the present state affords of the frailty of our nature; of the boundless extravagance of ungoverned passion; of the power which an infinite Being has over us, by the various capacities of misery which he has given us: in short, that kind and degree of experience which the present state affords us, that the constitution of nature is such as to admit the possibility, the danger, and the actual event, of creatures losing their innocence and happiness, and becoming vicious and wretched, hath a tendency to give us a practical sense of things very different from a mere speculative knowledge, that we are liable to vice, and capable of misery. And who knows, whether the security of creatures in the highest and most settled state of perfection may not in part arise from their having had such a sense of things as this, formed, and habitually fixed within them, in some state of probation? And passing through the present world with

[1] It is thus that partial evil becomes, or at least is overruled to, the general good of the human race. It may, indeed, be turned by us to a wrong end; but, if we duly reflect, we shall see that its real tendency is to good.— *Ed.*

that moral attention which is necessary to the acting a right part in it may leave everlasting impressions of this sort upon our minds. But to be a little more distinct: allurements to what is wrong; difficulties in the discharge of our duty; our not being able to act a uniform right part without some thought and care; and the opportunities which we have, or imagine we have, of avoiding what we dislike, or obtaining what we desire, by unlawful means, when we either cannot do it at all, or at least not so easily, by lawful ones,—these things, *i. e.*, the snares and temptations of vice, are what render the present world peculiarly fit to be a state of discipline, to those who will preserve their integrity, because they render being upon our guard, resolution, and the denial of our passions, necessary in order to that end. And the exercise of such particular recollection, intention of mind, and self-government, in the practice of virtue, has, from the make of our nature, a peculiar tendency to form habits of virtue, as implying, not only a real, but also a more continued and a more intense exercise of the virtuous principle, or a more constant and a stronger effort of virtue exerted into act. Thus, suppose a person to know himself to be in particular danger, for some time, of doing anything wrong, which yet he fully resolves not to do; continued recollection, and keeping upon his guard, in order to make good his resolution, is a *continued* exerting of that act of virtue in a *high degree*, which need have been, and perhaps would have been, only *instantaneous* and *weak* had the temptation been so. It is indeed ridiculous to assert, that self-denial is essential to virtue and piety; but it would have been nearer the truth, though not strictly the truth itself, to have said, that it is essential to discipline and improvement. For though actions materially virtuous, which have no sort of difficulty, but are perfectly agreeable to our particular inclinations, may possibly be done only from these particular inclinations, and so may not be any exercise of the principle of virtue, *i. e.*, not be virtuous actions at all; yet, on the contrary, they may be an exercise of that principle; and when they are, they have a tendency to form and fix the habit of virtue. But when the exercise of the virtuous principle is more continued, oftener repeated, and more intense, as it must be in circumstances of danger, temptation, and difficulty, of any kind and in any degree, this tendency is increased proportionably, and a more confirmed habit is the consequence.

This undoubtedly holds to a certain length; but how far it may hold, I know not. Neither our intellectual powers, nor our bodily strength can be improved beyond such a degree; and both may be over-wrought. Possibly there may be somewhat analogous to this, with respect to the moral character, which is scarce worth considering. And I mention it only, lest it should come into some persons' thoughts, not as an exception to the foregoing observations, which perhaps it is, but as a confutation of them, which it is not. And there may be several other exceptions. Observations of this kind cannot be supposed to hold minutely and in every case. It is enough that they hold in general. And these plainly hold so far, as that from them may be seen distinctly, which is all that is intended by them, that *the present world is peculiarly fit to be a state of discipline for our improvement in virtue and piety;* in the same sense as some sciences, by requiring and engaging the attention, not, to be sure, of such persons as will not, but of such as will set themselves to them, are fit to form the mind to habits of attention.

Indeed the present state is so far from proving, in event, a discipline of virtue to the generality of men, that, on the contrary, they seem to make it a discipline of vice. And the viciousness of the world is in different ways the great temptation which renders it a state of virtuous discipline, in the degree it is to good men. The whole end and the whole occasion of mankind's being placed in such a state as the present, is not pretended to be accounted for[1]. That which appears amidst the general corruption is, that there are some persons who, having within them the principle of amendment and recovery, attend to and follow the notices of virtue and religion, be they more clear or more obscure, which are afforded them; and that the present world is not

---

[1] In other words, "we do not pretend to account for the whole end for which mankind are placed in such a state as the present; but it is to be observed, that the very viciousness of the world adapts it peculiarly for a state of discipline to those who will amend; and that a state of society perfectly virtuous, or vicious in a less degree, would be less adapted to this purpose."—(*D.*)

only an exercise of virtue in these persons, but an exercise of it in ways and degrees peculiarly apt to improve it; apt to improve it, in some respects, even beyond what would be by the exercise of it required in a perfectly virtuous society, or in a society of equally imperfect virtue with themselves. But that the present world does not actually become a state of moral discipline to many, even to the generality, *i. e.*, that they do not improve or grow better in it, cannot be urged as a proof that it was not intended for moral discipline, by any who at all observe the analogy of nature. For, of the numerous seeds of vegetables and bodies of animals, which are adapted and put in the way to improve to such a point or state of natural maturity and perfection, we do not see perhaps that one in a million actually does. Far the greatest part of them decay before they are improved to it, and appear to be absolutely destroyed. Yet no one who does not deny all final causes will deny that those seeds and bodies which do attain to that point of maturity and perfection answer the end for which they were really designed by nature, and therefore that nature designed them for such perfection. And I cannot forbear adding, though it is not to the present purpose, that the *appearance* of such an amazing *waste* in nature, with respect to these seeds and bodies by foreign causes, is to us as unaccountable as, what is much more terrible, the present and future ruin of so many moral agents by themselves, *i. e.*, by vice.

Against this whole notion of moral discipline, it may be objected in another way, that so far as a course of behaviour materially virtuous proceeds from hope and fear, so far it is only a discipline and strengthening of self-love [1]. But doing what God commands, because he commands it, is obedience, though it proceeds from hope or fear. And a course of such obedience will form habits of it. And a constant regard to veracity, justice, and charity, may form distinct habits of these particular virtues, and will certainly form habits of self-government, and of denying our inclinations whenever veracity, justice, or charity requires it.

[1] Religion is so far from disowning the principle of self-love, that it often addresses itself to that very principle, and always to the mind in that state where reason presides; and there can be had no access to the understanding, but by convincing men that the course of life we would persuade them to is not contrary to their interest.—*Butler's Sermon* xiii.

Nor is there any foundation for this great nicety, with which
some affect to distinguish in this case, in order to depreciate
all Religion proceeding from hope or fear.  For veracity,
justice, and charity, regard to God's authority and to our
own chief interest, are not only all three coincident, but
each of them is, in itself, a just and natural motive or
principle of action.  And he who begins a good life from
any one of them, and perseveres in it, as he is already in
some degree, so he cannot fail of becoming more and more,
of that character which is correspondent to the constitution
of nature as moral, and to the relation which God stands
in to us as moral governor of it; nor, consequently, can he
fail of obtaining that happiness which this constitution and
relation necessarily suppose connected with that character[1].

These several observations, concerning the active principle of virtue and obedience to God's commands, are applicable to passive submission or resignation to his will[2];
which is another essential part of a right character connected with the former, and very much in our power to
form ourselves to.  It may be imagined, that nothing but
afflictions can give occasion for or require this virtue; that
it can have no respect to, nor be any way necessary to
qualify for, a state of perfect happiness; but it is not experience which can make us think thus.  Prosperity itself,
whilst anything supposed desirable is not ours, begets ex
travagant and unbounded thoughts.  Imagination is alto
gether as much a source of discontent as anything in our
external condition.  It is indeed true, that there can be no
scope for patience, when sorrow shall be no more; but there
may be need of a temper of mind which shall have been

[1] Butler's meaning is as follows:—Self-love, as an *active* principle,
aiming at our chief interest must uniformly coincide with the will of God;
for obedience to his will must ever be our chief interest.  But *self-love*, as a
passive feeling of desire for the gratification of our wishes and affections, may
not be more absolutely coincident with God's will than our particular affections are ; and as being, like them, subject to excitement, independent of the
approbation of the moral principle, they may require habits of resignation, as
those require habits of obedience.   At all events, both of them, as passive feelings, disturb the mind, and so need discipline in order to restrain
them.—(*D.*)

[2] Resignation to the will of God is the *whole of piety ;* it includes in it all
that is good, and is a source of the most settled quiet and composure of
mind.   It may be said to be perfect when our will is lost and resolved into
his.—*Serm.* xiv.   (*Ed.*)

formed by patience. For though self-love, considered merely
as an active principle leading us to pursue our chief interest,
cannot but be uniformly coincident with the principle of
obedience to God's commands, our interest being rightly
understood; because this obedience, and the pursuit of our
own chief interest, must be in every case one and the same
thing: yet it may be questioned whether self-love, considered merely as the desire of our own interest or happiness, can, from its nature, be thus absolutely and uniformly
coincident with the will of God, any more than particular
affections can[1]; coincident in such sort as not to be liable
to be excited upon occasions and in degrees impossible to
be gratified consistently with the constitution of things or
the divine appointments. So that *habits* of resignation may,
upon this account, be requisite for all creatures; habits,
I say, which signify what is formed by use. However,
in general it is obvious that both self-love and particular
affection in human creatures, considered only as passive
feelings, distort and rend the mind, and therefore stand in
need of discipline. Now denial of those particular affections, in a course of active virtue and obedience to God's
will, has a tendency to moderate them, and seems also to
have a tendency to habituate the mind to be easy and satisfied with that degree of happiness which is allotted us,
*i. e.*, to moderate self-love. But the proper discipline for
resignation is affliction. For a right behaviour under that
trial; recollecting ourselves so as to consider it in the view
in which Religion teaches us to consider it as from the hand
of God; receiving it as what he appoints or thinks proper
to permit in his world and under his government; this will
habituate the mind to a dutiful submission. And such
submission, together with the active principle of obedience[2],
make up the temper and character in us which answers to
his sovereignty, and which absolutely belongs to the condition of our being, as dependent creatures. Nor can it be
said that this is only breaking the mind to a submission to
mere power; for mere power may be accidental and precarious and usurped: but it is forming within ourselves the

[1] Page 149.
[2] The whole temper or character in us which answers to the sovereignty
of God and belongs to our dependent condition, is formed by the union of
the two principles of active obedience and passive submission.—(*D.*)

temper of resignation to his rightful authority, who is by
nature supreme over all.

Upon the whole : such a character and such qualifications are necessary for a mature state of life in the present
world, as nature alone does in no wise bestow, but has put
it upon us, in great part, to acquire in our progress from
one stage of life to another, from childhood to mature age ;
put it upon us to acquire them, by giving us capacities of
doing it, and by placing us in the beginning of life in a
condition fit for it. And this is a general analogy to our
condition in the present world as in a state of moral discipline for another. It is in vain, then, to object against the
credibility of the present life's being intended for this
purpose, that all the trouble and the danger unavoidably
accompanying such discipline might have been saved us by
our being made at once the creatures and the characters
*which we were to be.* For we experience, that *what we were to
be* was to be the effect of *what we would do ;* and that the
general conduct of nature is, not to save us trouble or
danger, but to make us capable of going through them,
and to put it upon us to do so. Acquirements of our own
experience and habits are the *natural* supply to our deficiencies and security against our dangers, since it is as
plainly natural to set ourselves to acquire the qualifications,
as the external things, which we stand in need of. In
particular, it is as plainly a general law of nature, that we
should, with regard to our temporal interest, form and
cultivate practical principles within us, by attention, use,
and discipline, as anything whatever is a natural law, chiefly
in the beginning of life, but also throughout the whole
course of it. And the alternative is left to our choice ;
either to improve ourselves, and better our condition, or, in
default of such improvement, to remain deficient and
wretched. It is therefore perfectly credible, from the analogy of nature, that the same may be our case, with respect
to the happiness of a future state, and the qualifications
necessary for it.

There is a third thing[1] which may seem implied in the

---

[1] A probation-state has been already regarded in a twofold light—first, as
implying trial, difficulties, and danger ; secondly, as implying moral discipline
and improvement. It remains to speak of it as a stage for the exhibition of
character.—*Ed.*

present world's being a state of probation; that it is a theatre of action for the manifestation of persons' characters with respect to a future one; not, to be sure, to an all-knowing Being, but to his creation, or part of it. This may, perhaps, be only a consequence of our being in a state of probation in the other senses. However, it is not impossible, that men's showing and making manifest what is in their heart, what their real character is, may have respect to a future life, in ways and manners which we are not acquainted with; particularly it may be a means, for the Author of Nature does not appear to do anything without means, of their being disposed of suitably to their characters, and of its being known to the creation, by way of example, that they are thus disposed of. But not to enter upon any conjectural account of this, one may just mention, that the manifestation of persons' characters contributes very much, in various ways, to the carrying on a great part of that general course of nature, respecting mankind, which comes under our observation at present. I shall only add, that probation, in both these senses, as well as in that treated of in the foregoing chapter, is implied in moral government; since by persons' behaviour under it, their characters cannot but be manifested, and, if they behave well, improved.

## CHAPTER VI.[1]

### OF THE OPINION OF NECESSITY, CONSIDERED AS INFLUENCING PRACTICE.

THROUGHOUT the foregoing Treatise it appears, that the condition of mankind, considered as inhabitants of this

[1] The analogy pursued in this treatise between the experienced constitution of nature and the expected dispensation taught by religion, suggests the following question :—If the opinion of necessity be reconcilable with the former, is it not also reconcilable with the latter? To answer this *hypothetical* question is the object of this chapter. But first an objection which, if valid, would subvert the very foundation of the whole treatise, must be answered. Butler's argument is throughout built on the assumption that there is an intelligent Author and Governor of nature; but the Fatalist destroys the proof of this assumption, by asserting that necessity will itself account for the origin and preservation of all things. This question, then, must first be answered; upon the supposition that the opinion of necessity is reconcilable

world only, and under the government of God which we experience, is greatly analogous to our condition, as designed for another world, or under that farther government which Religion teaches us. If, therefore, any assert, as a Fatalist must, that the opinion of universal Necessity is reconcilable with the former, there immediately arises a question in the way of analogy, whether he must not also own it to be reconcilable with the latter, i. e., with the system of Religion itself and the proof of it. The reader then will observe that the question now before us is not absolute. Whether the opinion of Fate be reconcilable with Religion; but hypothetical, Whether, upon supposition of its being reconcilable with the constitution of Nature, it be not reconcilable with Religion also; or, what pretence a Fatalist, not other persons, but a Fatalist, has to conclude from his opinion that there can be no such thing as Religion. And as the puzzle and obscurity, which must unavoidably arise from arguing upon so absurd a supposition as that of universal Necessity, will, I fear, easily be seen, it will, I hope, as easily be excused.

But since it has been all along taken for granted, as a thing proved, that there is an intelligent Author of Nature or natural Governor of the world, and since an objection may be made against the proof of this, from the opinion of universal Necessity, as it may be supposed that such Necessity will itself account for the origin and preservation of all things, it is requisite that this objection be distinctly answered, or that it be shown, that a Fatality supposed consistent with what we certainly experience does not destroy the proof of an intelligent Author and Governor of Nature, before we proceed to consider whether it destroys the proof of a moral Governor of it, or of our being in a state of Religion[1].

with the constitution of nature, does it destroy the proof of an intelligent Author and Governor of nature?—*Ed.*

[1] It is objected by a Fatalist, that theological writers speak of the *necessary* existence of God. We reply that the reason of their so speaking lies in the scantiness of language, and that something very different from 'the Fatalist's notion is intended by it. To establish our answer, we must show—1stly, our conception of the necessary existence of God; and 2ndly, how it differs from the opinion of the Fatalist.

1. When we are conscious of any idea in our minds, we intuitively discern that it must be related to something external to itself as its archetype; and

Now, when it is said by a Fatalist, that the whole constitution of Nature, and the actions of men, that everything,
and every mode and circumstance of everything, is necessary, and could not possibly have been otherwise; it is to
be observed, that this Necessity does not exclude deliberation, choice, preference, and acting from certain principles,
and to certain ends, because all this is matter of undoubted
experience acknowledged by all, and what every man may
every moment be conscious of. And from hence it follows
that Necessity alone and of itself, is in no sort an account
of the constitution of Nature, and how things came *to be*
and *to continue* as they are; but only an account of this *circumstance* relating to their origin and continuance, that they
could not have been otherwise than they are and have been.
The assertion that everything is by Necessity of Nature, is
not an answer to the question, Whether the world came into
being as it is by an intelligent Agent forming it thus, or
not, but to quite another question; Whether it came into
being as it is in that way and manner which we call *necessarily*, or in that way and manner which we call *freely*.   For
suppose farther, that one who was a Fatalist, and one who
kept to his natural sense of things, and believed himself a
Free Agent, were disputing together and vindicating their
respective opinions, and they should happen to instance in
a house, they would agree that it was built by an architect.
Their difference concerning Necessity and Freedom would
occasion no difference of judgment concerning this, but only
concerning another matter, whether the architect built it
necessarily or freely. Suppose, then, they should proceed to
inquire concerning the constitution of Nature, in a lax way
of speaking one of them might say it was by Necessity, and
the other by Freedom; but if they had any meaning to their

hence we infer that it must exist in some other way besides its abstract
shape, for every abstract implies a concrete.   Now we have within us an
idea of infinity; and we feel that this must imply some infinite Being corresponding to it; and hence we conclude that there must necessarily be an
infinite Being to whose existence design did not contribute, but was subsequent to it and excluded from it; and hence arose the expression that necessity is the account of the existence of God.

2. But this conception differs from that of the Fatalist; for this necessity
is antecedent in nature to design; but it cannot be meant that everything
exists by any such a necessity, for, in such a case, design could never alter
nature, but we daily see that design does have that effect.—(*D.*)

words, as the latter must mean a Free Agent, so the former must at length be reduced to mean an Agent, whether he would say one or more, acting by Necessity, for abstract notions can do nothing.   Indeed we ascribe to God a necessary existence [1], uncaused by any agent.   For we find within ourselves the idea of infinity, *i. e.*, immensity and eternity, impossible, even in imagination, to be removed out of being.   We seem to discern intuitively, that there must, and cannot but be, somewhat external to ourselves answering this idea or the archetype of it.   And from hence (for *this abstract*, as much as any other, implies a *concrete*) we conclude that there is, and cannot but be, an infinite and immense eternal Being existing prior to all design contributing to his existence and exclusive of it.   And from the scantiness of language a manner of speaking has been introduced; that Necessity is the foundation, the reason, the account of the existence of God.   But it is not alleged, nor can it be at all intended, that *everything* exists as it does by this kind of Necessity; a Necessity antecedent in nature to design; it cannot, I say, be meant that everything exists as it does, by this kind of Necessity, upon several accounts, and particularly because it is admitted that design in the actions of men contributes to many alterations in nature. For if any deny this, I shall not pretend to reason with them.

From these things it follows : *First*, That when a Fatalist asserts that everything is *by Necessity* he must mean *by an Agent acting necessarily;* he must, I say, mean this, for I am very sensible he would not choose to mean it; and *Secondly*, That the Necessity by which such an Agent is supposed to act, does not exclude intelligence and design.   So that were the system of Fatality admitted, it would just as much ac-

---

[1] As to the meaning of *necessary existence*, logicians have long since determined that there are but two modes according to which any being can be said to exist, or to be what it is ; and these are contingency and necessity. Where the non-existence of a being is possible, that is, where we can, without a contradiction, suppose it *not to exist*, that being exists *contingently*, or contingency is the *mode of its existence*.   But if there be any being who demonstrably *must exist*, and whose non-existence is therefore impossible and inconceivable, that being exists *necessarily*, or necessity is the *mode* of its existence.   But necessity can in no sense be considered as the cause, or even as the ground or reason of any existence, or of any effect whatever.—*Hamilton on the Existence of God.*   (*Ed.*)

count for the formation of the world as for the structure of a house, and no more. Necessity as much requires and supposes a Necessary Agent, as Freedom requires and supposes a Free Agent to be the former of the world. And the appearances of *design* and of *final causes* in the constitution of nature as really prove this acting Agent to be an *intelligent designer*, or to act from choice upon the scheme of Necessity, supposed possible, as upon that of Freedom.

It appearing thus, that the notion of Necessity does not destroy the proof that there is an intelligent Author of Nature and natural Governor of the world, the present question, which the analogy before mentioned suggests [1], and which I think it will answer, is this; Whether the opinion of Necessity supposed consistent with possibility, with the constitution of the world [2], and the natural government which we experience exercised over it, destroys all reasonable ground of belief that we are in a state of Religion, or whether that opinion be reconcilable with religion, with the system, and the proof of it.

Suppose, then, a Fatalist to educate any one, from his youth up, in his own principles [3] that the child should reason upon them and conclude that since he cannot possibly behave otherwise than he does, he is not a subject of blame or commendation, nor can deserve to be rewarded or punished; imagine him to eradicate the very perceptions of blame and commendation out of his mind by means of this system; to form his temper and character and behaviour to it; and from it to judge of the treatment he was to expect, say, from reasonable men upon his coming abroad into the world; as the Fatalist judges from this system what he is to expect from the Author of Nature, and with regard to a future state. I cannot forbear stopping here to ask, whether any one of common sense would think fit that a child should be put upon these speculations, and be left to apply them to

[1] P. 161.

[2] Fatalists are fond of inferring moral necessity from physical. Thus Voltaire in effect urges, that it would be very singular that all nature, all the planets, should obey eternal laws, and that there should be a little animal, five feet high, who, in contempt of these laws, could act as he pleased, solely according to his caprice.—(*H.*)

[3] The absurdity of the Fatalist's theory is next shown from experience. The attempt to educate a child in such a system would end in his final ruin; and we are but children in these things.—*Ed.*

practice. And a man has little pretence to reason who is not sensible that we are all children in speculations of this kind. However, the child would doubtless be highly delighted to find himself freed from the restraints of fear and shame with which his playfellows were fettered and embarrassed; and highly conceited in his superior knowledge, so far beyond his years. But conceit and vanity would be the least bad part of the influence which these principles must have, when thus reasoned and acted upon, during the course of his education. He must either be allowed to go on and be the plague of all about him, and himself too, even to his own destruction: or else correction must be continually made use of to supply the want of those natural perceptions of blame and commendation which we have supposed to be removed; and to give him a practical impression, of what he had reasoned himself out of the belief of, that he was in fact an accountable child, and to be punished for doing what he was forbid. It is therefore in reality impossible but that the correction which he must meet with, in the course of his education, must convince him that if the scheme he was instructed in were not false, yet that he reasoned inconclusively upon it, and somehow or other misapplied it to practice and common life; as what the Fatalist experiences of the conduct of Providence at present, ought in all reason to convince him that this scheme is misapplied when applied to the subject of Religion[1]. But supposing the child's temper could remain still formed to the system, and his expectation of the treatment he was to have in the world be regulated by it, so as to expect that no reasonable man would blame or punish him for anything which he should do, because he could not help doing it; upon this supposition it is manifest he would, upon his coming abroad into the world, be insupportable to society, and the treatment which he would receive from it would render it so to him; and he could not fail of doing somewhat, very soon, for which he would be delivered over into the hands of civil justice. And thus, in the end, he would be convinced of the obligations he was under to his wise instructor. Or suppose this scheme of Fatality in any other way applied to practice, such practical application of it will be found equally absurd—equally fallacious in a practical sense—for

[1] P. 162.

instance, that if a man be destined to live such a time, he shall live to it, though he take no care of his own preservation; or if he be destined to die before that time, no care can prevent it; therefore, all care about preserving one's life is to be neglected, which is the fallacy instanced in by the ancients. But now, on the contrary, none of these practical absurdities can be drawn from reasoning upon the supposition that we are free, but all such reasoning with regard to the common affairs of life is justified by experience. And therefore, though it were admitted that this opinion of Necessity were speculatively true, yet, with regard to practice, it is as if it were false, so far as our experience reaches; that is, to the whole of our present life. For the constitution of the present world, and the condition in which we are actually placed, is as if we were free. And it may perhaps justly be concluded that since the whole process of action, through every step of it, suspense, deliberation, inclining one way, determining, and at last doing as we determine, is as if we were free, therefore we are so. But the thing here insisted upon is that under the present natural government of the world, we find we are treated and dealt with as if we were free, prior to all consideration whether we are or not. Were this opinion, therefore, of Necessity admitted to be ever so true, yet such is in fact our condition and the natural course of things, that whenever we apply it to life and practice, this application of it always misleads us, and cannot but mislead us in a most dreadful manner with regard to our present interest. And how can people think themselves so very secure, then, that the same application of the same opinion may not mislead them also, in some analogous manner, with respect to a future, a more general, and more important interest? For Religion being a practical subject, and the analogy of nature showing us that we have not faculties to apply this opinion, were it a true one, to practical subjects, whenever we do apply it to the subject of Religion, and thence conclude that we are free from its obligations, it is plain this conclusion cannot be depended upon. There will still remain just reason to think, whatever appearances are, that we deceive ourselves in somewhat of a like manner as when people fancy they can draw contradictory conclusions from the idea of infinity.

From these things together, the attentive reader will see

it follows, that if upon supposition of Freedom the evidence of Religion be conclusive, it remains so, upon supposition of Necessity, because the notion of Necessity is not applicable to practical subjects; *i. e.*, with respect to them, is as if it were not true; nor does this contain any reflection upon reason, but only upon what is unreasonable; for to pretend to act upon reason, in opposition to practical principles, which the Author of our Nature gave us to act upon, and to pretend to apply our reason to subjects, with regard to which our own short views, and even our experience will show us, it cannot be depended upon; and such, at best, the subject of Necessity must be; this is vanity, conceit, and unreasonableness.

But this is not all. For we find within ourselves a will, and are conscious of a character. Now, if this in us be reconcilable with Fate, it is reconcilable with it, in the Author of Nature. And besides, natural government and final causes imply a character and a will in the Governor and Designer[1]; a will concerning the creatures whom he governs. The Author of Nature then being certainly of some character or other, notwithstanding Necessity[2]; it is evident this Necessity is as reconcilable with the particular character of benevolence, veracity, and justice in him which attributes are the foundation of Religion, as with any other character; since we find this Necessity no more hinders *men* from being benevolent than cruel; true, than faithless; just, than unjust; or, if the Fatalist pleases, what we call unjust. For it is said indeed, that what, upon supposition of Freedom, would be just punishment, upon supposition of Necessity becomes manifestly unjust[3]; because it is punishment inflicted for doing that which persons could

---

[1] By *will* and *character* is meant that which, in speaking of men, we should express, not only by these words, but also by the words *temper, taste, dispositions, practical principles; that whole frame of mind from whence we act in one manner rather than another.*

[2] Necessity, if it be reconcilable with anything, is reconcilable with that moral character of the great Author of Nature, which is the foundation of religion—the character, namely, of benevolence, truth, and justice.—( *W.*)

[3] The mention of justice here introduces a casual notice of the absurdity of the Fatalists, who deny the justice of a punishment, on the ground that the thing for which it is inflicted was unavoidable, overlooking that the same necessity which justifies the crime justifies the punishment likewise; and subsequently this remark is shown to have a direct bearing on the subject, by causing us to observe how the notions of justice and injustice still remain, even while we are putting forth theories destructive of them.—(*D.*)

not avoid doing; as if the Necessity, which is supposed to destroy the injustice of murder, for instance, would not also destroy the injustice of punishing it. However, as little to the purpose as this objection is in itself, it is very much to the purpose to observe from it how the notions of justice and injustice remain, even whilst we endeavour to suppose them removed; how they force themselves upon the mind, even whilst we are making suppositions destructive of them; for there is not, perhaps, a man in the world but would be ready to make this objection at first thought.

But though it is most evident that universal Necessity, if it be reconcilable with anything, is reconcilable with that character in the Author of Nature which is the foundation of Religion; "Yet, does it not plainly destroy the proof that he is of that character, and consequently the proof of Religion?" By no means. For we find that happiness and misery are not our fate in any such sense as not to be the consequences of our behaviour; but that they are the consequences of it [1]. We find God exercises the same kind of government over us, with that which a father exercises over his children, and a civil magistrate over his subjects. Now, whatever becomes of abstract questions concerning Liberty and Necessity, it evidently appears to us that veracity and justice must be the natural rule and measure of exercising this authority or government to a Being who can have no competitions or interfering of interests with his creatures and his subjects.

But as the doctrine of Liberty, though we experience its truth, may be perplexed with difficulties which run up into the most abstruse of all speculations, and as the opinion of Necessity seems to be the very basis upon which infidelity grounds itself, it may be of some use to offer a more particular proof of the obligations of Religion, which may distinctly be shown not to be destroyed by this opinion [2].

The proof from final causes of an intelligent Author of Nature is not affected by the opinion of Necessity, sup-

[1] Ch. ii.

[2] Though arguments drawn from the analogy of nature entirely refute the doctrine of Necessity, and though experience bears witness to the doctrine of Liberty, yet it is confessed that some theoretic difficulties remain. On this account, and because Necessity is the basis of infidel speculation, it is thought useful to append a list of some of the obligatory proofs of religion which are in no way affected by it.—(D.)

posing Necessity a thing possible in itself and reconcilable
with the constitution of things [1]. And it is a matter of
fact, independent on this or any other speculation, that he
governs the world by the method of rewards and punishments [2]; and also that he hath given us a moral faculty by
which we distinguish between actions, and approve some as
virtuous and of good desert, and disapprove others as
vicious and of ill desert [3]. Now this moral discernment
implies in the notion of it a rule of action, and a rule of a
very peculiar kind; for it carries in it authority and a right
of direction, authority in such a sense as that we cannot
depart from it without being self-condemned [4]. And that
the dictates of this moral faculty [5], which are by nature a
rule to us, are moreover the laws of God—laws in a sense
including sanctions—may be thus proved. Consciousness of
a rule or guide of action in creatures who are capable
of considering it as given them by their Maker, not only
raises immediately a sense of duty, but also a sense of
security in following it, and of danger in deviating from it.
A direction of the Author of Nature, given to creatures
capable of looking upon it as such, is plainly a command
from him; and a command from him necessarily includes
in it, at least, an implicit promise in case of obedience, or
threatening in case of disobedience. But then the sense or
perception of good and ill desert [6], which is contained in
the moral discernment, renders the sanction explicit, and
makes it appear, as one may say, expressed. For since his
method of government is to reward and punish actions, his
having annexed to some actions an inseparable sense of
good desert, and to others of ill, this surely amounts to
declaring upon whom his punishments shall be inflicted,
and his rewards be bestowed; for he must have given us
this discernment and sense of things as a presentiment of
what is to be hereafter; that is, by way of information beforehand, what we are finally to expect in this world. There

---

[1] P. 162, &c.    [2] Ch. ii.    [3] Dissert. II.    [4] Serm. II. at the *Rolls*.

[5] This moral faculty of which Butler speaks, namely conscience, implies a
practical rule of a very peculiar nature, in that it is *authoritative*, (for we
cannot disobey it without being self-condemned,) and as *carrying with it its
own sanction*, (for the knowledge that we have such a rule exposes us to
God's threats if we disobey it, and to His promises of reward if we listen to
its dictate.s)

[6] Dissert. II.

is then most evident ground to think, that the government of God, upon the whole, will be found to correspond to the nature which he has given us; and that, in the upshot and issue of things, happiness and misery shall, in fact and event, be made to follow virtue and vice respectively, as he has already in so peculiar a manner associated the ideas of them in our minds; and from hence might easily be deduced the obligations of religious worship, were it only to be considered as a means of preserving upon our minds a sense of this moral government of God, and securing our obedience to it, which yet is an extremely imperfect view of that most important duty.

Now, I say, no objection from Necessity can lie against this general proof of Religion? None against the proposition reasoned upon that we have such a moral faculty and discernment, because this is a mere matter of fact, a thing of experience, that human kind is thus constituted; none against the conclusion, because it is immediate and wholly from this fact. For the conclusion, that God will finally reward the righteous and punish the wicked, is not here drawn from its appearing to us fit [1] that *he should*, but from its appearing that he has told us *he will*. And this he hath certainly told us, in the promise and threatening which it hath been observed the notion of a command implies, and the sense of good and ill desert which he has given us more distinctly expresses. And this reasoning from fact is confirmed, and in some degree even verified, by other facts, by the natural tendencies of virtue and

[1] However, I am far from intending to deny that the will of God is determined by what is fit, by the right and reason of the case ; though one chooses to decline matters of such abstract speculation, and to speak with caution when one does speak of them. But if it be intelligible to say, that *it is fit and reasonable for every one to consult his own happiness*, then *fitness of action, or the right and reason of the case*, is an intelligible manner of speaking. And it seems as inconceivable to suppose God to approve one course of action, or one end, preferably to another, which yet his acting at all from design implies that he does, without supposing somewhat prior in that end to be the ground of the preference, as to suppose him to discern an abstract proposition to be true, without supposing somewhat prior in it to be the ground of the discernment. It doth not therefore appear that moral right is any more relative to perception than abstract truth is, or that it is any more improper to speak of the fitness and rightness of actions and ends, as founded in the nature of things, than to speak of abstract truth as thus founded.

of vice [1]; and by this, that God, in the natural course of his providence, punishes vicious actions as mischievous to society, and also vicious actions as such in the strictest sense [2]; so that the general proof of Religion is unanswerably real, even upon the wild supposition which we are arguing upon.

It must likewise be observed further, that natural Religion hath, besides this, an external evidence, which the doctrine of Necessity, if it could be true, would not affect. For suppose a person, by the observations and reasoning above, or by any other, convinced of the truth of Religion, that there is a God who made the world, who is the moral Governor and Judge of mankind, and will upon the whole deal with every one according to his works; I say, suppose a person convinced of this by reason, but to know nothing at all of antiquity, or the present state of mankind, it would be natural for such a one to be inquisitive what was the history of this system of doctrine, at what time, and in what manner, it came first into the world, and whether it were believed by any considerable part of it. And were he upon inquiry to find that a particular person, in a late age, first of all proposed it, as a deduction of reason, and that mankind were before wholly ignorant of it; then, though its evidence from reason would remain, there would be no additional probability of its truth from the account of its discovery. But instead of this being the fact of the case, on the contrary, he would find what could not but afford him a very strong confirmation of its truth: *First*. That somewhat of this system, with more or fewer additions and alterations, hath been professed in all ages and countries, of which we have any certain information relating to this matter. *Secondly*. That it is certain historical fact, so far as we can trace things up, that this whole system of belief, that there is one God, the Creator and moral Governor of the world, and that mankind is in a state of Religion, was received in the first ages. And *Thirdly*. That as there is no hint or intimation in history, that this system was first reasoned out; so there is express historical or traditional evidence, as ancient as history, that it was taught first by revelation. Now these things must be allowed to be of great weight. The first of them, general consent, shows this system to

[1] P. 121.                    [2] P. 114, &c.

be conformable to the common sense of mankind [1]. The second, namely, that Religion was believed in the first ages of the world, especially as it does not appear that there were then any superstitious or false additions to it, cannot but be a further confirmation of its truth. For it is a proof of this alternative; either that it came into the world by revelation, or that it is natural, obvious, and forces itself upon the mind. The former of these is the conclusion of learned men; and whoever will consider how unapt for speculation rude and uncultivated minds are, will, perhaps from hence alone, be strongly inclined to believe it the truth. And as it is shown in the Second Part [2] of this Treatise that there is nothing of such peculiar presumption against a revelation in the beginning of the world, as there is supposed to be against subsequent ones; a sceptic could not, I think, give any account which would appear more probable even to himself of the early pretences to revelation, than by supposing some real original one from whence they were copied. And the third thing above mentioned, that there is express historical or traditional evidence as ancient as history of the system of Religion being taught mankind by revelation; this must be admitted as some degree of real proof that it was so taught; for why should not the most ancient tradition be admitted as some additional proof of a fact, against which there is no presumption? And this proof is mentioned here, because it has its weight to show, that Religion came into the world by revelation, prior to all consideration of the proper authority of any book supposed to contain it, and even prior to all consideration whether the revelation itself be uncorruptly handed down and related, or mixed and darkened with fables. Thus the historical account, which we have of the origin of Religion, taking in all circumstances, is a real confirmation of its truth, no way affected by the opinion of Necessity. And the *external* evidence, even of natural Religion, is by no means inconsiderable.

[1] The external evidence for religion is summed up here into three heads: 1stly, general consent; 2ndly, early belief; 3rdly, most ancient tradition. We should use a practical caution in these probable proofs of religion. As our reason is liable to prejudice, so is our moral discernment to perversion. And this should be a serious warning, again, as to our decisions with respect to religion, and particularly lest we substitute the world's fashions in the place of that moral rule which God has given us.—(*W.*)

[2] Ch. ii.

But it is carefully to be observed, and ought to be recol-
lected after all proofs of virtue and religion, which are only
general, that as speculative reason may be neglected, prejudiced, and deceived, so also may our moral understanding
be impaired and perverted, and the dictates of it not impar-
tially attended to.  This indeed proves nothing against the
reality of our speculative or practical faculties of perception,
against' their being intended by nature to inform us in the
theory of things, and instruct us how we are to behave, and
what we are to expect in consequence of our behaviour. Yet
our liableness in the degree we are liable to prejudice and
perversion, is a most serious admonition to us to be upon
our guard with respect to what is of such consequence as
our determinations concerning virtue and religion, and particularly not to take custom, and fashion, and slight notions
of honour, or imaginations of present ease, use, and convenience to mankind, for the only moral rule [1].

The foregoing observations drawn from the nature of the
thing and the history of Religion, amount, when taken
together, to a real practical proof of it not to be confuted ;
such a proof as, considering the infinite importance of the
thing, I apprehend would be admitted fully sufficient in
reason to influence the actions of men who act upon thought
and reflection, if it were admitted that there is no proof of
the contrary.  But it may be said, " There are many probabilities which cannot indeed be confuted, i. e., shown to be
no probabilities, and yet may be overbalanced by greater
probabilities on the other side ; much more by demonstration.  And there is no occasion to object against particular
arguments alleged for an opinion when the opinion itself
may be clearly shown to be false, without meddling with
such arguments at all, but leaving them just as they are [2]
Now the method of government by rewards and punishments, and especially rewarding and punishing good and il
desert as such respectively, must go upon supposition, that
we are Free and not Necessary Agents.  And it is incredibl
that the Author of Nature should govern us upon a suppo
sition as true which he knows to be false [3], and therefor

---

[1] Dissert. II.                         [2] Pp. 73, 76.
[3] Hume goes so far as to affirm that, though man in truth is a Necessar
Agent, having all his actions fixed by determinate laws, yet, this being co
cealed from him, he acts with the conviction of being a Free Agent.—(W
But can such a position as this be maintained without doing dishonour

absurd to think he will reward or punish us for our actions hereafter, especially that he will do it under the notion that they are of good or ill desert." Here then the matter is brought to a point. And the answer to all this is full, and not to be evaded; that the whole constitution and course of things, the whole analogy of providence shows beyond possibility of doubt, that the conclusion from this reasoning is false, wherever the fallacy lies[1]. The doctrine of freedom indeed clearly shows where, in supposing ourselves Necessary, when in truth we are Free Agents. But upon the supposition of Necessity, the fallacy lies in taking for granted that it is incredible Necessary Agents should be rewarded and punished. But that somehow or other the conclusion now mentioned is false, is most certain[2]. For it is fact that God does govern even brute creatures by the method of rewards and punishments, in the natural course of things. And men are rewarded and punished for their actions, punished for actions mischievous to society as being so, punished for vicious actions as such, by the natural instrumentality of each other under the present conduct of Providence. Nay, even the affection of gratitude, and the passion of resentment, and the rewards and punishments following from them, which in general are to be considered as natural, *i. e.*, from the Author of Nature; these rewards and punishments being naturally[3] annexed to actions considered as implying good intention and good desert, ill intention and ill desert—these natural rewards and punishments, I say, are as much a contradiction to the conclusion above, and show its falsehood, as a more exact and complete rewarding and

God, by attributing to Him the governing us upon a supposition which he knows to be false? Would it not be dishonouring our fellow-man to attribute to him such conduct without full proof? and is it a less dishonour to the God of truth, to Him who is the truth itself? Surely if we are treated by God as Free Agents, it is but right to conclude that we *are* such.—*Ed.*

[1] For even a number of arguments, which, taken severally, are confessedly inconclusive, when taken together, amount to a real practical proof of any moral point, and such a proof as cannot be set aside except by a counterbalance of probable arguments on the other side.—*Ed.*

[2] The Fatalist argument may be stated in syllogistic form: Necessary Agents cannot be punished by God; we are Necessary Agents; therefore we cannot be punished by God. Now if we are Free Agents, the minor premiss here is false; if we are Necessary Agents, then the major is false; for as a matter of fact we *are* punished and rewarded.

[3] Serm. viii. at the *Rolls*.

punishing of good and ill desert as such. So that if it be incredible that Necessary Agents should be thus rewarded and punished, then men are not necessary but free, since it is matter of fact that they are thus rewarded and punished. But if on the contrary, which is the supposition we have been arguing upon, it be insisted that men are Necessary Agents; then there is nothing incredible in the further supposition of Necessary Agents being thus rewarded and punished, since we ourselves are thus dealt with.

From the whole, therefore, it must follow that a Necessity supposed possible, and reconcilable with the constitution of things, does in no sort prove that the Author of Nature will not, nor destroy the proof that he will, finally and upon the whole, in his eternal government, render his creatures happy or miserable, by some means or other, as they behave well or ill. Or, to express this conclusion in words conformable to the title of the chapter, the analogy of nature shows us that the opinion of Necessity, considered as practical, is false. And if Necessity, upon the supposition above mentioned, doth not destroy the proof of natural Religion, it evidently makes no alteration in the proof of revealed.

From these things, likewise, we may learn in what sense to understand that general assertion, that the opinion of Necessity is essentially destructive of all religion. First, in a practical sense, that by this notion atheistical men pretend to satisfy and encourage themselves in vice, and justify to others their disregard to all religion. And secondly, in the strictest sense, that it is a contradiction to the whole constitution of nature, and to what we may every moment experience in ourselves, and so overturns everything. But by no means is this assertion to be understood as if Necessity, supposing it could possibly be reconciled with the constitution of things and with what we experience, were not also reconcilable with Religion, for upon this supposition it demonstrably is so.

# CHAPTER VII.

## OF THE GOVERNMENT OF GOD, CONSIDERED AS A SCHEME OR CONSTITUTION, IMPERFECTLY COMPREHENDED.

THOUGH it be, as it cannot but be, acknowledged that the analogy of nature gives a strong credibility to the general doctrine of Religion, and to the several particular things contained in it considered as so many matters of fact; and likewise that it shows this credibility not to be destroyed by any notions of Necessity: yet still objections may be insisted upon against the wisdom, equity, and goodness of the divine government implied in the notion of Religion, and against the method by which this government is conducted; to which objections analogy can be no direct answer[1]. For the credibility or the certain truth of a matter of fact does not immediately prove anything concerning the wisdom or goodness of it; and analogy can do no more, immediately or directly, than show such and such things to be true or credible considered only as matters of fact. But still, if, upon supposition of a moral constitution of nature and a moral government over it, analogy suggests and makes it credible that this government must be a scheme, system, or constitution of government, as distinguished from a number of single unconnected acts of distributive justice and goodness, and likewise that it must be a scheme, so imperfectly comprehended, and of such a sort in other respects, as to afford a direct general answer to all objections against the justice and goodness of it; then analogy is remotely of great service in answering those objections, both by suggesting the answer and showing it to be a credible one.

[1] In chap. iii. objections were urged against the *fact* of God's moral government in respect of rewards and punishments, and they were directly answered from analogy by showing that the *seeds*, as it were, of a moral government, are discernible in the world around us. But objections may be raised, not only against the fact of God's moral government, but also against its *perfect moral character*. Admitting that government as a *fact*, it still may be urged that it is not *wise, just,* and *good*. Can analogy answer such an objection? Not directly, indeed, but indirectly, by suggesting as the proper answer our present imperfect comprehension of so vast a scheme. Two arguments are urged in support of this position: the one drawn from the *general* analogy existing between God's natural and moral governments; the other from *particular* points of analogy between them.—*Ed.*

Now this, upon inquiry, will be found to be the case.
For, *First*, Upon supposition that God exercises a moral
government over the world, the analogy of his natural
government suggests and makes it credible that his moral
government must be a scheme quite beyond our comprehension; and this affords a general answer to all objections
against the justice and goodness of it. And, *Secondly*, A
more distinct observation of some particular things contained in God's scheme of natural government, the like
things being supposed, by analogy, to be contained in his
moral government, will further show how little weight is to
be laid upon these objections.

I. Upon supposition that God exercises a moral government over the world, the analogy of his natural government
suggests and makes it credible that his moral government
must be a scheme quite beyond our comprehension, and
this affords a general answer to all objections against the
justice and goodness of it[1]. It is most obvious, analogy
renders it highly credible, that, upon supposition of a
moral government, it must be a scheme; for the world, and
the whole natural government of it, appears to be so; to be
a scheme, system, or constitution, whose parts correspond
to each other, and to a whole, as really as any work of art,
or as any particular model of a civil constitution and
government. In this great scheme of the natural world
individuals have various peculiar relations to other individuals of their own species. And whole species are, we
find, variously related to other species upon this earth.
Nor do we know how much further these kinds of relations
may extend. And, as there is not any action or natural
event which we are acquainted with so single and unconnected as not to have a respect to some other actions
and events, so possibly each of them, when it has not an
immediate, may yet have a remote, natural relation to other
actions and events much beyond the compass of this present
world. There seems indeed nothing from whence we can
so much as make a conjecture whether all creatures, actions,
and events, throughout the whole of nature have relations
to each other. But as it is obvious that all events have

[1] This argument was evidently a favourite instrument in the hands of
Butler; he draws it out at greater length in Serm. xv. upon the "Ignorance
of Man."

future unknown consequences, so if we trace any, as far as we can go, into what is connected with it, we shall find that if such event were not connected with somewhat further in nature unknown to us, somewhat both past and present, such event could not possibly have been at all. Nor can we give the whole account of any one thing whatever; of all its causes, ends, and necessary adjuncts, those adjuncts, I mean, without which it could not have been. By this most astonishing connection, these reciprocal correspondences and mutual relations, everything which we see in the course of nature is actually brought about. And things seemingly the most insignificant imaginable are perpetually observed to be necessary conditions to other things of the greatest importance; so that any one thing whatever may, for aught we know to the contrary, be a necessary condition to any other. The natural world, then, and natural government of it, being such an incomprehensible scheme, so incomprehensible that a man must, really in the literal sense, know nothing at all who is not sensible of his ignorance in it; this immediately suggests and strongly shows the credibility, that the moral world and government of it may be so too. Indeed the natural and moral constitution and government of the world are so connected, as to make up together but one scheme; and it is highly probable that the first is formed and carried on merely in subserviency to the latter, as the vegetable world is for the animal, and organized bodies for minds[1]. But the thing intended here is, without inquiring how far the administration of the natural world is subordinate to that of the moral, only to observe the credibility that one should be analogous or similar to the other; that therefore every act of divine justice and goodness may be supposed to look much beyond itself and its immediate object, may have some reference to other parts of God's moral administration, and to a general moral plan; and that every circumstance of this his moral

[1] There is no manner of absurdity in supposing a veil, on purpose, drawn over some scenes of infinite power, wisdom, and goodness, the sight of which might, some way or other, strike us too strongly; or that better ends are designed and served by their being concealed, than could be by their being exposed to our knowledge. The Almighty may cast clouds and darkness round about Him for reasons and purposes of which we have not the least glimpse or conception.—*Butler's Sermon* xv. (*Ed.*)

government may be adjusted beforehand with a view to the whole of it. Thus for example : the determined length of time, and the degrees and ways in which virtue is to remain in a state of warfare and discipline, and in which wickedness is permitted to have its progress; the times appointed for the execution of justice, the appointed instruments of it, the kinds of rewards and punishments, and the manners of their distribution; all particular instances of divine justice and goodness, and every circumstance of them, may have such respects to each other as to make up altogether a whole, connected and related in all its parts; a scheme or system, which is as properly one as the natural world is, and of the like kind. And supposing this to be the case, it is most evident that we are not competent judges of this scheme from the small parts of it which come within our view in the present life, and therefore no objections against any of these parts can be insisted upon by reasonable men.

This our ignorance, and the consequence here drawn from it, are universally acknowledged upon other occasions, and though scarce denied, yet are universally forgot when persons come to argue against Religion. And it is not perhaps easy, even for the most reasonable men, always to bear in mind the degree of our ignorance, and make due allowances for it. Upon these accounts it may not be useless to go on a little further, in order to show more distinctly how just an answer our ignorance is to objections against the scheme of Providence. Suppose, then, a person boldly to assert that the things complained of, the origin and continuance of evil, might easily have been prevented by repeated interpositions [1]; interpositions so guarded and circumstanced as would preclude all mischief arising from them; or, if this were impracticable, that a *scheme* of government is itself an imperfection; since more good might have been produced without any scheme, system, or constitution at all, by continued single unrelated acts of distributive justice and goodness, because these would have occasioned no irregularities. And farther than this, it is presumed, the objections will not be carried. Yet the answer is obvious; that were these assertions true, still the observations above, concerning our ignorance in the scheme of divine govern-

[1] Pp. 183, 184.

ment and the consequence drawn from it, would hold in great measure, enough to vindicate Religion against all objections from the disorders of the present state.    Were these assertions true, yet the government of the world might be just and good notwithstanding; for, at the most, they would infer nothing more than that it might have been better.    But indeed they are mere arbitrary assertions; no man being sufficiently acquainted with the possibilities of things, to bring any proof of them to the lowest degree of probability.    For however possible what is asserted may seem, yet many instances may be alleged in things much less out of our reach, of suppositions absolutely impossible and reducible to the most palpable self-contradictions, which not every one by any means would perceive to be such, nor perhaps any one at first sight suspect.    From these things it is easy to see distinctly how our ignorance, as it is the common, is really a satisfactory answer to all objections against the justice and goodness of Providence.    If a man, contemplating any one providential dispensation which had no relation to any others, should object, that he discerned in it a disregard to justice or a deficiency of goodness; nothing would be less an answer to such objection than our ignorance in other parts of providence, or in the possibilities of things no way related to what he was contemplating. But when we know not but the parts objected against may be relative to other parts unknown to us, and when we are unacquainted with what is, in the nature of the thing, practicable in the case before us, then our ignorance is a satisfactory answer, because some unknown relation, or some unknown impossibility, may render what is objected against just and good; nay, good in the highest practicable degree.

II. And how little weight is to be laid upon such objections will further appear by a more distinct observation of some particular things contained in the natural government of God, the like to which may be supposed, from analogy, to be contained in his moral government.

*First.* As in the scheme of the natural world, no ends appear to be accomplished without means, so we find that means very undesirable often conduce to bring about ends in such a measure desirable as greatly to overbalance the disagreeableness of the means; and in cases where such means are conducive to such ends, it is not reason, but experience which shows us that they are thus conducive. Experience also shows many means to be conducive and necessary to accomplish ends, which means, before experience, we should have thought would have had even a contrary tendency. Now from these observations relating to the natural scheme of the world, the moral being supposed analogous to it, arises a great credibility that the putting our misery in each other's power to the degree it is, and making men liable to vice to the degree we are, and in general, that those things which are objected against the moral scheme of Providence, may be, upon the whole, friendly and assistant to virtue, and productive of an overbalance of happiness; *i. e.*, the things objected against may be means by which an overbalance of good will, in the end, be found produced; and from the same observations, it appears to be no presumption against this, that we do not, if indeed we do not, see those means to have any such tendency, or that they seem to us to have a contrary one. Thus those things, which we call irregularities, may not be so at all; because they may be means of accomplishing wise and good ends more considerable; and it may be added, as above, that they may also be the only means by which these wise and good ends are capable of being accomplished.

After these observations it may be proper to add, in order to obviate an absurd and wicked conclusion from any of them, that though the constitution of our nature from whence we are capable of vice and misery may, as it undoubtedly does, contribute to the perfection and happiness of the world; and though the actual permission of evil may be beneficial to it (*i. e.*, it would have been more mischievous, not that a wicked person had himself abstained from his own wickedness, but that any one had forcibly prevented it, than that it was permitted): yet, notwithstanding, it might have been much better for the world if this very evil had never been done. Nay, it is most clearly conceivable, that the very commission of wickedness may be beneficial to the world, and yet, that it would be infinitely more beneficial for men to refrain from it. For thus, in the wise and good constitution of the natural world, there are disorders which bring their own cures; diseases which are themselves remedies. Many a man would have died, had it not been for the gout or a fever; yet it would be thought madness to assert that sickness is a better or more perfect state than health; though the like, with regard to the moral world, has been asserted. But,

*Secondly.* The natural government of the world is carried on by general laws. For this there may be wise and good reasons; the wisest and best, for aught we know to the contrary. And that there are such reasons is suggested to our thoughts by the analogy of nature; by our being made to experience good ends to be accomplished, as indeed all the good which we enjoy is accomplished, by this means, that the laws, by which the world is governed, are general. For we have scarce any kind of enjoyments, but what we are, in some way or other, instrumental in procuring ourselves, by acting in a manner which we foresee likely to procure them; now this foresight could not be at all, were not the government of the world carried on by general laws. And though, for aught we know to the contrary, every single case may be, at length, found to have been provided for even by these: yet to prevent all irregularities, or remedy them as they arise, by the wisest and best general laws, may be impossible in the nature of things; as we see it is absolutely impossible in civil government. But then we are ready to think that the constitution of nature remaining as it is, and the course of things being permitted to go on in other respects as it does, there might be interpositions to prevent irregularities, though they could not have been prevented or remedied by any general laws. And there would indeed be reason to wish, which, by the way, is very different from a right to claim, that all irregularities were prevented or remedied by present interpositions, if these interpositions would have no other effect than this. But it is plain they would have some visible and immediate bad effects; for instance, they would encourage idleness and negligence, and they would render doubtful the natural rule of life, which is ascertained by this very thing, that the course of the world is carried on by general laws. And further, it is certain they would have distant effects, and very great ones too, by means of the wonderful connections before mentioned[1]; so that we cannot so much as guess what would be the whole result of the interpositions desired.

[1] P. 179, &c.

It may be said, any bad result might be prevented by
further interpositions whenever there was occasion for
them; but this again is talking quite at random, and in the
dark [1]. Upon the whole, then, we see wise reasons why the
course of the world should be carried on by general laws,
and good ends accomplished by this means; and, for aught
we know, there may be the wisest reasons for it, and the
best ends accomplished by it. We have no ground to
believe that all irregularities could be remedied as they
arise, or could have been precluded by general laws. We
find that interpositions would produce evil and prevent
good; and, for aught we know, they would produce greater
evil than they would prevent; and prevent greater good
than they would produce. And if this be the case, then
the not interposing is so far from being a ground of complaint, that it is an instance of goodness. This is intelligible and sufficient; and going further seems beyond the
utmost reach of our faculties.

But it may be said, that "after all, these supposed impossibilities and relations are what we are unacquainted
with; and we must judge of Religion, as of other things,
by what we do know, and look upon the rest as nothing;
or, however, that the answers here given to what is objected
against Religion may equally be made use of to invalidate
the proof of it, since their stress lies so very much upon
our ignorance." But,

*First*. Though total ignorance in any matter does indeed
equally destroy, or rather preclude, all proof concerning it,
and objections against it, yet partial ignorance does not.
For we may in any degree be convinced that a person is of
such a character, and consequently will pursue such ends;
though we are greatly ignorant what is the proper way of
acting, in order the most effectually to obtain those ends;
and, in this case, objections against his manner of acting,
as seemingly not conducive to obtain them, might be
answered by our ignorance; though the proof that such
ends were intended might not at all be invalidated by it.
Thus the proof of Religion is a proof of the moral character
of God, and consequently that his government is moral,
and that every one upon the whole shall receive according
to his deserts; a proof that this is the designed end of his

[1] P. 181.

government. But we are not competent judges what is the proper way of acting in order the most effectually to accomplish this end[1]. Therefore our ignorance is an answer to objections against the conduct of Providence, in permitting irregularities, as seeming contradictory to this end. Now, since it is so obvious that our ignorance may be a satisfactory answer to objections against a thing, and yet not affect the proof of it, till it can be shown, it is frivolous to assert, that our ignorance invalidates the proof of Religion, as it does the objections against it.

*Secondly.* Suppose unknown impossibilities, and unknown relations, might justly be urged to invalidate the proof of Religion, as well as to answer objections against it; and that in consequence of this the proof of it were doubtful: yet still, let the assertion be despised, or let it be ridiculed, it is undeniably true, that moral obligations would remain certain, though it were not certain what would, upon the whole, be the consequences of observing or violating them[2]. For these obligations arise immediately and necessarily from the judgment of our own mind, unless perverted, which we cannot violate without being self-condemned. And they would be certain too, from considerations of interest. For though it were doubtful what will be the future consequences of virtue and vice, yet it is, however, credible, that they may have those consequences which Religion teaches us they will; and this credibility is a certain[3] obligation in point of prudence to abstain from all wickedness, and to live in the conscientious practice of all that is good. But,

*Thirdly.* The answers above given to the objections[4] against Religion cannot equally be made use of to invalidate the proof of it. For, upon suspicion that God exercises a moral government over the world, analogy does most strongly lead us to conclude that this moral government

[1] P. 76.

[2] Even if arguing upon our ignorance did invalidate the proof of God's moral government, still there would remain certain moral obligations which would lead us to believe it to be a fact, and there would be certain considerations of interest besides.—*Ed.*

[3] P. 73, and Part ii. chap. vi.

[4] The argument from ignorance, however, cannot be equally adduced to invalidate the proof of God's moral government, as it can to overthrow objections against it, for it is not applicable in the one case as in the other.—*Ed.*

must be a scheme, or constitution, beyond our comprehension. And a thousand particular analogies show us that parts of such a scheme, from their relation to other parts, may conduce to accomplish ends which we should have thought they had no tendency at all to accomplish, nay, ends, which, before experience, we should have thought such parts were contradictory to, and had a tendency to prevent. And therefore all these analogies show that the way of arguing made use of in objecting against Religion is delusive; because they show it is not at all incredible that, could we comprehend the whole, we should find the permission of the disorders objected against to be consistent with justice and goodness, and even to be instances of them. Now this is not applicable to the proof of Religion, as it is to the objections against it[1], and therefore cannot invalidate that proof, as it does these objections.

*Lastly.* From the observation now made, it is easy to see that the answers above given to the objections against Providence, though, in a general way of speaking, they may be said to be taken from our ignorance; yet are by no means taken merely from that, but from somewhat which analogy shows us concerning it. For analogy shows us positively, that our ignorance in the possibilities of things, and the various relations in nature, renders us incompetent judges, and leads us to false conclusions, in cases similar to this, in which we pretend to judge and to object. So that the things above insisted upon are not mere suppositions of unknown impossibilities and relations, but they are suggested to our thoughts, and even forced upon the observation of serious men, and rendered credible too, by the analogy of nature. And therefore to take these things into the account is to judge by experience and what we do know; and it is not judging so, to take no notice of them[2].

[1] Serm. at the *Rolls.*

[2] The answers to objections above are not drawn in reality from our ignorance, but from something positive which analogy shows us concerning it; namely, that we are incompetent judges of a divine scheme. Hence, to proceed upon a confession of this our incompetency is not to proceed upon ignorance, but upon knowledge.—(*W.*)

## CONCLUSION.

THE observations of the last Chapter lead us to consider this little scene of human life in which we are so busily engaged, as having a reference of some sort or other to a much larger plan of things. Whether we are any way related to the more distant parts of the boundless universe into which we are brought, is altogether uncertain. But it is evident that the course of things which comes within our view is connected with somewhat past, present, and future, beyond it[1]. So that we are placed, as one may speak, in the middle of a scheme, not a fixed but a progressive one, every way incomprehensible; incomprehensible in a manner equally with respect to what has been, what now is, and what shall be hereafter. And this scheme cannot but contain in it somewhat as wonderful, and as much beyond our thought and conception[2], as anything in that of Religion. For will any man in his senses say that it is less difficult to conceive how the world came to be and to continue as it is without than with an intelligent Author and Governor of it[3]? or admitting an intelligent Governor of it, that there is some other rule of government more natural and of easier conception than that which we call moral? Indeed, without an intelligent Author and Governor of Nature, no account at all can be given how this universe or the part of it particularly in which we are concerned came to be, and the course of it to be carried on as it is; nor any of its general end and design, without a moral Governor of it. That there is an intelligent Author of Nature and natural Governor of the world is a principle gone upon in the foregoing treatise as proved, and generally known and confessed to be proved. And the very notion of an intelligent Author of Nature proved by particular final causes, implies a will

[1] P. 178, &c.     [2] See Part ii. ch. ii.

[3] The religious mind of Herodotus, which saw God in everything around him, is constantly inferring that nature exhibits marks of design, and these imply to him an intelligent Author of Nature. Thus, in iii., 108, ne instances, as a proof of the πρόνοια of Nature, or of Nature's Author, the Deity, the fact that ravenous beasts are comparatively rare and have but few young at a birth, while the opposite is the case with the tame creatures. But it is clear that the induction of particular instances might be multiplied till it becomes as wide as nature itself.

and a character[1]. Now as our whole nature, the nature which he has given us, leads us to conclude his will and character to be moral, just, and good; so we can scarce in imagination conceive what it can be otherwise. However, in consequence of this his will and character, whatever it be, he formed the universe as it is, and carries on the course of it as he does rather than in any other manner, and has assigned to us and to all living creatures a part and a lot in it. Irrational creatures act this their part, and enjoy and undergo the pleasures and the pains allotted them without any reflection. But one would think it impossible that creatures endued with reason could avoid reflecting sometimes upon all this, reflecting, if not from whence we came, yet at least, whither we are going, and what the mysterious scheme in the midst of which we find ourselves will at length come out and produce—a scheme in which it is certain we are highly interested, and in which we may be interested even beyond conception; for many things prove it palpably absurd to conclude that we shall cease to be at death. Particular analogies do most sensibly show us that there is nothing to be thought strange in our being to exist in another state of life. And that we are now living beings affords a strong probability that we shall *continue* so; unless there be some positive ground, and there is none from reason or analogy, to think death will destroy us. Were a persuasion of this kind ever so well grounded, there would surely be little reason to take pleasure in it. But indeed it can have no other ground than some such imagination as that of our gross bodies being ourselves, which is contrary to experience. Experience too most clearly shows us the folly of concluding from the body and the living agent affecting each other mutually, that the dissolution of the former is the destruction of the latter. And there are remarkable instances of their not affecting each other, which lead us to a contrary conclusion. The supposition, then, which in all reason we are to go upon, is that our living nature will *continue* after death. And it is infinitely unreasonable to form an institution of life, or to act upon any other supposition. Now all expectation of immortality, whether more or less certain, opens an unbounded prospect to our hopes and our fears; since we see the

[1] P. 16$.

constitution of nature is such as to admit of misery as well as to be productive of happiness, and experience ourselves to partake of both in some degree, and since we cannot but know what higher degrees of both we are capable of. And there is no presumption against believing further that our future interest depends upon our present behaviour; for we see our present interest doth, and that the happiness and misery which are naturally annexed to our actions, very frequently do not follow till long after the actions are done, to which they are respectively annexed. So that were speculation to leave us uncertain, whether it were likely that the Author of Nature in giving happiness and misery to his creatures hath regard to their actions or not; yet, since we find by experience that he hath such regard, the whole sense of things which he has given us plainly leads us at once and without any elaborate inquiries to think that it may, indeed must be to good actions chiefly that he hath annexed happiness, and to bad actions misery, or that he will upon the whole reward those who do well, and punish those who do evil. To confirm this from the constitution of the world, it has been observed that some sort of moral government is necessarily implied in that natural government of God which we experience ourselves under; that good and bad actions at present are naturally rewarded and punished, not only as beneficial and mischievous to society, but also as virtuous and vicious; and that there is in the very nature of the thing, a tendency to their being rewarded and punished in a much higher degree than they are at present. And though this higher degree of distributive justice which nature thus points out and leads towards is prevented for a time from taking place, it is by obstacles which the state of this world unhappily throws in its way, and which therefore are in their nature temporary. Now, as these things in the natural conduct of Providence are observable on the side of virtue, so there is nothing to be set against them on the side of vice. A moral scheme of government, then, is visibly established, and in some degree carried into execution; and this, together with the essential tendencies of virtue and vice duly considered, naturally raise in us an apprehension that it will be carried on further towards perfection in a future state, and that every one shall there receive according to his deserts. And if this be so, then our future and general interest, under the moral government of God, is appointed to depend upon our behaviour, notwithstanding the difficulty which this may occasion of securing it, and the danger of losing it; just in the same manner as our temporal interest, under his natural government, is appointed to depend upon our behaviour, notwithstanding the like difficulty and danger. For, from our original constitution, and that of the world which we inhabit, we are naturally trusted with ourselves, with our own conduct and our own interest. And from the same constitution of nature, especially joined with that course of things which is owing to men, we have temptations to be unfaithful in this trust; to forfeit this interest, to neglect it, and run ourselves into misery and ruin. From these temptations arise the difficulties of behaving so as to secure our temporal interest, and the hazard of behaving so as to miscarry in it. There is therefore nothing incredible in supposing there may be the like difficulty and hazard with regard to that chief and final good which Religion lays before us. Indeed the whole account, how it came to pass that we were placed in such a condition as this, must be beyond our comprehension; but it is in part accounted for by what Religion teaches us, that the character of virtue and piety must be a necessary qualification for a future state of security and happiness under the moral government of God; in like manner, as some certain qualifications or other are necessary for every particular condition of life, under his natural government; and that the present state was intended to be a school of discipline for improving in ourselves that character. Now this intention of nature is rendered highly credible by observing that we are plainly made for improvement of all kinds; that it is a general appointment of Providence that we cultivate practical principles, and form within ourselves habits of action in order to become fit for what we were wholly unfit for before; that, in particular, childhood and youth is naturally appointed to be a state of discipline for mature age; and that the present world is peculiarly fitted for a state of moral discipline; and, whereas objections are urged against the whole notion of moral government and a probationary state from the opinion of Necessity, it has been shown that God has given us the evidence, as it were, of experience, that all objections against Religion on this head are vain and delusive. He has also, in his natural government, suggested an answer to all our short-sighted objections against the equity and goodness of his moral government, and' in general he has exemplified to us the latter by the former.

These things, which, it is to be remembered, are matters of fact, ought in all common sense to awaken mankind, to induce them to consider in earnest their condition, and what they have to do. It is absurd, absurd to the degree of being ridiculous, if the subject were not of so serious a kind, for men to think themselves secure in a vicious life, or even in that immoral thoughtlessness, which far the greatest part of them are fallen into. And the credibility of Religion, arising from experience and facts here considered, is fully sufficient in reason to engage them to live in the general practice of all virtue and piety, under the serious apprehension, though it should be mixed with some doubt[1], of a righteous administration established in nature, and a future judgment in consequence of it; especially when we consider how very questionable it is whether anything at all can be gained by vice[2], how unquestionably little as well as precarious the pleasures and profits of it are at the best, and how soon they must be parted with at the longest. For in the deliberations of reason concerning what we are to pursue and what to avoid, as temptations to anything from mere passion are supposed out of the case, so inducements to vice from cool expectations of pleasure and interest so small and uncertain and short are really so insignificant, as in the view of reason to be almost nothing in themselves, and in comparison with the importance of Religion they quite disappear and are lost. Mere passion indeed may be alleged, though not as a reason, yet as an excuse for a vicious course of life. And how sorry an excuse it is will be manifest by observing that we are placed in a condition in which we are unavoidably inured to govern our passions by being necessitated to govern them; and to lay ourselves under the same kind of restraints, and as great ones too from temporal regards, as virtue and piety in the ordinary course of things require. The plea of ungovernable passion, then, on the side of vice is the poorest of all things; for it is no reason, and but a poor excuse. But the proper motives to

[1] Part ii. ch. vi.                    [2] P. 112.

religion are the proper proofs[1] of it from our moral nature,
from the presages of conscience, and our natural apprehension of God under the character of a righteous Governor
and Judge; a nature and conscience and apprehension
given us by him, and from the confirmation of the dictates
of reason, by *life and immortality brought to light by the Gospel; and the wrath of God revealed from heaven against all
ungodliness and unrighteousness of men.*

[1] St. Paul commences his Epistle to the Romans with the professed acknowledgment, or rather the authoritative assertion, of the two great
evidences of natural religion—the one legible in the book of the creation,
the other indigenous in the soul of man. This latter is the *moral constitution of our souls,* which is the transcript, obscured and defaced indeed,
but still the transcript, of the great law of God; that law which the very
heathen know, and cannot avoid knowing, because "they have the work of
it written in their hearts," and their thoughts "accusing or excusing" them
by its dictates. And when St. Paul charges the Gentiles with the knowledge of this law, it is such a knowledge as, in his mind, was sufficient to
bring them under the *capacity* and consequent *obligation* of some *obedience;*
otherwise his whole doctrine and inculcation of that law, as subjecting them
to judgment, would be a lifeless argument.—*Davison on Primitive Sacrifice.* (*Ed.*)

# PART II

## OF REVEALED RELIGION

# CHAPTER I.

## OF THE IMPORTANCE OF CHRISTIANITY[1].

SOME persons, upon pretence of the sufficiency of the light of nature, avowedly reject all revelation, as in its very notion incredible, and what must be fictitious. And indeed it is certain no revelation would have been given, had the light of nature been sufficient in such a sense as to render one not wanting and useless[2]. But no man, in seriousness and

---

[1] An inquiry into the *importance* of Christianity is obviously a proper introduction to a treatise on its credibility. There are, moreover, two classes of persons who require to have this proved to them. Some avowedly *reject* all revelation, as in its very notion incredible; while others *neglect* or overlook it, without examining its evidence, without indeed rejecting it, and even upon supposition of its truth. The ground, both of rejection and neglect, is the assumed sufficiency of the light of nature; and against both it is maintained that the light of nature has been proved insufficient by the state of religion among heathens, whether before or after revelation; by the doubts which the greatest men have entertained on things of the utmost moment; by the natural inattention and ignorance of mankind in general, who neither could nor would reason out natural religion; by the need felt even by the better sort of supernatural instruction and assistance. Now, on a first and general view, this may be said:—If God has given us a revelation, it must be important, unless we are assured (as we cannot be, for our ignorance proves nothing) that all the reasons for it have ceased.—(*W.*)

[2] That the principles of natural religion have come to be so far understood and admitted as they are, may fairly be taken for one of the effects of the gospel revelation; *a proof of its actual* influence on opinions at the least, instead of a disproof of its necessity or use.—*Davison on Prophecy.* (*Ed.*)

simplicity of mind, can possibly think it so, who considers
the state of Religion in the heathen world before revelation,
and its present state in those places which have borrowed
no light from it; particularly the doubtfulness of some of
the greatest men concerning things of the utmost importance, as well as the natural inattention and ignorance of
mankind in general. It is impossible to say who would
have been able to have reasoned out that whole system,
which we call natural religion, in its genuine simplicity,
clear of superstition; but there is certainly no ground to
affirm that the generality could. If they could, there is no
sort of probability that they would. Admitting there were,
they would highly want a standing admonition to remind
them of it, and inculcate it upon them.

And further still, were they as much disposed to attend
to religion as the better sort of men are, yet even upon
this supposition there would be various occasions for supernatural instruction and assistance[1], and the greatest advantages might be afforded by them. So that to say revelation is a thing superfluous, what there was no need of, and
what can be of no service, is, I think, to talk quite wildly
and at random. Nor would it be more extravagant to
affirm, that mankind is so entirely at ease in the present
state, and life so completely happy, that it is a contradiction
to suppose our condition capable of being in any respect
better.

There are other persons, not to be ranked with these,
who seem to be getting into a way of neglecting and, as it
were, overlooking revelation as of small importance, provided natural Religion be kept to. With little regard either
to the evidence of the former, or to the objections against it,
and even upon supposition of its truth; "the only design
of it," say they, "must be, to establish a belief of the moral
system of nature, and to enforce the practice of natural
piety and virtue. The belief and practice of these things.

---

[1] Even admitting that the heathens of the better sort did not want the
power or the inclination to reason out the principles of natural religion clear
of superstition, and so might have partly found it out for themselves; still revelation might even then be required to aid their reasonings, and might afford
them the greatest assistance and advantage. Socrates, Plato, Confucius, and
other bright lights of antiquity, have given their authority to the necessity
and the anterior probability of a revelation from God.—*Ed.*

were, perhaps, much promoted by the first publication of Christianity; but whether they are believed and practised, upon the evidence and motives of nature or of revelation, is no great matter."[1]  This way of considering revelation, though it is not the same with the former, yet borders nearly upon it, and very much, at length, runs up into it, and requires to be particularly considered with regard to the persons who seem to be getting into this way.  The consideration of it will likewise further show the extravagance of the former opinion, and the truth of the observations in answer to it just mentioned.  And an inquiry into the importance of Christianity cannot be an improper introduction to a treatise concerning the credibility of it.

Now if God has given a revelation to mankind, and commanded those things which are commanded in Christianity, it is evident, at first sight, that it cannot in any wise be an indifferent matter, whether we obey or disobey those commands; unless we are certainly assured that we know all the reasons for them, and that all those reasons are now ceased with regard to mankind in general, or to ourselves in particular.  And it is absolutely impossible we can be assured of this.  For our ignorance of these reasons proves nothing in the case; since the whole analogy of nature shows, what is indeed in itself evident, that there may be infinite reasons for things with which we are not acquainted.

But the importance of Christianity will more distinctly appear by considering it more distinctly: *First*, as a republication and external institution of natural or essential Religion, adapted to the present circumstances of mankind, and intended to promote natural piety and virtue; and *Secondly*, as containing an account of a dispensation of things not discoverable by reason, in consequence of which several distinct precepts are enjoined us.  For though natural Religion is the foundation and principal part of Christianity, it is not in any sense the whole of it.

---

[1] Invenis multos ———— propterea nolle fieri Christianos, quia quasi sufficiunt sibi de bonâ vitâ suâ. Bene vivere opus est, ait. Quid mihi præcepturus est Christus? Ut bene vivam? Jam bene vivo. Quid mihi necessarius est Christus? Nullum homicidium, nullum furtum, nullam rapinam facio, res alienas non concupisco, nullo adulterio contaminor? Nam inveniatur in vitâ meâ aliquid quod reprehendatur, et qui reprehenderit faciat Christianum.—*Aug. in Psal.* xxxi.

I. Christianity is a republication of natural Religion[1]. It instructs mankind in the moral system of the world: that it is the work of an infinitely perfect Being, and under his government, that virtue is his law, and that he will finally judge mankind in righteousness, and render to all according to their works in a future state; and, which is very material, it teaches natural Religion in its genuine simplicity, free from those superstitions with which it was totally corrupted, and under which it was in a manner lost.

Revelation is further an authoritative publication of natural Religion, and so affords the evidence of testimony for the truth of it. Indeed the miracles and prophecies recorded in Scripture were intended to prove a particular dispensation of Providence, the redemption of the world by the Messiah; but this does not hinder but that they may also prove God's general providence over the world as our moral Governor and Judge. And they evidently do prove it, because this character of the Author of Nature is necessarily connected with and implied in that particular revealed dispensation of things; it is likewise continually taught expressly and insisted upon by those persons who wrought the miracles and delivered the prophecies. So that indeed natural Religion seems as much proved by the Scripture revelation as it would have been had the design of revelation been nothing else than to prove it.

But it may possibly be disputed how far miracles can prove natural Religion, and notable objections may be urged against this proof of it, considered as a matter of speculation; but considered as a practical thing there can be none[2]. For

[1] Christianity is indeed a republication of natural religion in the genuine *simplicity* of its leading doctrines, such as the existence of God, his character as a natural and a moral governor. It is all this; but at the same time it is something much higher also; it is an *authoritative* republication of natural religion with new proofs from miracles and prophecy; which, while they are the *direct* evidence of revealed religion, are also an *additional* evidence of natural religion.—*Ed.*

It has been admitted by infidels that Christianity is a republication of the law of nature; but they deny that there are any advantages arising out of this republication. So that, if they do not themselves draw the conclusion, they leave us to infer that Christianity is useless. The latter is the method and design of the author of "Christianity as old as the Creation."—(*H.*)

[2] Miracles not only contain a new demonstration of God's existence, but strengthen the proofs it draws from the frame of the world, and clear them

suppose a person to teach natural Religion to a nation who
had lived in total ignorance or forgetfulness of it, and to
declare he was commissioned by God so to do: suppose
him, in proof of his commission, to foretell things future
which no human foresight could have guessed at; to divide
the sea with a word; feed great multitudes with bread from
heaven; cure all manner of diseases; and raise the dead,
even himself, to life: would not this give additional credibility to his teaching, a credibility beyond what that of a
common man would have, and be an authoritative publication of the law of nature, *i. e.*, a new proof of it? It would
be a practical one of the strongest kind, perhaps, which
human creatures are capable of having given them. The
Law of Moses then, and the Gospel of Christ, are authoritative publications of the religion of nature; they afford a proof of God's general providence as Governor of
the world, as well as of his particular dispensations of providence towards sinful creatures revealed in the Law and
the Gospel. As they are the only evidence of the latter,
so they are an additional evidence of the former.

To show this further, let us suppose a man of the greatest
and most improved capacity, who had never heard of revelation, convinced upon the whole, notwithstanding the disorders of the world, that it was under the direction and
moral government of an infinitely-perfect Being; but ready
to question whether he were not got beyond the reach of his
faculties: suppose him, brought by this suspicion, into great
danger of being carried away by the universal bad example of
almost every one around him, who appeared to have no sense,
no practical sense at least, of these things; and this, perhaps,
would be as advantageous a situation with regard to Religion,
as nature alone ever placed any man in. What a confirmation now must it be to such a person all at once to find
that this moral system of things was revealed to mankind
in the name of that infinite Being whom he had from principles of reason believed in; and that the publishers of the
revelation proved their commission from him by making it
appear that he had entrusted them with a power of suspend-
ing and changing the general laws of nature.

from the two principal objections of atheism; viz., either that the world is
eternal, or that it owes its existence to a fortuitous concourse of atoms.—(*H.*)
See *Farmer on Miracles.*

Nor must it by any means be omitted, for it is a thing of the utmost importance, that life and immortality are eminently brought to light by the Gospel. The great doctrines of a future state, the danger of a course of wickedness, and the efficacy of repentance, are not only confirmed in the Gospel, but are taught, especially the last is, with a degree of light to which that of nature is but darkness.

Further: As Christianity served these ends and purposes when it was first published by the miraculous publication itself; so it was intended to serve the same purposes in future ages by means of the settlement of a visible church: of a society distinguished from common ones, and from the rest of the world, by peculiar religious institutions; by an instituted method of instruction, and an instituted form of external Religion. Miraculous powers were given to the first preachers of Christianity, in order to their introducing it into the world: *a visible church was established, in order to continue it and carry it on successively throughout all ages*[1]. Had Moses and the Prophets, Christ and his Apostles, only taught, and by miracles proved Religion to their contemporaries, the benefits of their instructions would have reached but to a small part of mankind. Christianity must have been in a great degree sunk and forgot in a very few ages. To prevent this appears to have been one reason why a visible church was instituted; to be like a city upon a hill, a standing memorial to the world of the duty which we owe our Maker; to call men continually both by example and instruction to attend to it, and by the form of Religion ever before their eyes remind them of the reality; to be the repository of the oracles of God; to hold up the light of revelation in aid to that of nature, and propagate it throughout all generations to the end of the world—the light of revelation, considered here in no other

---

[1] Compare Pearson on the Creed (Art. ix.) :—" The necessity of believing the *holy Catholic Church* appeareth first in this, that Christ hath appointed it as the only way unto eternal life. We read at the first that ' the Lord added to the church daily such as should be saved.'—(Acts ii. 47.) And what was then daily done, hath been done since continually. Christ never appointed two ways to heaven ; nor did he build a church to save some, and make another institution for other men's salvation. ' There is none other name under heaven given among men whereby we must be saved, but the name of Jesus.'—(Acts iv. 12.) And that name is no otherwise given under heaven than in the church." (*Ed.*)

view, than as designed to enforce natural Religion. And in proportion as Christianity is professed and taught in the world, Religion, natural or essential Religion, is thus distinctly and advantageously laid before mankind, and brought again and again to their thoughts as a matter of infinite importance. A visible church[1] has also a further tendency to promote natural Religion, as being an instituted method of education, originally intended to be of more peculiar advantage to those who conform to it. For one end of the institution was, that by admonition and reproof, as well as instruction; by a general regular discipline, and public exercises of religion, *the body of Christ*, as the Scripture speaks, should be *edified*, *i. e.*, trained up in piety and virtue for a higher and better state. This settlement, then, appearing thus beneficial, tending in the nature of the thing to answer, and in some degree actually answering, those ends; it is to be remembered, that the very notion of it implies positive institutions, for the visibility of the church consists in them[2]. Take away everything of this kind, and you lose the very notion itself. So that if the things now mentioned are advan· tages, the reason and importance of positive institutions in general is most obvious, since without them these advantages could not be secured to the world. And it is mere idle wantonness to insist upon knowing the reasons why such particular ones were fixed upon rather than others.

The benefit arising from this supernatural assistance, which Christianity affords to natural Religion, is what some persons are very slow in apprehending. And yet it is a thing distinct in itself, and a very plain obvious one. For will any in good earnest really say, that the bulk of

[1] The visibility of the church consists in its positive institutions, and the advantages of a visible church show the reason and importance of positive institutions in general. The reasons for the preference given in the Christian church to certain particular positive institutions over others, it is idle and wanton to inquire.—( *W.*)

[2] From these things appears the weakness of all pleas for neglecting the public service of the church. For though a man prays with as much devotion and less interruption at home, and reads better sermons there, yet that will by no means excuse the neglect of his appointed part in keeping up the ofession of Christianity among mankind. This neglect, were it universal, must be the dissolution of the whole visible church.—*Butler's Sermon before the Society for the Propagation of the Gospel.* (*Ed.*)

mankind in the heathen world were in as advantageous a situation with regard to natural Religion as they are now amongst us; that it was laid before them, and enforced upon them, in a manner as distinct, and as much tending to influence their practice?

The objections against all this, from the perversion of Christianity, and from the supposition of its having had but little good influence, however innocently they may be proposed, yet cannot be insisted upon as conclusive, upon any principles but such as lead to downright Atheism; because the manifestation of the law of nature by reason, which, upon all principles of Theism, must have been from God, has been perverted and rendered ineffectual in the same manner. It may indeed, I think, truly be said, that the good effects of Christianity have not been small; nor its supposed ill effects, any effects at all of it, properly speaking[1]. Perhaps, too, the things themselves done have been aggravated; and if not, Christianity hath been often only a pretence; and the same evils in the main would have been done upon some other pretence. However, great and shocking as the corruptions and abuses of it have really been, they cannot be insisted upon as arguments against it, upon principles of Theism. For one cannot proceed one step in reasoning upon natural Religion, any more than upon Christianity, without laying it down as a first principle, that the dispensations of Providence are not to be judged of by their perversions, but by their genuine tendencies: not by what they do actually seem to effect, but by what they would effect if mankind did their part—that part which is justly put and left upon them. It is altogether as much the language of one as of the other: *He that is unjust, let him be unjust still: and he that is holy, let him be holy still*[2]. The light of reason does not, any more than that of revelation, force men to submit to its authority; both admonish them of what they ought to do and avoid, together with the consequences of each, and after this, leave them at full liberty to act just as they please till the appointed time of judgment. Every moment's experience shows that this is God's general rule of government.

To return, then: Christianity being a promulgation of

[1] See Paley's Evidences, part iii. chap. vii.
[2] Rev. xxii. 11.

the law of nature; being moreover an authoritative promulgation of it, with new light and other circumstances
of peculiar advantage adapted to the wants of mankind;
these things fully show its importance.   And it is to be observed further, that as the nature of the case requires, so all
Christians are commanded to contribute, by their profession
of Christianity, to preserve it in the world, and render it
such a promulgation and enforcement of Religion.   For it
is the very scheme of the Gospel, that each Christian
should, in his degree, contribute towards continuing and
carrying it on: all by uniting in the public profession and
external practice of Christianity, some by instructing, by
having the oversight and taking care of this religious community, the Church of God.   Now this further shows the
importance of Christianity; and, which is what I chiefly
intend, its importance in a practical sense, or the high obligations we are under to take it into our most serious
consideration, and the danger there must necessarily be, not
only in treating it despitefully, which I am not now speaking of, but in disregarding and neglecting it.   For this is
neglecting to do what is expressly enjoined us, for continu
ing those benefits to the world, and transmitting them
down to future times.   And all this holds, even though the
only thing to be considered in Christianity were its sub
serviency to natural Religion.   But,

II. Christianity is to be considered in a further view; as
containing an account of a dispensation of things, not at all
discoverable by reason, in consequence of which several distinct precepts are enjoined us[1].   Christianity is not only an
external institution of natural Religion, and a new promul
gation of God's general providence, as righteous Governor
and Judge of the world; but it contains also a revelation of
a particular dispensation of Providence, carrying on by his
Son and Spirit for the recovery and salvation of mankind,
who are represented in Scripture to be in a state of ruin.
And in consequence of this revelation being made, we are

[1] Butler here insists that Christianity not merely is a new dispensation
beyond the discovery of reason, but also that it reveals to us certain new
relations to the Divine Persons, and hence imposes upon us certain duties
before unknown.   These duties become obligatory on us from the moment
that our relation to these Divine Persons is made known to us.   They are
anterior to, and independent of, any external command, and arise simply and
directly out of the very nature of their offices and relations toward us.—*Ed.*

commanded *to be baptized*, not only *in the name of the Father*, but also *of the Son, and of the Holy Ghost;* and other obligations of duty, unknown before, to the Son and the Holy Ghost, are revealed. Now the importance ·of· these duties may be judged of, by observing that they arise, not from positive command merely, but also from the offices, which appear, from Scripture, to belong to those divine persons in the Gospel dispensation, or from the relations which we are there informed they stand in to us. By reason is revealed the relation which God the Father stands in to us. Hence arises the obligation of duty which we are under to him. In Scripture are revealed the relations which the Son and Holy Spirit stand in to us. Hence arise the obligations of duty which we are under to them. The truth of the case, as one may speak, in each of these three respects being admitted: that God is the governor of the world upon the evidence of reason; that Christ is the mediator between God and man, and the Holy Ghost our guide and sanctifier, upon the evidence of revelation: the truth of the case, I say, in each of these respects being admitted, it is no more a question why it should be commanded that we be baptized in the name of the Son and of the Holy Ghost, than that we be baptized in the name of the Father. This matter seems to require to be more fully stated [1].

Let it be remembered, then, that Religion comes under the twofold consideration of internal and external; for the latter is as real a part of Religion, of true Religion, as the former. Now when Religion is considered under the first notion, as an inward principle, to be exerted in such and such inward acts of the mind and heart, the essence of natural Religion may be said to consist in religious regards to *God the Father Almighty;* and the essence of revealed Religion, as distinguished from natural, to consist in religious regards to *the Son* and to *the Holy Ghost*. And the obligation we are under, of paying these religious regards to each of these divine persons respectively, arises from the respective relations which they each stand in to us. How these relations are made known, whether by reason or revelation, makes no alteration in the case; because the duties arise out of the relations

[1] See The Nature, Obligation, and Efficacy of the Christian Sacraments, &c., and Colliber of revealed Religion, as there quoted.

themselves, not out of the manner in which we are informed of them. The Son and Spirit have each his proper office in that great dispensation of Providence, the redemption of the world; the one our mediator, the other our sanctifier. Does not, then, the duty of religious regards to both these divine persons as immediately arise, to the view of reason, out of the very nature of these offices and relations, as the inward good-will and kind intention which we owe to our fellow-creatures arises out of the common relations between us and them? But it will be asked, " What are the inward religious regards, appearing thus obviously due to the Son and Holy Spirit, as arising, not merely from command in Scripture, but from the very nature of the revealed relations, which they stand in to us?" I answer, the religious regards of reverence, honour, love, trust, gratitude, fear, hope. In what external manner this inward worship is to be expressed, is a matter of pure revealed command; as perhaps the external manner, in which God the Father is to be worshipped may be more so than we are ready to think; but the worship [1], the internal worship itself, to the Son and Holy Ghost, is no further matter of pure revealed command, than as the relations they stand in to us are matter of pure revelation; for the relations being known, the obligations to such internal worship are obligations of reason, arising out of those relations themselves. In short, the history of the Gospel as immediately shows us the reason of these obligations, as it shows us the meaning of the words Son and Holy Ghost.

If this account of the Christian Religion be just, those persons who can speak lightly of it, as of little consequence, provided natural Religion be kept to, plainly forget, that Christianity, even what is peculiarly so called, as distinguished from natural Religion, has yet somewhat

---

[1] The obligation of paying religious worship to the eternal Son or the Holy Ghost is as much *moral* as the duty of charity to mankind; for both obligations arise, independent of any external command, from our relations to both the one and the other, immediately that they are made known to us. It is because God stands to us in the relation of our Creator, our Redeemer, and our Sanctifier, that we owe him religious regards, independent of any express command; and it is because mankind already stand to us in the relation of brethren, that we owe them the duty of charity, even apart from any precept.—*Ed.*

very important, even of a moral nature. For the office of
our Lord being made known, and the relation he stands
in to us, the obligation of religious regards to him is
plainly moral, as much as charity to mankind is; since
this obligation arises, before external command, immediately out of that his office and relation itself. Those
persons appear to forget, that revelation is to be considered, as informing us of somewhat new in the state of
mankind, and in the government of the world; as ac-
quainting us with some relations we stand in, which could
not otherwise have been known. And these relations
being real (though before revelation we could be under no
obligations from them, yet upon their being revealed),
there is no reason to think, but that neglect of behaving
suitably to them will be attended with the same kind of
consequences under God's government, as neglecting to
behave suitably to any other relations made known to us
by reason. And ignorance, whether unavoidable or voluntary, so far as we can possibly see, will just as much, and
just as little, excuse in one case as in the other; the
ignorance being supposed equally unavoidable, or equally
voluntary, in both cases.

If therefore Christ be indeed the mediator between God
and man, *i. e.*, if Christianity be true; if he be indeed our
Lord, our Saviour, and our God, no one can say what may
follow, not only the obstinate but the careless disregard
to him in those high relations. Nay, no one can say what
may follow such disregard, even in the way of natural consequence [1]. For as the natural consequences of vice in
this life are doubtless to be considered as judicial punishments inflicted by God, so likewise, for aught we know,
the judicial punishments of the future life may be, in a
like way or a like sense, the natural consequence of vice [2],
of men's violating or disregarding the relations which God
has placed them in here, and made known to them.

Again : If mankind are corrupted and depraved in their
moral character, and so are unfit for that state which Christ
is gone to prepare for his disciples ; and if the assistance
of God's Spirit be necessary to renew their nature in the
degree requisite to their being qualified for that state,—all
which is implied in the express though figurative declara-

[1] Pp. 97, 98.                    [2] Ch. v.

tion, *Except a man be born of the Spirit, he cannot enter into the kingdom of God*[1],—supposing this, is it possible any serious person can think it a slight matter, whether or no he makes use of the means expressly commanded by God for obtaining this divine assistance? especially since the whole analogy of nature shows, that we are not to expect any benefits without making use of the appointed means for obtaining or enjoying them. Now reason shows us nothing of the particular immediate means of obtaining either temporal or spiritual benefits. This, therefore, we must learn, either from experience or revelation. And experience the present case does not admit of.

The conclusion from all this evidently is, that, Christianity being supposed either true or credible, it is unspeakable irreverence, and really the most presumptuous rashness, to treat it as a light matter. It can never justly be esteemed of little consequence, till it be positively supposed false. Nor do I know a higher and more important obligation which we are under than that of examining most seriously into the evidence of it, supposing its credibility; and of embracing it upon supposition of its truth.

The two following deductions may be proper to be added, in order to illustrate the foregoing observations, and to prevent their being mistaken.

*First*. Hence we may clearly see where lies the distinction between what is positive and what is moral in Religion. Moral *precepts* are precepts, the reasons of which we see; positive *precepts* are precepts, the reasons of which we do not see[2]. Moral *duties*[3] arise out of the nature of

[1] John iii. 5.

[2] This is the distinction between moral and positive precepts considered respectively as such. But yet, since the latter have somewhat of a moral nature, we may see the reason of them considered in this view. Moral and positive precepts are in some respects alike, in other respects different. So far as they are alike, we discern the reasons of both; so far as they are different, we discern the reasons of the former, but not of the latter. See p. 198, &c., and p. 206.

[3] Moral duties are superior to positive duties, for, 1stly, they are prior in point of time, flowing directly from some acknowledged relation of ourselves to another; 2ndly, they are, as it were, ends, to which positive duties are means. But, on the other hand, it must be remembered that a positive duty becomes a moral duty directly we know it to come from one to whom we stand in a particular relation. Thus the external worship of God is a moral duty, though *sacrifice*, as a particular form of worship, is only a positive duty; but when we come to know that it has been commanded by God himself, it rises from a mere positive to a moral duty.—*Ed.*

the case itself, prior to external command. Positive *duties* do not arise out of the nature of the case, but from external command; nor would they be duties at all, were it not for such command received from him whose creatures and subjects we are. But the manner in which the nature of the case, or the fact of the relation, is made known, this doth not denominate any duty either positive or moral. That we be baptized in the name of the Father is as much a positive duty as that we baptized in the name of the Son, because both arise equally from revealed command; though the relation which we stand in to God the Father is made known to us by reason, the relation we stand in to Christ by revelation only. On the other hand, the dispensation of the Gospel admitted, gratitude as immediately becomes due to Christ, from his being the voluntary minister of this dispensation, as it is due to God the Father, from his being the fountain of all good; though the first is made known to us by revelation only, the second by reason. Hence also we may see, and for distinctness' sake it may be worth mentioning, that positive institutions come under a twofold consideration. They are either institutions founded on natural Religion, as baptism in the name of the Father; though this has also a particular reference to the Gospel dispensation, for it is in the name of God, as the Father of our Lord Jesus Christ: or they are external institutions founded on revealed Religion, as baptism in the name of the Son and of the Holy Ghost.

*Secondly.* From the distinction between what is moral and what is positive in Religion, appears the ground of that peculiar preference which the Scripture teaches us to be due to the former.

The reason of positive institutions in general is very obvious, though we should not see the reason why such particular ones are pitched upon rather than others. Whoever, therefore, instead of cavilling at words, will attend to the thing itself, may clearly see that positive institutions in general, as distinguished from this or that particular one, have the nature of moral commands, since the reasons of them appear. Thus, for instance, the *external* worship of God is a moral duty, though no particular mode of it be so. Care, then, is to be taken, when a comparison is made between positive and moral duties, that they be compared no further than as they are different:

no further than as the former are positive, or arise out of mere external command, the reasons of which we are not acquainted with; and as the latter are moral, or arise out of the apparent reason of the case, without such external command. Unless this caution be observed, we shall run into endless confusion.

Now this being premised, suppose two standing precepts enjoined by the same authority; that, in certain conjunctures, it is impossible to obey both; that the former is moral, *i. e.*, a precept of which we see the reasons, and that they hold in the particular case before us; but that the latter is positive, *i. e.*, a precept of which we do not see the reasons : it is indisputable that our obligations are to obey the former[1], because there is an apparent reason for this preference, and none against it. Further, positive institutions—I suppose all those which Christianity enjoins—are means to a moral end, and the end must be acknowledged more excellent than the means. Nor is observance of these institutions any religious obedience at all, or of any value, otherwise than as it proceeds from a moral principle. This seems to be the strict logical way of stating and determining this matter; but will, perhaps, be found less applicable to practice than may be thought at first sight.

And therefore, in a more practical though more lax way of consideration, and taking the words *moral law* and *positive institutions* in the popular sense, I add, that the whole moral law is as much matter of revealed command as positive institutions are, for the Scripture enjoins every moral virtue. In this respect, then, they are both upon a level. But the moral law is, moreover, written upon our hearts; interwoven into our very nature. And this is a plain intimation of the Author of it, which is to be preferred when they interfere.

But there is not altogether so much necessity for the determination of this question as some persons seem to think. Nor are we left to reason alone to determine it. For, *First*, though mankind have, in all ages, been greatly

---

[1] But we are not to suppose, because we cannot see the reasons for them, that God has not the wisest and best reasons for imposing them. This would not be worth remarking, if deistical writers, who deny the possibility of such precepts, did not confound *positive* with *arbitrary* precepts.—(*H.*)

prone to place their religion in peculiar positive rites, by
way of equivalent for obedience to moral precepts, yet,
without making any comparison at all between them, and
consequently without determining which is to have the
preference, the nature of the thing abundantly shows all
notions of that kind to be utterly subversive of true religion, as they are, moreover, contrary to the whole general
tenor of Scripture; and likewise to the most express particular declarations of it, that nothing can render us accepted of God without moral virtue. *Secondly*, upon the
occasion of mentioning together positive and moral duties,
the Scripture always puts the stress of Religion upon the
latter, and never upon the former, which, though no sort
of allowance to neglect the former, when they do not interfere with the latter, yet is a plain intimation that when
they do, the latter are to be preferred. And further, as
mankind are for placing the stress of their religion any-
where rather than upon virtue, lest both the reason of the
thing, and the general spirit of Christianity, appearing in
the intimation now mentioned, should be ineffectual against
this prevalent folly, our Lord himself, from whose command alone the obligation of positive institutions arises,
has taken occasion to make the comparison between them
and moral precepts; when the Pharisees censured him for
*eating with publicans and sinners*, and also when they censured his disciples for *plucking the ears of corn on the Sabbath day*. Upon this comparison he has determined expressly, and in form, which shall have the preference when
they interfere. And by delivering his authoritative determination in a proverbial manner of expression, he has
made it general: *I will have mercy, and not sacrifice*[1]. The
propriety of the word *proverbial* is not the thing insisted
upon, though I think the manner of speaking is to be
called so. But that the manner of speaking very remark-
ably renders the determination general, is surely indisputable. For had it, in the latter case, been said only that
God preferred mercy to the rigid observance of the Sabbath, even then, by parity of reason, most justly might
we have argued, that he preferred mercy likewise to the
observance of other ritual institutions, and, in general,
moral duties to positive ones. And thus the determina-

[1] Matt. ix. 13, and xii. 7.

tion would have been general, though its being so were inferred and not expressed. But as the passage really stands in the Gospel, it is much stronger. For the sense and the very literal words of our Lord's answer are as applicable to any other instance of a comparison between positive and moral duties as to this upon which they were spoken. And if, in case of competition, mercy is to be preferred to positive institutions, it will scarce be thought that justice is to give place to them. It is remarkable, too, that as the words are a quotation from the Old Testament, they are introduced, on both the forementioned occasions, with a declaration that the Pharisees did not understand the meaning of them. This, I say, is very remarkable. For, since it is scarce possible for the most ignorant person not to understand the literal sense of the passage in the Prophet[1], and since understanding the literal sense would not have prevented their *condemning the guiltless*[2], it can hardly be doubted that the thing which our Lord really intended in that declaration was, that the Pharisees had not learned from it, as they might, wherein the *general* spirit of Religion consists : that it consists in moral piety and virtue, as distinguished from forms and ritual observances. However, it is certain we may learn this from his divine application of the passage in the Gospel.

But as it is one of the peculiar weaknesses of human nature, when upon a comparison of two things one is found to be of greater importance than the other, to consider this other as of scarce any importance at all[3], it is highly necessary that we remind ourselves, how great presumption it is to make light of any institutions of divine appointment; that our obligations to obey all God's commands whatever are absolute and indispensable; and that commands merely positive, admitted to be from him, lay us under a moral obligation to obey them, an obligation moral in the strictest and most proper sense.

[1] Hosea vi.        [2] See Matt. xii. 7.

[3] A neglect of the ordinances of religion of Divine appointment is the sure symptom of a criminal indifference about those *higher* duties by which men pretend to atone for the omission. It is too often found to be the beginning of a licentious life, and for the most part ends in the highest excesses of profligacy and irreligion.—*Horsley's Sermons on the Sabbath.* (*Ed.*)

To these things I cannot forbear adding, that the account now given of Christianity most strongly shows and
enforces upon us the obligation of searching the Scriptures, in order to see what the scheme of revelation really
is, instead of determining beforehand, from reason, what
the scheme of it must be[1]. Indeed, if in Revelation there
be found any passages the seeming meaning of which is
contrary to natural Religion, we may most certainly conclude such seeming meaning not to be the real one.
But it is not any degree of a presumption against an interpretation of Scripture, that such interpretation contains
a doctrine which the light of nature cannot discover[2], or a
precept which the law of nature does not oblige to.

# CHAPTER II.

## OF THE SUPPOSED PRESUMPTION AGAINST A REVELATION, CONSIDERED AS MIRACULOUS.

HAVING shown the importance of the Christian revelation
and the obligations which we are under seriously to attend
to it, upon supposition of its truth or its credibility, the
next thing in order, is to consider the supposed presumptions against revelation in general, which shall be the
subject of this chapter, and the objections against the
Christian in particular, which shall be the subject of some
following ones[3]. For it seems the most natural method,
to remove these prejudices against Christianity, before we
proceed to the consideration of the positive evidence for it,
and the objections against that evidence[4].

It is, I think, commonly supposed that there is some
peculiar presumption[5], from the analogy of nature, against

[1] See ch. iii.                     [2] Pp. 193, 194.
[3] Ch. iii. iv. v. vi.              [4] Ch. vii.

[5] Hume has gone further; he asserts that " the credit we give to testimony
is derived solely from experience," while, he adds, "a miracle is contrary to
experience. No testimony should ever gain credit to an event, unless it is
more extraordinary that it should be false than that the event should have
happened. . . . It is contrary to experience that a miracle should be
true; but not contrary to experience that testimony should be false." In
short, he considers miracles as *impossible ;* for, speaking of the Abbé de
Paris's miracles, he says, " What have we now to oppose to such a cloud of
witnesses, but *the absolute impossibility or miraculous nature of the events
they relate ?*" Besides the answers here given, see the introduction to the

the Christian scheme of things, at least against miracles, so as that stronger evidence is necessary to prove the truth and reality of them, than would be sufficient to convince us of other events, or matters of fact.   Indeed the consideration of this supposed presumption cannot but be thought very insignificant by many persons.   Yet, as it belongs to the subject of this Treatise, so it may tend to open the mind, and remove some prejudices, however needless the consideration of it be upon its own account[1].

I. I find no appearance of a presumption, from the analogy of nature, against the general scheme of Christianity, that God created and invisibly governs the world by Jesus Christ; and by him also will hereafter judge it in righteousness, *i. e.*, render to every one according to his works, and that good men are under the secret influence of his Spirit.   Whether these things are or are not to be called miraculous, is perhaps only a question about words; or, however, is of no moment in the case.   If the analogy of nature raises any presumption against this general scheme of Christianity, it must be either because it is not discoverable by reason or experience, or else because it is unlike that course of nature which is.   But analogy raises

"Analogy" above ; and that to Paley's "Evidences." The fallacy of Hume's reasoning consists in this, that he argues from the laws of matter and motion established in the world; which laws being confessedly arbitrary constitutions of the Creator, the manner of their operation cannot be drawn from any previous reasoning, but must be drawn solely from experience; but if we admit the existence of a God, we must admit that we can discover, by reasoning *à priori*, a connection between an almighty Cause and every effect which is the object of power.   To establish his position, it is necessary to prove that nothing is possible but what is established in the usual course of nature.   And as to his objection from *testimony*—for he opposes the uncertainty of testimony to the certainty of contrary experience—this is answered below (ch. iii.).   Further, that the evidence of testimony is superior to that of experience, and that they are somewhat connected, so that the weakening of the one weakens the other, is shown in Price's "Dissertation," p. 400, and in Dr. Adam's "Essay on Miracles," p. 5.—*Ed.*

[1] After showing the importance of Christianity, it seems the most natural method to remove an objection against revelation in general, and objections against the Christian revelation in particular, before considering the positive evidence for Christianity and the objections against that evidence.   The objection against revelation in general is, that it is *miraculous*.   In obviating the supposed presumption against the *particular* instance of miraculous power displayed in a revelation, the supposed presumption against *miracles in general* will be considered.—*Ed.*

no presumption against the truth of this scheme, upon either of these accounts.

*First.* There is no presumption, from analogy, against the truth of it, upon account of its not being discoverable by reason or experience [1]. For suppose one who never heard of revelation, of the most improved understanding, and acquainted with our whole system of natural philosophy and natural religion; such a one could not but be sensible that it was but a very small part of the natural and moral system of the universe which he was acquainted with  He could not but be sensible that there must be innumerable things in the dispensations of Providence past, in the invisible government over the world at present carrying on, and in what is to come, of which he was wholly ignorant [2], and which could not be discovered without revelation. Whether this scheme of nature be, in the strictest sense, infinite or not, it is evidently vast, even beyond all possible imagination. And doubtless that part of it which is opened to our view is but as a point, in comparison of the whole plan of Providence, reaching throughout eternity past and future; in comparison of what is even now going on in the remote parts of the boundless universe; nay, in comparison of the whole scheme of this world. And, therefore, that things lie beyond the natural reach of our faculties, is no sort of presumption against the truth and reality of them; because it is certain there are innumerable things, in the constitution and government of the universe, which are thus beyond the natural reach of our faculties. *Secondly.* Analogy raises no presumption against any of the things contained in this general doctrine of Scripture now mentioned, upon account of their being unlike the known course of nature. For there is no presumption at all from analogy, that the *whole* course of things, or divine government, naturally unknown to us, and *everything* in it, is like to anything in that which is known,

---

[1] There is *no* presumption against the scheme of Christianity on the ground of its not being discoverable by reason; for many things in the universe are so also. *None* on the ground of its being unlike the known course of nature; for in the known course of nature we see many dissimilarities, and the general scheme of Christianity is not entirely unlike the known course of nature.—*Ed.*

[2] Pp. 177, 178.

and therefore no peculiar presumption against anything in the former, upon account of its being unlike to anything in the latter. And in the constitution and natural government of the world, as well as in the moral government of it, we see things in a great degree unlike one another, and therefore ought not to wonder at such unlikeness between things visible and invisible. However, the scheme of Christianity is by no means entirely unlike the scheme of nature, as will appear in the following part of this Treatise.

The notion of a miracle, considered as a proof of a divine mission, has been stated with great exactness by divines, and is, I think, sufficiently understood by every one. There are also invisible miracles, the Incarnation of Christ, for instance, which, being secret, cannot be alleged as a proof of such a mission, but require themselves to be proved by visible miracles. Revelation itself, too, is miraculous, and miracles are the proof of it ; and the supposed presumption against these shall presently be considered. All which I have been observing here is, that, whether we choose to call everything in the dispensations of Providence, not discoverable without revelation, nor like the known course of things, miraculous ; and whether the general Christian dispensation now mentioned is to be called so or not ; the foregoing observations seem certainly to shew, that there is no presumption against it from the analogy of nature.

II. There is no presumption, from analogy, against some operations which we should now call miraculous [1], particularly none against a revelation at the beginning of the world—nothing of such presumption against it as is supposed to be implied or expressed in the word *miraculous* [2].

[1] A revelation would be called miraculous ; and by "miraculous" we mean an infringement on the ordinary course of nature. Now there is no presumption from the analogy of nature against a revelation as miraculous at the beginning of the world : for at that time there was no established course of nature, and hence there could be no miracle. Nor could there be any such presumption after the course of nature was established, because we know of no other parallel, such as another world, from which to argue.—*Ed.*

[2] A miracle is defined by Hume as "a violation of a law of nature by a particular volition of the Deity, or by the interposing of an invisible agent." It is defined by others as "an extraordinary work, in which the interposition of Divine power is clear and indisputable."—(*H.*)

For a miracle, in its very notion, is relative to a course of nature, and implies somewhat different from it, considered as being so. Now, either there was no course of nature at the time which we are speaking of, or if there were, we are not acquainted what the course of nature is, upon the first peopling of worlds. And therefore the question, whether mankind had a revelation made to them at that time, is to be considered, not as a question concerning a miracle, but as a common question of fact. And we have the like reason, be it more or less, to admit the report of tradition concerning this question, and concerning common matters of fact of the same antiquity; for instance, what part of the earth was first peopled.

Or thus: When mankind was first placed in this state, there was a power exerted, totally different from the present course of nature. Now, whether this power, thus wholly different from the present course of nature, for we cannot properly apply to it the word *miraculous;* whether this power stopped immediately after it had made man, or went on, and exerted itself further in giving him a revelation, is a question of the same kind as whether an ordinary power exerted itself in such a particular degree and manner, or not.

Or suppose the power exerted in the formation of the world be considered as miraculous, or rather be called by that name, the case will not be different, since it must be acknowledged that such a power was exerted. For supposing it acknowledged that our Saviour spent some years in a course of working miracles, there is no more presumption, worth mentioning, against his having exerted this miraculous power in a certain degree greater, than in a certain degree less—in one or two more instances, than in one or two fewer—in this, than in another manner.

It is evident, then, that there can be no peculiar presumption, from the analogy of nature, against supposing a revelation, when man was first placed upon earth.

Add, that there does not appear the least intimation in history or tradition that Religion was first reasoned out; but the whole of history and tradition makes for the other side—that it came into the world by revelation. Indeed the state of Religion in the first ages of which we have any account seems to suppose and imply that this was the original of it amongst mankind. And these reflections together, without taking in the peculiar authority of Scripture, amount to real and a very material degree of evidence that there was a revelation at the beginning of the world. Now this, as it is a confirmation of natural Religion, and therefore mentioned in the former part of this Treatise[1]; so likewise it has a tendency to remove any prejudices against a subsequent revelation.

III. But still it may be objected, that there is some peculiar presumption from analogy against miracles; particularly against revelation, after the settlement and during the continuance of a course of nature.

Now with regard to this supposed presumption, it is to be observed in general, that before we can have ground for raising what can, with any propriety, be called an *argument* from analogy, for or against revelation considered as somewhat miraculous, we must be acquainted with a similar or parallel case[2]. But the history of some other world, seemingly in like circumstances with our own, is no more than a parallel case; and therefore nothing short of this can be so. Yet, could we come at a presumptive proof, for or against a revelation, from being informed whether such world had one or not, such a proof, being drawn from one single instance only, must be infinitely precarious. More particularly: *First* of all, there is a very strong presumption against common speculative truths, and against the most ordinary facts before the proof of them, which yet is overcome by almost any proof. There is a presumption of millions to one against the story of Cæsar, or of any other man. For suppose a number of common facts so and so circumstanced, of which one had no kind of proof, should happen to come into one's thoughts, every one would, without any possible doubt, conclude them to be false. And the like may be said of a single common fact; and from hence it appears, that the question of importance, as to the matter before us, is con-

---

[1] P. 172, &c.

[2] There can be no argument from analogy without two distinct ratios. "The ratio of God's dealing with this world is similar to the ratio of God's dealings with another world," would be a fair analogical argument. But we know of no such other world; and even if we did, to argue from one analogous case would be infinitely precarious.—(*W.*)

cerning the degree of the peculiar presumption supposed against miracles; not whether there be any peculiar presumption at all against them. For, if there be the presumption [1] of millions to one against the most common facts, what can a small presumption additional to this amount to, though it be peculiar? It cannot be estimated, and is as nothing. The only material question is, whether there be any such presumption against miracles as to render them in any sort incredible. *Secondly.* If we leave out the consideration of Religion, we are in such total darkness upon what causes, occasions, reasons, or circumstances, the present course of nature depends, that there does not appear any improbability for or against supposing that five or six thousand years may have given scope for causes, occasions, reasons, or circumstances, from whence miraculous interpositions may have arisen; and from this, joined with the foregoing observation, it will follow, that there must be a presumption, beyond all comparison greater, against the *particular* common facts just now instanced in, than against miracles *in general*, before any evidence of either. But, *Thirdly.* Take in the consideration of Religion, or the moral system of the world, and then we see distinct particular reasons for miracles: to afford mankind instruction additional to that of nature, and to attest the truth of it. And this gives a real credibility to the supposition, that it might be part of the original plan

---

[1] As this has been controverted, and as it does not appear to have been Locke's opinion (for in his chapter on Probability, he says, that in things happening indifferently, there is nothing for or against them), it may be useful to confirm the account of Butler by a passage from Price's " Dissertations." " In many cases of particular histories, which are immediately believed upon the slightest testimony, there would have appeared to us, previously to this testimony, an improbability of almost infinity to one against their reality, as any one must perceive who will think how sure he is of the falsehood of all facts that have *no* evidence to support them, or which he has only imagined to himself. It is, then, very common for the slightest testimony to overcome an almost infinite improbability. In order to discover whether there is this improbability, let the connection of such facts with testimony be withdrawn, and then let it be considered what they are. If upon doing this, *i. e.*, upon making these objects of imagination, unsupported by any proof, they become improbable, the point, I should think, will be determined; for to find that a fact, when its connection with testimony is withdrawn, becomes improbable, is the same as to find that, independently of testimony, it is improbable."—(*H.*)

of things, that there should be miraculous interpositions.
Then, *Lastly*. Miracles must not be compared to common
natural events, or to events which, though uncommon, are
similar to what we daily experience, but to the extraordinary
phenomena of nature; and then the comparison will be
between the presumption against miracles, and the presumption against such uncommon appearances, suppose,
as comets, and against there being any such powers in
nature as magnetism and electricity, so contrary to the
properties of other bodies not endued with these powers.
And before any one can determine whether there be any
peculiar presumption against miracles, more than against
other extraordinary things, he must consider what, upon
first hearing, would be the presumption against the last-
mentioned appearances and powers to a person acquainted
only with the daily, monthly, and annual course of nature
respecting this earth, and with those common powers of
matter which we every day see.

Upon all this I conclude, that there certainly is no such
presumption against miracles as to render them in any
wise incredible; that, on the contrary, our being able to
discern reasons for them gives a positive credibility to the
history of them, in cases where those reasons hold; and
that it is by no means certain that there is any peculiar
presumption at all, from analogy, even in the lowest
degree, against miracles, as distinguished from other extraordinary phenomena; though it is not worth while to
perplex the reader with inquiries into the abstract nature
of evidence, in order to determine a question which,
without such inquiries, we see[1] is of no importance.

## CHAPTER III.

OF OUR INCAPACITY OF JUDGING WHAT WERE TO BE EXPECTED
IN A REVELATION; AND THE CREDIBILITY, FROM ANALOGY,
THAT IT MUST CONTAIN THINGS APPEARING LIABLE TO
OBJECTIONS[2].

BESIDES the objections against the evidence for Christianity, many are alleged against the scheme of it; against

[1] P. 215.
[2] Having shown the importance of Christianity, and having removed an
bjection against revelation in general, as miraculous, Butler proceeds to

the whole manner in which it is put and left with the
world, as well as against several particular relations in
Scripture—objections drawn from the deficiencies of revelation; from things in it appearing to men *foolishness*[1];
from its containing matters of offence which have led, and
it must have been foreseen would lead, into strange enthusiasm and superstition, and be made to serve the purposes of tyranny and wickedness; from its not being universal; and, which is a thing of the same kind, from its
evidence not being so convincing and satisfactory as it
might have been: for this last is sometimes turned into a
positive argument against its truth[2]. It would be tedious,
indeed impóssible, to enumerate the several particulars
comprehended under the objections here referred to; they
being so various, according to the different fancies of men.
There are persons who think it a strong objection against
the authority of Scripture, that it is not composed by rules
of art, agreed upon by critics, for polite and correct writing.
And the scorn is inexpressible with which some of the prophetic parts of Scripture are treated; partly through the
rashness of interpreters[3], but very much also on account
of the hieroglyphical and figurative language in which
they are left us. Some of the principal things of this sort

consider objections against the Christian revelation in particular, as distinguished from objections against its evidence, against the whole manner in
which it is put and left with the world, as well as against particular relations
in Scripture, against its deficiencies, against the "foolishness" of its doctrine
of redemption (1 Cor. i. 23), against its offences, against its want of
universality, and the supposed deficiency of its proof, and even against the
style of Scripture. In this chapter the general answer to such objections is
made, viz., that objections against the scheme of Christianity, as distinct from
objections against its evidence, are frivolous, because we are incompetent
judges of a scheme of revelation. This incompetency of judgment is probable
from the following analogical argument: as we are incompetent judges, before
experience, of the *scheme of nature*, which contains many things different
from what might have been expected, and liable to great apparent objections;
so it is probable that we are incompetent judges of the *scheme of revelation*,
which contains many things different from what might have been expected,
and liable to great apparent objections; in other words, the ratio of our
incompetent judgment to the natural scheme is similar to, and renders probable, the ratio of our incompetent judgment to the revealed scheme.—(*W.*)

[1] 1 Cor. i. 28.          [2] See ch. vi.

[3] Thus Voltaire pretended to believe that Ezekiel eat the roll of parch-
ment in reality, which the prophet expressly asserts to have been a mere
vision.—(*H.*)

shall be particularly considered in the following chapters. But my design at present is to observe in general, with respect to this whole way of arguing, that, upon supposition of a revelation, it is highly credible beforehand, we should be incompetent judges of it to a great degree; and that it would contain many things appearing to us liable to great objections, in case we judge of it otherwise than by the analogy of nature. And, therefore, though objections against the evidence of Christianity are most seriously to be considered, yet objections against Christianity itself are, in a great measure, frivolous; almost all objections against it, excepting those which are alleged against the particular proofs of its coming from God. I express myself with caution, lest I should be mistaken to vilify reason; which is indeed the only faculty we have wherewith to judge concerning anything, even revelation itself: or be misunderstood to assert, that a supposed revelation cannot be proved false from internal characters. For, it may contain clear immoralities or contradictions; and either of these would prove it false. Nor will I take upon me to affirm, that nothing else can possibly render any supposed revelation incredible. Yet still the observation above, is, I think, true beyond doubt, that objections against Christianity, as distinguished from objections against its evidence, are frivolous. To make out this, is the general design of the present chapter. And with regard to the whole of it, I cannot but particularly wish that the proofs might be attended to, rather than the assertions cavilled at, upon account of any unacceptable consequences, whether real or supposed, which may be drawn from them. For, after all, that which is true must be admitted, though it should show us the shortness of our faculties, and that we are in no wise judges of many things of which we are apt to think ourselves very competent ones. Nor will this be any objection with reasonable men, at least upon second thought it will not be any objection with such, against the justness of the following observations.

As God governs the world and instructs his creatures according to certain laws or rules in the known course of nature, known by reason together with experience; so the

Scripture informs us of a scheme of divine Providence[1]
additional to this. It relates, that God has, by revelation,
instructed men in things concerning his government which
they could not otherwise have known, and reminded them
of things which they might otherwise know, and attested
the truth of the whole by miracles. Now if the natural
and the revealed dispensation of things are both from God,
if they coincide with each other, and together make up one
scheme of Providence; our being incompetent judges of
one, must render it credible that we may be incompetent
judges also of the other. Since, upon experience, the
acknowledged constitution and course of nature is found
to be greatly different from what, before experience, would
have been expected, and such as men fancy there lie great
objections against; this renders it beforehand highly
credible, that they may find the revealed dispensation likewise, if they judge of it as they do of the constitution of
nature, very different from expectations formed beforehand, and liable, in appearance, to great objections; objections against the scheme itself, and against the degrees
and manners of the miraculous interpositions by which it
was attested and carried on. Thus, suppose a prince to
govern his dominions in the wisest manner possible by
common known laws, and that upon some exigencies he
should suspend these laws, and govern, in several instances, in a different manner; if one of his subjects were
not a competent judge beforehand, by what common rules
the government should or would be carried on; it could
not be expected that the same person would be a competent judge in what exigencies, or in what manner, or to
what degree, those laws commonly observed would be
suspended or deviated from. If he were not a judge of
the wisdom of the ordinary administration, there is no
reason to think he would be a judge of the wisdom of the
extraordinary. If he thought he had objections against
the former, doubtless it is highly supposable he might
think also that he had objections against the latter. And
thus, as we fall into infinite follies and mistakes whenever

---

[1] There is one great scheme of Providence, made up of two parts, God's
natural and revealed dispensations. And if we are incompetent judges of
the one part, which we do see, it is probable that we are incompetent judges
of the other, which we cannot see.—*Ed.*

we pretend otherwise than from experience and analogy to judge of the constitution and course of nature, it is evidently supposable beforehand that we should fall into as great in pretending to judge, in like manner, concerning revelation; nor is there any more ground to expect that this latter should appear to us clear of objections, than that the former should.

These observations, relating to the whole of Christianity, are applicable to inspiration in particular. As we are in no sort judges beforehand, by what laws or rules, in what degree, or by what means it were to have been expected that God would naturally instruct us; so upon supposition of his affording us light and instruction by revelation, additional to what he has afforded us by reason and experience, we are in no sort judges by what methods and in what proportion it were to be expected that this supernatural light and instruction would be afforded us [1]. We know not beforehand what degree or kind of natural information it were to be expected God would afford men, each by his own reason and experience; nor how far he would enable and effectually dispose them to communicate it, whatever it should be, to each other; nor whether the evidence of it would be certain, highly probable, or doubtful; nor whether it would be given with equal clearness and conviction to all. Nor could we guess, upon any good ground I mean, whether natural knowledge, or even the faculty itself by which we are capable of attaining it, reason would be given us at once, or gradually. In like manner we are wholly ignorant what degree of new knowledge it were to be expected God would give mankind by revelation, upon supposition of his affording one; or how far, or in what way, he would interpose miraculously to qualify them to whom he should originally make the revelation for communicating the knowledge given by it, and to secure their doing it to the age in which they should live, and to secure its being transmitted to posterity. We are equally ignorant whether the evidence of it would be certain or highly probable, or doubtful [2]; or whether all

[1] The argument may be briefly stated thus. As, before experience, we are incompetent judges of natural instruction, so it is probable that we are incompetent judges of supernatural instruction.—(W.)

[2] See ch. vi.

who should have any degree of instruction from it, and any degree of evidence of its truth, would have the same; or whether the scheme would be revealed at once, or unfolded gradually. Nay, we are not in any sort able to judge whether it were to have been expected that the revelation should have been committed to writing, or left to be handed down, and consequently corrupted by verbal tradition, and at length sunk under it, if mankind so pleased, and during such time as they are permitted, in the degree they evidently are, to act as they will.

But it may be said, "that a revelation in some of the above-mentioned circumstances—one, for instance, which was not committed to writing, and thus secured against danger of corruption—would not have answered its purpose." I ask, what purpose? It would not have answered all the purposes which it has now answered, and in the same degree, but it would have answered others, or the same in different degrees. And which of these were the purposes of God, and best fell in with his general government, we could not at all have determined beforehand.

Now since it has been shown that we have no principles of reason upon which to judge beforehand, how it were to be expected revelation should have been left, or what was most suitable to the divine plan of government in any of the forementioned respects, it must be quite frivolous to object afterwards as to any of them, against its being left in one way rather than another, for this would be to object against things upon account of their being different from expectations, which have been shown to be without reason. And thus we see that the only question concerning the truth of Christianity is, whether it be a real revelation, not whether it be attended with every circumstance which we should have looked for; and concerning the authority of Scripture, whether it be what it claims to be—not whether it be a book of such sort, and so promulged, as weak men are apt to fancy a book containing a divine revelation should. And, therefore, neither obscurity nor seeming inaccuracy of style, nor various readings, nor early disputes about the authors of particular parts, nor any other things of the like kind, though they had been much more considerable in degree than they are, could overthrow the authority of the Scripture; unless the Prophets, Apostles, or our Lord had promised that the book containing the divine revelation should be secure from those things. Nor indeed can any objections overthrow such a kind of revelation as the Christian claims to be, since there are no objections against the morality of it[1] but such as can show that there is no proof of miracles wrought originally in attestation of it, no appearance of anything miraculous in its obtaining in the world, nor any of prophecy, that is, of events foretold, which human sagacity could not foresee. If it can be shown that the proof alleged for all these is absolutely none at all, then is revelation overturned. But were it allowed that the proof of any one or all of them is lower than is allowed, yet, whilst any proof of them remains, revelation will stand upon much the same foot it does at present, as to all the purposes of life and practice, and ought to have the like influence upon our behaviour.

From the foregoing observations, too, it will follow, and those who will thoroughly examine into revelation will find it worth remarking, that there are several ways of arguing, which, though just with regard to other writings, are not applicable to Scripture, at least, not to the prophetic parts of it. We cannot argue, for instance, that this cannot be the sense or intent of such a passage of Scripture, for if it had it would have been expressed more plainly, or have been represented under a more apt figure or hieroglyphic; yet we may justly argue thus with respect to common books. And the reason of this difference is very evident[2]; that in Scripture we are not competent judges, as we are in common books, how plainly it were to have been expected, what is the true sense should have been expressed, or under how apt an image figured. The only question is, what appearance there is that this is the sense; and scarce at all, how much more determinately or accurately it might have been expressed or figured.

---

[1] P. 229.

[2] Other books have men ignorant and fallible as ourselves for their authors; but the holy Bible is the word of One who is infinitely above us. We need then, as it were, to stand on a much higher elevation than we do at present, before we can look down on holy Scripture in such a way as to judge what was to be expected in it beforehand.—*Ed.*

"But it is not self-evident that internal improbabilities of all kinds weaken external probable proof?" Doubtless. But to what practical purpose can this be alleged here, when it has been proved before [1] that real internal improbabilities, which rise even to moral certainty, are overcome by the most ordinary testimony; and when it now has been made appear that we scarce know what are improbabilities as to the matter we are here considering; as it will further appear from what follows.

For though from the observations above made it is manifest that we are not in any sort competent judges what supernatural instruction were to have been expected, and though it is self-evident that the objections of an incompetent judgment must be frivolous; yet it may be proper to go one step further, and observe that if men will be regardless of these things, and pretend to judge of the Scripture by preconceived expectations, the analogy of nature shows beforehand, not only that it is highly credible they may, but also probable that they will, imagine they have strong objections against it, however really unexceptionable; for so, prior to experience, they would think they had, against the circumstances, and degrees, and the whole manner of that instruction, which is afforded by the ordinary course of nature. Were the instruction which God affords to brute creatures by instincts and mere propensions, and to mankind by these together with reason, matter of probable proof and not of certain observation, it would be rejected as incredible, in many instances of it, only upon account of the means by which this instruction is given, the seeming disproportions, the limitations, necessary conditions, and circumstances of it. For instance, would it not have been thought highly improbable that men should have been so much more capable of discovering, even to certainty, the general laws of matter, and the magnitudes, paths, and revolutions of the heavenly bodies, than the occasions and cures of distempers and many other things in which human life seems so much more nearly concerned than in astronomy? How capricious and irregular a way of information, would it be said, is that of *invention*, by means of which nature instructs us in matters of science, and in many things upon which the affairs of

[1] P. 213.

the world greatly depend : that a man should, by this faculty, be made acquainted with a thing in an instant, when perhaps he is thinking of somewhat else, which he has in vain been searching after, it may be, for years. So likewise the imperfections attending the only method by which nature enables and directs us to communicate our thoughts to each other, are innumerable. Language is, in its very nature, inadequate, ambiguous, liable to infinite abuse, even from negligence, and so liable to it from design, that every man can deceive and betray by it. And to mention but one instance more : that brutes without reason should act, in many respects, with a sagacity and foresight vastly greater than what men have in those respects, would be thought impossible. Yet it is certain they do act with such superior foresight; whether it be their own, indeed, is another question. From these things it is highly credible beforehand, that upon supposition God should afford men some additional instruction by revelation, it would be with circumstances, in manners, degrees, and respects which we should be apt to fancy we had great objections against the credibility of. Nor are the objections against the Scripture, nor against Christianity in general, at all more or greater than the analogy of nature would beforehand—not perhaps give ground to expect ; for this analogy may not be sufficient, in some cases, to ground an expectation upon ; but no more nor greater than analogy would show it beforehand to be supposable and credible, that there might seem to lie against revelation.

By applying these general observations to a particular objection, it will be more distinctly seen how they are applicable to others of the like kind, and indeed to almost all objections against Christianity, as distinguished from objections against its evidence. It appears from Scripture that, as it was not unusual in the apostolic age for persons, upon their conversion to Christianity, to be endued with miraculous gifts, so some of those persons exercised these gifts in a strangely irregular and disorderly manner[1];

[1] Butler here alludes more especially to the case of the Corinthian church, whose members are rebuked by St. Paul for their ill use of the spiritual gifts bestowed upon them, and at the same time are warned of their proper use. See 1 Cor. xii. 1–11. If it be objected that the " gifts " spoken of in the apostolic times were not really miraculous, because abused, we answer

and this is made an objection against their being really
miraculous[1].   Now the foregoing observations quite remove this objection, how considerable soever it may appear at first sight.   For, consider a person endued with
any of these gifts; for instance, that of tongues : it is to
be supposed that he had the same power over this miraculous gift as he would have had over it had it been the
effect of habit, of study and use, as it ordinarily is, or the
same power over it as he had over any other natural en-
dowment.   Consequently he would use it in the same
manner he did any other, either regularly and upon pro
per occasions only, or irregularly, and upon improper
ones, according to his sense of decency and his character
of prudence.   Where then is the objection?   Why, if this
miraculous power was indeed given to the world to propagate Christianity and attest the truth of it, we might, it
seems, have expected that other sort of persons should
have been chosen to be invested with it; or that these
should at the same time have been endued with prudence,
or that they should have been continually restrained and
directed in the exercise of it, *i. e.*, that God should have
miraculously interposed, if at all, in a different manner
or higher degree.   But, from the observations made above,
it is undeniably evident that we are not judges in what
degrees and manners it were to have been expected he
should miraculously interpose, upon supposition of his
doing it in some degree and manner.   Nor, in the natural
course of Providence, are superior gifts of memory, elo-
quence, knowledge, and other talents of great influence,
conferred only on persons of prudence and decency,
or such as are disposed to make the properest use of
them.   Nor is the instruction and admonition naturally
afforded us for the conduct of life, particularly in our education, commonly given in a manner the most suited to

that the possessors of such gifts had the same power over them that we have
over our natural gifts, and so were able to use them regularly or irregularly.
—(*W.*)

[1] It is an objection of the same kind, and therefore to be answered in the
same way, that the Apostles were ignorant of the true nature of demoniacs;
for, even if their ignorance be admitted on this or any other point of the like
kind, it cannot be concluded that they could not be taught divine truth,
without a knowledge of bodily diseases, or of other points equally extraneous
to the design of their mission.—(*H.*)

recommend it, but often with circumstances apt to prejudice us against such instruction.

One might go on to add, that there is a great resemblance between the light of nature and of revelation in several other respects. Practical Christianity, or that faith and behaviour which renders a man a Christian, is a plain and obvious thing, like the common rules of conduct with respect to our ordinary temporal affairs. The more distinct and particular knowledge of those things, the study of which the Apostle calls *going on unto perfection*[1], and of the prophetic parts of revelation, like many parts of natural and even civil knowledge, may require very exact thought and careful consideration. The hindrances, too, of natural and of supernatural light and knowledge have been of the same kind. And as it is owned the whole scheme of Scripture is not yet understood, so, if it ever comes to be understood before the *restitution of all things*[2], and without miraculous interpositions, it must be in the same way as natural knowledge is come at: by the continuance and progress of learning and of liberty, and by particular persons attending to, comparing, and pursuing intimations scattered up and down it, which are overlooked and disregarded by the generality of the world. For this is the way in which all improvements are made, by thoughtful men's tracing on obscure hints, as it were, dropped us by nature accidentally, or which seem to come into our minds by chance. Nor is it at all incredible that a book, which has been so long in the possession of mankind, should contain many truths as yet undiscovered. For, all the same phenomena and the same faculties of investigation from which such great discoveries in natural knowledge have been made in the present and last age, were equally in the possession of mankind several thousand years before. And possibly it might be intended that events, as they come to pass, should open and ascertain the meaning of several parts of Scripture.

It may be objected that this analogy fails in a material respect, for that natural knowledge is of little or no consequence. But I have been speaking of the general instruction which nature does or does not afford us. And besides, some parts of natural knowledge, in the more

[1] Heb. vi. 1.     [2] Acts iii. 21.

common restrained sense of the words, are of the greatest
consequence to the ease and convenience of life.   But
suppose the analogy did, as it does not, fail in this respect, yet it might be abundantly supplied from the whole
constitution and course of nature, which shows that God
does not dispense his gifts according to our notions of the
advantage and consequence they would be of to us.   And
this in general, with his method of dispensing knowledge
in particular, would together make out an analogy full to
the point before us.

But it may be objected still further and more generally,
" The Scripture represents the world as in a state of ruin,
and Christianity as an expedient to recover it, to help in
these respects where nature fails; in particular, to supply
the deficiencies of natural light.   Is it credible, then, that
so many ages should have been let pass before a matter of
such a sort, of so great and so general importance, was
made known to mankind; and then that it should be made
known to so small a part of them?   Is it conceivable that
this supply should be so very deficient, should have the
like obscurity and doubtfulness, be liable to the like perversions, in short, lie open to all the like objections, as the
light of nature itself? [1]   Without determining how far this,
in fact, is so, I answer, it is by no means incredible that it
might be so, if the light of nature and of revelation be
from the same hand.   Men are naturally liable to diseases, for which God, in his good providence, has provided natural remedies [2].   But remedies existing in nature
have been unknown to mankind for many ages—are known
but to few now; probably many valuable ones are not
known yet.   Great has been and is the obscurity and
difficulty in the nature and application of them.   Circumstances seem often to make them very improper,
where they are absolutely necessary.   It is after long
labour and study, and many unsuccessful endeavours, that
they are brought to be as useful as they are, after high
contempt and absolute rejection of the most useful we
have, and after disputes and doubts which have seemed
to be endless.   The best remedies too, when unskilfully,
much more if dishonestly applied, may produce new diseases; and with the rightest application the success of

[1] Ch. vi.                    [2] Ch. v.

them is often doubtful.  In many cases they are not at all effectual; where they are, it is often very slowly, and the application of them, and the necessary regimen accompanying it, is not uncommonly so disagreeable, that some will not submit to them, and satisfy themselves with the excuse, that if they would, it is not certain whether it would be successful.  And many persons who labour under diseases for which there are known natural remedies, are not so happy as to be always, if ever, in the way of them. In a word, the remedies which nature has provided for diseases are neither certain, perfect, nor universal.  And, indeed, the same principles of arguing which would lead us to conclude that they must be so, would lead us likewise to conclude that there could be no occasion for them, *i. e.*, that there could be no diseases at all.  And therefore our experience that there are diseases shows that it is credible beforehand, upon supposition nature has provided remedies for them, that these remedies may be, as by experience we find they are, not certain, nor perfect, nor universal, because it shows that the principles upon which we should expect the contrary are fallacious.

And now, what is the just consequence from all these things?  Not that reason is no judge of what is offered to us as being of divine revelation.  For this would be to infer that we are unable to judge of anything because we are unable to judge of all things.  Reason can, and it ought to judge, not only of the meaning, but also of the morality and the evidence of revelation[1].  *First.* It is the province of reason to judge of the morality of the Scripture; *i. e.*, not whether it contains things different from what we should have expected from a wise, just, and good Being; for objections from hence have been now obviated: but whether it contains things plainly contradictory to wisdom, justice, or goodness; to what the light of nature teaches us of God[2].  And I know nothing of this sort objected against

[1] Our conclusion is, not that reason is no judge at all of things belonging to revelation; that would be to infer a universal conclusion from a particular premiss; but that there are some things of which it is, and others of which it is not, a fit judge.  For example, reason ought to and can judge not only of the *meaning* of Scripture, but also of its *morality* and its *evidence.—Ed.*

[2] For example, the command given by God to the Israelites to destroy all the nations of Canaan.  For an answer on this head, see " Graves on the Pentateuch."—*Ed.*

Scripture, excepting such objections as are formed upon suppositions, which would equally conclude that the constitution of nature is contradictory to wisdom, justice, or goodness, which most certainly it is not. Indeed there are some particular precepts in Scripture given to particular persons, requiring actions which would be immoral and vicious were it not for such precepts. But it is easy to see that all these are of such a kind, as that the precept changes the whole nature of the case and of the action, and both constitutes and shows that not to be unjust or immoral, which, prior to the precept, must have appeared and really have been so; which may well be, since none of these precepts are contrary to immutable morality. If it were commanded to cultivate the principles, and act from the spirit of treachery, ingratitude, cruelty, the command would not alter the nature of the case or of the action in any of these instances. But it is quite otherwise in precepts which require only the doing an external action: for instance, taking away the property or life of any. For men have no right to either life or property, but what arises solely from the grant of God: when this grant is revoked, they cease to have any right at all in either; and when this revocation is made known, as surely it is possible it may be, it must cease to be unjust to deprive them of either. And though a course of external acts, which without command would be immoral, must make an immoral habit, yet a few detached commands have no such natural tendency. I thought proper to say thus much of the few Scripture precepts, which require, not vicious actions, but actions which would have been vicious, had it not been for such precepts; because they are sometimes weakly urged as immoral, and great weight is laid upon objections drawn from them. But to me there seems no difficulty at all in these precepts but what arises from their being offences, *i. e.*, from their being liable to be perverted, as indeed they are, by wicked designing men, to serve the most horrid purposes, and, perhaps, to mislead the weak and enthusiastic. And objections from this head are not objections against revelation, but against the whole notion of religion, as a trial, and against the general constitution of nature. *Secondly*. Reason is able to judge, and must, of the evidence of revelation, and of the objections urged against that evidence; which shall be the subject of a following chapter[1].

But the consequence of the foregoing observations is, that the question upon which the truth of Christianity depends is scarce at all what objections there are against its scheme, since there are none against the morality of it, but *what objections there are against its evidence; or, what proof there remains of it after due allowances made for the objections against that proof:* because it has been shown that the *objections against Christianity, as distinguished from objections against its evidence, are frivolous.* For surely very little weight, if any at all, is to be laid upon a way of arguing and objecting, which, when applied to the general constitution of nature, experience shows not to be conclusive; and such, I think, is the whole way of objecting treated of throughout this chapter. It is resolvable into principles, and goes upon suppositions, which mislead us to think that the Author of Nature would not act as we experience he does; or would act, in such and such cases, as we experience he does not in like cases. But the unreasonableness of this way of objecting will appear yet more evidently from hence, that the chief things thus objected against are justified, as shall be further shown[2], by distinct, particular, and full analogies, in the constitution and course of nature.

But it is to be remembered, that, as frivolous as objections of the foregoing sort against revelation are, yet, when a supposed revelation is more consistent with itself, and has a more general and uniform tendency to promote virtue, than, all circumstances considered, could have been expected from enthusiasm and political views, this is a presumptive proof of its not proceeding from them, and so of its truth: because we are competent judges, what might have been expected from enthusiasm and political views.

Ch. vii.                    [2] Ch. iv. latter part, and v. vi.

# CHAPTER IV.

### OF CHRISTIANITY, CONSIDERED AS A SCHEME OR CONSTITUTION, IMPERFECTLY COMPREHENDED [1].

It hath been now shown [2] that the analogy of nature renders it highly credible beforehand, that, supposing a revelation to be made, it must contain many things very different from what we should have expected, and such as appear open to great objections; and that this observation, in good measure, takes off the force of those objections, or rather precludes them. But it may be alleged that this is a very partial answer to such objections, or a very unsatisfactory way of obviating them; because it doth not show at all that the things objected against can be wise, just, and good, much less that it is credible they are so. It will therefore be proper to show this distinctly, by applying to these objections against the wisdom, justice, and goodness of Christianity, the answer above [3] given to the like objections against the constitution of Nature; before we consider the particular analogies in the latter, to the particular things objected against in the former. Now that which affords a sufficient answer to objections against the wisdom, justice, and goodness of the constitution of Nature, is its being a constitution, a system, or scheme imperfectly comprehended; a scheme in which means are made use of to accomplish ends, and which is carried on by general laws; for from these things it has been proved not only to be possible, but also to be credible, that those things which are objected against may be consistent with wisdom, jus-

---

[1] In the preceding chapter it has been shown that we are not competent judges of the scheme of revelation; and so objections against the Christian scheme, as a fact, have been obviated. But objections may be made not only against the fact of the Christian scheme, but also against its *perfection,* against its wisdom, justice, and goodness. To this class of objections it is answered, in the former part of this chapter (as it was answered in part I. chap. vii. to like objections against the moral character of God's government) by a triple analogical argument (in which the truth of Christianity, as a fact, is assumed), that Christianity, like God's natural government, is a scheme or constitution imperfectly comprehended, that it uses means to accomplish ends, and that it is carried on by general laws.—(*W.*)

[2] In the foregoing chapter.

[3] Part I. ch. vii., to which this all along refers.

tice, and goodness; nay, may be instances of them; and even that the constitution and government of Nature may be perfect in the highest possible degree. If Christianity then be a scheme, and of the like kind, it is evident the like objections against it must admit of the like answer. And,

I. Christianity is a scheme quite beyond our comprehension[1]. The moral government of God is exercised by gradually conducting things so in the course of his providence, that every one, at length and upon the whole, shall receive according to his deserts, and neither fraud nor violence, but truth and right, shall finally prevail. Christianity is a particular scheme under this general plan of Providence, and a part of it, conducive to its completion with regard to mankind; consisting itself also of various parts, and a mysterious economy which has been carrying on from the time the world came into its present wretched state, and is still carrying on, for its recovery, by a divine person, the Messiah, who is to *gather together in one the children of God that are scattered abroad*[2], and establish *an everlasting kingdom, wherein dwelleth righteousness*[3]. And in order to it, after various manifestations of things relating

---

[1] The following outline may serve here to draw out Butler's argument more clearly.

Like God's natural government, so Christianity is an incomprehensible scheme.
i. Christianity is a scheme.
   1. A particular scheme under the general scheme of God's moral government, to the final perfection of which it conduces, according to the rule of distributive justice.
   2. Which has been carrying on from the fall of man, and is now carrying on for his recovery.
   3. Which consists of the following parts:—
     *A.* A divine Messiah, who, that He might found an universal kingdom, in fulness of time took flesh, endured the cross, and is highly exalted.
     *B.* A divine sanctifier.
     *C.* The invisible government of Christ over his church.
     *D.* His preparation of a heavenly place for his followers.
     *E.* His future return to judge the world and to settle his kingdom.
ii. Christianity is a scheme incomprehensible; for
   1. Scripture expressly calls it the "mystery of godliness."
   2. Its revealed particulars always run up into something of which we are ignorant.
   3. A great part of this scheme is evidently unrevealed.—*Ed.*

[2] John xi. 52.        [3] 2 Pet. iii. 13.

to this great and general scheme of Providence, through a succession of many ages; (for *the Spirit of Christ which was in the prophets, testified beforehand his sufferings, and the glory that should follow: unto whom it was revealed, that not unto themselves, but unto us, they did minister the things which are now reported unto us by them that have preached the Gospel, which things the angels desire to look into*[1];)—after various dispensations looking forward and preparatory to this final salvation; *in the fulness of time,* when infinite wisdom thought fit; He, *being in the form of God,—made himself of no reputation, and took upon him the form of a servant, and was made in the likeness of men; and being found in fashion as a man, he humbled himself, and became obedient unto death, even the death of the cross; wherefore God also hath highly exalted him, and given him a name which is above every name: that at the name of Jesus every knee should bow, of things in heaven, and things in earth, and things under the earth, and that every tongue should confess that Jesus Christ is Lord, to the glory of God the Father*[2]. Parts likewise of this economy are the miraculous mission of the Holy Ghost, and his ordinary assistances given to good men; the invisible government which Christ at present exercises over his church; that which he himself refers to in these words: *In my Father's house are many mansions—I go to prepare a place for you*[3]; and his future return to *judge the world in righteousness,* and completely re-establish the kingdom of God. *For the Father judgeth no man, but hath committed all judgment unto the Son; that all men should honour the Son, even as they honour the Father*[4] *All power is given unto him in heaven and in earth*[5]. *And he must reign, till he hath put all enemies under his feet. Then cometh the end, when he shall have delivered up the kingdom to God, even the Father; when he shall have put down all rule, and all authority and power. And when all things shall be subdued unto him, then shall the Son also himself be subject unto him that put all things under him, that God may be all in all*[6]. Now little, surely, need be said to show that this system or scheme of things is but imperfectly comprehended by us. The Scripture expressly asserts it to be so; and indeed one cannot read a passage relating to this *great mystery of godliness*[7], but what immediately runs up into something which

[1] 1 Pet. i. 11, 12.    [2] Phil. ii. 6—11    [3] John xiv. 2.    [4] John v. 22, 23.
[5] Matt. xxviii. 18.    [6] 1 Cor. xv. 25, 24, 28.    [7] 1 Tim. iii. 16.

shows us our ignorance in it, as everything in nature shows us our ignorance in the constitution of nature. And whoever will seriously consider that part of the Christian scheme which is revealed in Scripture will find so much more unrevealed, as will convince him, that, to all the purposes of judging and objecting, we know as little of it as of the constitution of nature. Our ignorance, therefore, is as much an answer to our objections against the perfection of one, as against the perfection of the other [1].

II. It is obvious, too, that in the Christian dispensation, as much as in the natural scheme of things, means are made use of to accomplish ends. And the observation of this furnishes us with the same answer to objections against the perfection of Christianity, as to objections of the like kind against the constitution of nature. It shows the credibility that the things objected against, how *foolish* [2] soever they appear to men, may be the very best means of accomplishing the very best ends. And their appearing *foolishness* is no presumption against this, in a scheme so greatly beyond our comprehension [3].

III. The credibility, that the Christian dispensation may have been all along carried on by general laws [4], no less than the course of nature, may require to be more distinctly made out. Consider, then, upon what ground it is we say that the whole common course of nature is carried on according to general fore-ordained laws. We know indeed several of the general laws of matter; and a great part of the natural behaviour of living agents is reducible to general laws. But we know in a manner nothing by what laws storms and tempests, earthquakes, famine, pestilence, become the instruments of destruction to mankind. And the laws, by which persons born into the world at such a time and place are of such capacities, geniuses, tempers; the laws, by which thoughts come into our mind in a multitude of cases; and by which innumerable things happen of the greatest influence upon the affairs and state of the world ; these laws are so wholly unknown to us, that we call the events, which come to pass by them accidental; though all reasonable men know certainly, that there cannot in reality be any such thing as chance; and conclude that the things which

---

[1] P. 184.          [2] 1 Cor. i.
[3] Pp. 185, 186.    [4] P. 187.

have this appearance are the result of general laws, and may be reduced into them. It is then but an exceeding little way, and in but a very few respects, that we can trace up the natural course of things before us to general laws. And it is only from analogy that we conclude the whole of it to be capable of being reduced into them; only from our seeing that part is so. It is from our finding that the course of nature, in some respects and so far, goes on by general laws, that we conclude this of the rest [1]. And if that be a just ground for such a conclusion, it is a just ground also, if not to conclude, yet to apprehend, to render it supposable and credible, which is sufficient for answering objections, that God's miraculous interpositions may have been all along in like manner by *general* laws of wisdom. Thus, that miraculous powers should be exerted at such times, upon such occasions, in such degrees and manners, and with regard to such persons rather than others; that the affairs of the world being permitted to go on in their natural course so far, should, just at such a point, have a new direction given them by miraculous interpositions; that these interpositions should be exactly in such degrees and respects only; all this may have been by general laws. These laws are unknown indeed to us; but no more unknown than the laws from whence it is that some die as soon as they are born, and others live to extreme old age; that one man is so superior to another in understanding; with innumerable more things, which, as was before observed, we cannot reduce to any laws or rules at all, though it is taken for granted they are as much reducible to general ones as gravitation. Now, if the revealed dispensations of Providence, and miraculous interpositions, be by general laws, as well as God's ordinary government in the course of nature made known by reason and experience, there is no more reason to expect that every exigence, as it arises, should be provided for by these general laws or miraculous interpositions, than that every exigence in nature should by the general laws of nature; yet there

[1] The course of nature is reducible to general laws in a very small part only; numberless events of the highest importance are called accidental, *i. e.*, are not reducible by us to general laws; and yet we conclude from analogy, that, as part of the course of nature is reducible to general laws, so also is the whole.—(*W.*)

might be wise and good reasons that miraculous interpositions should be by general laws, and that these laws
should not be broken in upon or deviated from by other
miracles.

Upon the whole, then, the appearance of deficiencies
and irregularities in nature is owing to its being a scheme
but in part made known, and of such a certain particular
kind in other respects.   Now we see no more reason why
the frame and course of nature should be such a scheme,
than why Christianity should.   And that the former is such
a scheme, renders it credible, that the latter, upon supposition of its truth, may be so too.   And as it is manifest
that Christianity is a scheme revealed but in part, and a
scheme in which means are made use of to accomplish ends, like to that of nature ; so the credibility that it
may have been all along carried on by general laws, no less
than the course of nature, has been distinctly proved.
And from all this it is beforehand credible that there might,
I think probable that there would, be the like appearance
of deficiencies and irregularities in Christianity as in
nature ; *i. e.*, that Christianity would be liable to the like
objections as the frame of nature.   And these objections
are answered by these observations concerning Christianity ;
as the like objections against the frame of nature are
answered by the like observations concerning the frame of
nature.

The objections against Christianity, considered as a
matter of fact[1], having, in general, been obviated in the
preceding chapter ; and the same, considered as made
against the wisdom and goodness of it, having been obviated in this ; the next thing, according to the method proposed, is to show that the principal objections, in particular,
against Christianity, may be answered by particular and
full analogies in nature.   And as one of them is made
against the whole scheme of it together, as just now
described, I choose to consider it here, rather than in a
distinct chapter by itself.   The thing objected against this
scheme of the Gospel is, " that it seems to suppose God
was reduced to the necessity of a long series of intricate
means, in order to accomplish his ends, the recovery and

[1] Pp. 217, &c.

salvation of the world; in like sort as men, for want of
understanding or power, not being able to come at their
ends directly, are forced to go roundabout ways and make
use of many perplexed contrivances to arrive at them."
Now everything which we see shows the folly of this, considered as an objection against the truth of Christianity.
For, according to our manner of conception, God makes
use of a variety of means, what we often think tedious
ones, in the natural course of providence for the accom-
plishment of all his ends. Indeed it is certain there is somewhat in this matter quite beyond our comprehension, but
the mystery is as great in nature as in Christianity. We
know what we ourselves aim at as final ends, and what
courses we take, merely as means conducing to those
ends. But we are greatly ignorant how far things are considered by the Author of Nature under the single notion
of means and ends, so as that it may be said this is merely
an end, and that merely means in his regard. And whether there be not some peculiar absurdity in our very
manner of conception concerning this matter, somewhat
contradictory arising from our extremely imperfect views
of things, it is impossible to say. However, thus much is
manifest, that the whole natural world and government of
it is a scheme or system, not a fixed, but a progressive
one; a scheme in which the operation of various means
takes up a great length of time before the ends they tend
to can be attained. The change of seasons, the ripening of
the fruits of the earth, the very history of a flower, is an
instance of this, and so is human life. Thus vegetable
bodies, and those of animals, though possibly formed at
once, yet grow up by degrees to a mature state. And thus
rational agents, who animate these latter bodies, are naturally directed to form each his own manners and character
by the gradual gaining of knowledge and experience, and
by a long course of action. Our existence is not only
successive, as it must be of necessity; but one state
of our life and being is appointed by God to be a
preparation for another, and that to be the means of attaining to another succeeding one; infancy to childhood, childhood to youth, youth to mature age. Men are impatient
and for precipitating things; but the Author of Nature
appears deliberate throughout his operations, accomplish-

ing his natural ends by slow successive steps. And there is a plan of things beforehand laid out, which, from the nature of it, requires various systems of means, as well as length of time, in order to the carrying on its several parts into execution. Thus, in the daily course of natural providence, God operates in the very same manner as in the dispensation of Christianity, making one thing subservient to another; this, to somewhat further; and so on, through a progressive series of means, which extend both backward and forward, beyond our utmost view. Of this manner of operation, everything we see in the course of nature is as much an instance as any part of the Christian dispensation.

## CHAPTER V.

OF THE PARTICULAR SYSTEM OF CHRISTIANITY; THE APPOINTMENT OF A MEDIATOR [1], AND THE REDEMPTION OF THE WORLD BY HIM [2].

THERE is not, I think, anything relating to Christianity which has been more objected against than the mediation of Christ in some or other of its parts. Yet upon thorough consideration there seems nothing less justly liable to it. For,

[1] One of the chief particular objections against the Christian scheme is the foolishness of the mediation of Christ and the redemption of the world by him. The removal of this objection is the point of the present chapter. —Ed.

[2] The view of the situation of man and of the attributes of the Creator, which the Christian revelation unfolds, is complete and consistent, and while it accounts for all the phenomena of our state, contains but two that are beyond our reason, and none that are contrary to it. It is above our reason, why we should be subjected to so much hazard; it is also above our reason how the sacrifice of Christ should expiate human transgressions. But it is not, therefore, contrary to reason that God should have chosen to create a being who should form and display his character in a probationary state, before he was admitted to the scene of his ulterior destination; or that he should mercifully have appointed a mean by which, consistently with his own justice, the risk incurred by that being should be diminished. Admit this, and the moral world, which is sometimes treated as a scene of confusion in which an unequal contest between reason and passion, between duty and transgression, is constantly carried on, will appear a comprehensive plan of harmony and intelligible design.—*Sumner's Records of the Creation.*

I. The whole analogy of nature removes all imagined presumption against the general notion of *a Mediator between God and man*[1]. For we find all living creatures are brought into the world, and their life in infancy is preserved, by the instrumentality of others; and every satisfaction of it, some way or other, is bestowed by the like means. So that the visible government which God exercises over the world is by the instrumentality and mediation of others. And how far his invisible government be or be not so, it is impossible to determine at all by reason. And the supposition that part of it is so appears, to say the least, altogether as credible as the contrary. There is then no sort of objection, from the light of nature, against the general notion of a mediator[2] between God and man, considered as a doctrine of Christianity, or as an appointment in this dispensation; since we find by experience that God does appoint mediators to be the instruments of good and evil to us—the instruments of his justice and his mercy. And the objection here referred to is urged, not against mediation in that high, eminent, and peculiar sense in which Christ is our mediator, but absolutely against the whole notion itself of a mediator at all.

II. As we must suppose that the world is under the proper moral government of God, or in a state of religion, before we can enter into consideration of the revealed doctrine, concerning the redemption of it by Christ, so that supposition is here to be distinctly taken notice of. Now the divine moral government which religion teaches us implies that the consequence of vice shall be misery in some future state by the righteous judgment of God.

[1] 1 Tim. ii. 5.

[2] The instances of Codrus, the last Athenian king, exposing himself to *inevitable* death, and Marcus Curtius, a noble Roman, leaping into the gulf, have been both considered, from the certainty of the offering, and the feelings of their respective nations, as proofs of a disposition in mankind to think that the voluntary and certain death of a person reputed noble and innocent, (Pliny says of Curtius " *virtute ac pietate ac morte præclarâ* expleverat,") may prevent impending and divinely-threatened calamities. Vide the Epistle to the Romans, v. 7, 8 : "For scarcely for a *righteous* man will one die, yet peradventure for a *good* man some would even dare to die. But God commendeth his love towards us, in that while we were yet *sinners* Christ died for us."—*Ed.*

That such consequent punishment shall take effect by his appointment, is necessarily implied. But, as it is not in any sort to be supposed, that we are made acquainted with all the ends or reasons for which it is fit future punishments should be inflicted, or why God has appointed such and such consequent misery should follow vice; and as we are altogether in the dark how or in what manner it shall follow, by what immediate occasions, or by the instrumentality of what means; there is no absurdity in supposing it may follow in a way analogous to that in which many miseries follow such and such courses of action at present— poverty, sickness, infamy, untimely death by diseases, death from the hands of civil justice. There is no absurdity in supposing future punishment may follow wickedness of course, as we speak, or in the way of natural consequence from God's original constitution of the world; from the nature he has given us, and from the condition in which he places us; or, in a like manner, as a person rashly trifling upon a precipice, in the way of natural consequence, falls down; in the way of natural consequence, breaks his limbs, suppose; in the way of natural consequence of this, without help, perishes.

Some good men may perhaps be offended with hearing it spoken of as a supposable thing that future punishments of wickedness may be in the way of natural consequence; as if this were taking the execution of justice out of the hands of God, and giving it to nature. But they should remember, that when things come to pass according to the course of nature, this does not hinder them from being his doing who is the God of nature, and that the Scripture ascribes those punishments to divine justice which are known to be natural, and which must be called so, when distinguished from such as are miraculous. But after all, this supposition, or rather this way of speaking, is here made use of only by way of illustration of the subject before us. For since it must be admitted, that the future punishment of wickedness is not a matter of arbitrary appointment, but of reason, equity, and justice, it comes, for aught I see, to the same thing, whether it is supposed to be inflicted in a way analogous to that in which the temporal punishments of vice and folly are inflicted, or in any other way. And though there were a difference, it is allowable, in the present case, to make this supposition, plainly not an incredible one, that future punishment may follow wickedness in the way of natural consequence, or according to some general laws of government already established in the universe.

III. Upon this supposition, or even without it, we may observe somewhat much to the present purpose in the constitution of nature or appointments of Providence; the provision which is made, that all the bad natural consequences of men's actions should not always actually follow, or that such bad consequences as, according to the settled course of things, would inevitably have followed if not prevented, should, in certain degrees, be prevented[1]. We are apt presumptuously to imagine that the world might have been so constituted as that there would not have been any such thing as misery or evil. On the contrary, we find the Author of Nature permits it; but then he has provided reliefs, and in many cases perfect remedies for it, after some pains and difficulties; reliefs and remedies even for that evil which is the fruit of our own misconduct, and which, in the course of nature, would have continued and ended in our destruction, but for such remedies. And this is an instance both of severity and indulgence in the constitution of nature. Thus all the bad consequences now mentioned of a man's trifling upon a precipice might be prevented. And though all were not, yet some of them might, by proper interposition, if not rejected, by another's coming to the rash man's relief, with his own laying hold on that relief in such sort as the case required. Persons may do a great deal themselves towards preventing the bad consequences of their follies, and more may be done by themselves, together with the assistance of others their fellow-creatures; which assistance nature re-

---

[1] This is one of the favourite topics of Butler. In his preface he urges the appeal from facts and from experience as that which ought to over-rule any mere abstract theories or suppositions, as what might have been the case, and how things might have been better than they are. Compare part I. chap. i. (p. 96.) " But if, as was above intimated, leaving off the delusive custom of substituting imagination in the room of experience, we would confine ourselves to what we do know and understand; if we would only argue from that, and from that form our expectations," &c.

And again, in part I. chap. iii., after discussing his ideal perfect state Butler resumes his argument thus: " But let us return to the earth our habitation, and we shall see," &c.—*Ed.*

quires and prompts us to. This is the general constitution of the world. Now, suppose it had been so constituted that, after such actions were done as were foreseen naturally to draw after them misery to the doer, it should have been no more in human power to have prevented that naturally consequent misery, in any instance, than it is in all; no one can say whether such a more severe constitution of things might not yet have been really good. But that, on the contrary, provision is made by nature that we may and do, to so great degree, prevent the bad natural effects of our follies; this may be called mercy or compassion in the original constitution of the world, compassion as distinguished from goodness in general. And the whole known constitution and course of things affording us instances of such compassion, it would be according to the analogy of nature to hope that, however ruinous the natural consequences of vice might be, from the general laws of God's government over the universe, yet provision might be made, possibly might have been originally made, for preventing those ruinous consequences from inevitably following; at least from following universally, and in all cases.

Many, I am sensible, will wonder at finding this made a question, or spoken of as in any degree doubtful. The generality of mankind are so far from having that awful sense of things which the present state of vice and misery and darkness seems to make but reasonable, that they have scarce any apprehension or thought at all about this matter any way; and some serious persons may have spoken unadvisedly concerning it. But let us observe what we experience to be, and what, from the very constitution of nature, cannot but be, the consequences of irregular and disorderly behaviour, even of such rashness, wilfulness, neglects, as we scarce call vicious. Now, it is natural to apprehend that the bad consequences of irregularity will be greater, in proportion as the irregularity is so. And there is no comparison between these irregularities and the greater instances of vice, or a dissolute, profligate disregard to all religion, if there be anything at all in religion. For, consider what it is for creatures, moral agents, presumptuously to introduce that confusion and misery into the kingdom of God which mankind have, in fact, introduced; to blaspheme the Sovereign Lord of all, to contemn his authority, to be injurious, to the degree they are, to their fellow-creatures, the creatures of God.   Add, that the effects of vice in the present world are often extreme misery, irretrievable ruin, and even death; and upon putting all this together, it will appear that as no one can say in what degree fatal the unprevented consequences of vice may be, according to the general rule of divine government; so it is by no means intuitively certain how far these consequences could possibly, in the nature of the thing, be prevented, consistently with the eternal rule of right, or with what is, in fact, the moral constitution of nature.   However, there would be large ground to hope, that the universal government was not so severely strict, but that there was room for pardon, or for having those penal consequences prevented.   Yet,

· IV. There seems no probability that anything we could do would alone and of itself prevent them: prevent their following or being inflicted.   But one would think at least it were impossible that the contrary should be thought certain.   For we are not acquainted with the whole of the case.   We are not informed of all the reasons which render it fit that future punishments should be inflicted; and therefore cannot know, whether anything we could do would make such an alteration, as to render it fit that they should be remitted.   We do not know what the whole natural or appointed consequences of vice are, nor in what way they would follow, if not prevented; and therefore can in no sort say, whether we could do anything which would be sufficient to prevent them.   Our ignorance being thus manifest, let us recollect the analogy of Nature or Providence.   For, though this may be but a slight ground to raise a positive opinion upon in this matter, yet it is sufficient to answer a mere arbitrary assertion, without any kind of evidence, urged by way of objection against a doctrine, the proof of which is not reason, but revelation.   Consider then: people ruin their fortunes by extravagance; they bring diseases upon themselves by excess; they incur the penalties of civil laws; and surely civil government is natural; will sorrow for these follies past, and behaving well for the future, alone and of itself prevent the natural consequences of them?   On the contrary, men's natural abilities of helping themselves are often impaired; or if not, yet they are forced to be beholden to the assistance of others, upon several accounts, and in different ways; assistance which they would have had no occasion for, had it not been for their misconduct; but which, in the disadvantageous condition they have reduced themselves to, is absolutely necessary to their recovery, and retrieving their affairs. Now since this is our case, considering ourselves merely as inhabitants of this world, and as having a temporal interest here, under the natural government of God, which however has a great deal moral in it; why is it not supposable that this may be our case also, in our more important capacity, as under his perfect moral government, and having a more general and future interest depending? If we have misbehaved in this higher capacity, and rendered ourselves obnoxious to the future punishment which God has annexed to vice, it is plainly credible, that behaving well for the time to come may be—not useless, God forbid—but wholly insufficient, alone and of itself, to prevent that punishment; or to put us in the condition which we should have been in had we preserved our innocence.

And though we ought to reason with all reverence, whenever we reason concerning the divine conduct, yet it may be added, that it is clearly contrary to all our notions of government, as well as to what is, in fact, the general constitution of nature, to suppose, that doing well for the future should, in all cases, prevent all the judicial bad consequences of having done evil, or all the punishment annexed to disobedience [1]. And we have manifestly nothing from whence to determine, in what degree, and in what cases, reformation would prevent this punishment, even supposing that it would in some [2]. And though the efficacy

[1] If it be said that this would not be proper in human governments, because they may easily be deceived by false shows of repentance, we answer that, supposing human governors could certainly distinguish a true repentance from a false one, the inconvenience of such a constitution to the public would still be the same; for it would encourage persons to commit crimes, in hopes of doing it with impunity, since every criminal would think that, in order to escape punishment, he had nothing to do but repent, and this alone would satisfy the law; and he would be apt to flatter himself that this was at any time in his power.—*Leland against Tindal.* (*Ed.*)

[2] The case of *penitence* is clearly different from that of *innocence.* It

of repentance itself alone, to prevent what mankind had
rendered themselves obnoxious to, and recover what they
had forfeited, is now insisted upon, in opposition to Christianity; yet, by the general prevalence of propitiatory sacrifices over the heathen world, this notion of repentance
alone being sufficient to expiate guilt, appears to be contrary to the general sense of mankind[1].

Upon the whole, then, had the laws, the general laws, of
God's government been permitted to operate without any
interposition in our behalf, the future punishment, for
aught we know to the contrary, or have any reason to
think, must inevitably have followed, notwithstanding anything we could have done to prevent it.  Now,

V. In this darkness, or this light of nature, call it which
you please, revelation comes in, confirms every doubting
fear which could enter into the heart of man concerning
the future unprevented consequence of wickedness; supposes the world to be in a state of ruin (a supposition
which seems the very ground of the Christian dispensation,
and which, if not provable by reason, yet is in no wise
contrary to it); teaches us too that the rules of divine
government are such as not to admit of pardon immediately and directly upon repentance, or by the sole efficacy
of it; but then teaches at the same time, what nature
might justly have hoped, that the moral government of the
universe was not so rigid but that there was room for an

---

implies a mixture of guilt pre-contracted, and punishment proportionably
deserved; it is consequently inconsistent with *rectitude* that both should be
treated alike by God. The present conduct of the penitent will receive God's
approbation; but the reformation of the sinner cannot have a retrospective
effect; the agent may be changed, but his former sins cannot be thereby
cancelled.  The convert and the sinner are the same individual person, and
the agent must be answerable for his whole conduct.—*Balguy's Essay on
Redemption.*  Cicero goes no farther on this head than to assert, "Quem
pœnitet peccâsse, *pene* est innocens."—*Dr. Shuckford.*  (*Ed.*)

[1] Our notions of moral government and the wide-spread belief of the world
in propitiatory sacrifices, are both of them against the supposition that mere
reformation and repentance will prevent the penal consequences of sin.  That
the heathen believed their animal sacrifices to be not only of an *expiatory*
but of a *vicarious* nature, might be shown from a variety of passages.  For
instance,

> " Cor pro corde, precor; pro fibris sumite fibras.
> Hanc animam vobis pro meliore damus."

OVID, *Fasti*, vi.  (*Ed.*)

interposition to avert the fatal consequences of vice, which therefore, by this means, does admit of pardon. Revelation teaches us, that the unknown laws of God's more general government, no less than the particular laws by which we experience he governs us at present, are compassionate[1], as well as good in the more general notion of goodness; and that he hath mercifully provided that there should be an interposition to prevent the destruction of human kind, whatever that destruction unprevented would have been. *God so loved the world, that he gave his only begotten Son, that whosoever believeth,* not, to be sure, in a speculative, but in a practical sense, *that whosoever believeth in him, should not perish*[2] : gave his Son in the same way of goodness to the world, as he affords particular persons the friendly assistance of their fellow-creatures; when without it their temporal ruin would be the certain consequence of their follies; in the same way of goodness I say, though in a transcendent and infinitely higher degree. And the Son of God *loved us, and gave himself for us,* with a love which he himself compares to that of human friendship; though, in this case, all comparisons must fall infinitely short of the thing intended to be illustrated by them. He interposed in such a manner as was necessary and effectual to prevent that execution of justice upon sinners, which God had appointed should otherwise have been executed upon them; or in such a manner as to prevent that punishment from actually following, which, according to the general laws of divine government, must have followed the sins of the world, had it not been for such interposition.[3]

---

[1] P. 242.        [2] John iii. 16.

[3] It cannot, I suppose, be imagined, even by the most cursory reader, that it is, in any sort, affirmed or implied in anything said in this chapter, that none can have the benefit of the general redemption but such as have the advantage of being made acquainted with it in the present life. But it may be needful to mention that several questions, which have been brought into the subject before us and determined, are not in the least entered into here; questions which have been, I fear, rashly determined, and perhaps with equal rashness contrary ways. For instance, whether God could have saved the world by other means than the death of Christ, consistently with the general laws of his government. And had not Christ come into the world, what would have been the future condition of the better sort of men; those just persons over the face of the earth for whom Manasses in his prayer asserts repentance was not appointed. The meaning of the first of these questions is greatly ambiguous, and neither of them can properly be answered

If anything here said should appear, upon first thought, inconsistent with divine goodness, a second, I am persuaded, will entirely remove that appearance. For were we to suppose the constitution of things to be such as that the whole creation must have perished, had it not been for somewhat which God had appointed should be, in order to prevent that ruin; even this supposition would not be inconsistent in any degree with the most absolutely perfect goodness. But still it may be thought that this whole manner of treating the subject before us, supposes mankind to be naturally in a very strange state. And truly so it does. But it is not Christianity which has put us into this state. Whoever will consider the manifold miseries, and the extreme wickedness of the world, that the best have great wrongnesses within themselves, which they complain of, and endeavour to amend; but that the generality grow more profligate and corrupt with age; that even moralists thought the present state to be a state of punishment; and, what might be added, that the earth our habitation has the appearances of being a ruin: whoever, I say, will consider all these, and some other obvious things, will think he has little reason to object against the Scripture account, that mankind is in a state of degradation [1], against this being the fact, how difficult soever he may think it to account for, or even to form a distinct conception of, the occasions and circumstances of it. But that the crime of our first parents was the occasion of our being placed in a more disadvantageous condition, is a thing throughout and particularly analogous to what we see in the daily course of natural providence, as the recovery of the world by the interposition of Christ has been shown to be so in general.

without going upon that infinitely absurd supposition that we know the whole of the case. And perhaps the very inquiry, *What would have followed if God had not done as he has,* may have in it some very great impropriety, and ought not to be carried on any further than is necessary to help our partial and inadequate conceptions of things.

[1] Here arises the objection that the doctrine which represents man as being in a lost and fallen state is inconsistent with the divine goodness. Our answer is that even the supposition that not only man but the whole creation must have been lost but for God's remedial interference, would not have been inconsistent with God's goodness. And if so, then much less the former.

VI. The particular manner in which Christ interposed in the redemption of the world, or his office as *Mediator,* in the largest sense, *between God and man,* is thus represented to us in the Scripture. *He is the light of the world*[1] the revealer of the will of God in the most eminent sense. He is a propitiatory sacrifice[2]; *the Lamb of God*[3]: and, as he voluntarily offered himself up, he is styled our High Priest[4]. And, which seems of peculiar weight, he is described beforehand in the Old Testament under the same characters of a priest, and an expiatory victim[5]. And whereas it is objected that all this is merely by way of allusion to the sacrifices of the Mosaic law; the Apostle on the contrary affirms, that the *law was a shadow of good things to come, and not the very image of the things*[6]: and that *the priests that offer gifts according to the law—serve unto the example and shadow of heavenly things, as Moses was admonished of God when he was about to make the tabernacle. For see (saith he) that thou make all things according to the pattern showed to thee in the mount*[7]: *i. e.,* the Levitical priesthood was a shadow of the priesthood of Christ; in like manner as the tabernacle made by Moses was according to that showed him in the mount. The priesthood of Christ, and the tabernacle in the mount, were the originals; of the former of which the Levitical priesthood was a type, and of the latter the tabernacle made by Moses was a copy. The doctrine of this epistle then plainly is, that the legal sacrifices were allusions to the great and final atonement to be made by the blood of Christ, and not that this was an allusion to those. Nor can anything be more express or determinate than the following passage. *It is not possible that the blood of bulls and of goats should take away sins. Wherefore, when he cometh into the world, he saith, Sacrifice and offering,* i. e., of bulls and of goats, *thou wouldest not, but a body hast thou prepared me. Lo, I come to do thy will, O God. By the which will we are sanctified through the offering of the body of Jesus Christ once for all*[8]. And to add one passage more of the like kind:

---

[1] John i. and viii. 12.

[2] Rom. iii. 25, v. 11; 1 Cor. v. 7; Eph. v. 2; 1 John ii. 2; Matt. xxvi. 28.

[3] John i. 29, 36, and throughout the book of Revelation.

[4] Throughout the epistle to the Hebrews.

[5] Isa. liii.; Dan. ix. 24; Ps. cx. 4.          [6] Heb. x. 1.

[7] Heb. viii. 4, 5.          [8] Heb. x. 4, 5, 7, 9, 10.

*Christ was once offered to bear the sins of many; and unto them that look for him shall he appear the second time, without sin;* i. e., without bearing sin, as he did at his first coming, by being an offering for it, without having our *iniquities* again *laid upon him,* without being any more a sin-offering:— *unto them that look for him shall he appear the second time, without sin, unto salvation*[1]. Nor do the inspired writers at all confine themselves to this manner of speaking concerning the satisfaction of Christ; but declare an efficacy in what he did and suffered for us, additional to and beyond mere instruction, example, and government, in great variety of expression: *That Jesus should die for that nation,* the Jews, *and not for that nation only, but that also,* plainly by the efficacy of his death, *he should gather together in one the children of God that were scattered abroad*[2]: that *he suffered for sins, the just for the unjust*[3]: that *he gave his life, himself, a ransom*[4]: that *we are bought, bought with a price*[5]: that *he redeemed us with his blood: redeemed us from the curse of the law, being made a curse for us*[6]: that he is our *advocate, intercessor,* and *propitiation*[7]: that *he was made perfect,* or consummate, *through sufferings; and being* thus *made perfect, he became the author of salvation*[8]: that *God was in Christ reconciling the world to himself, by the death of his Son by the cross, not imputing their trespasses unto them*[9]: and lastly, that *through death he destroyed him that had the power of death*[10]. Christ then, having thus *humbled himself, and become obedient unto death, even the death of the cross; God also hath highly exalted him, and given him a name which is above every name, hath given all things into his hands, hath committed all judgment unto him; that all men should honour the Son, even as they honour the Father*[11]. For *worthy is the Lamb that was slain to receive power, and riches, and wisdom, and strength, and honour, and glory, and blessing. And every creature which is in heaven, and on the earth, heard I saying, Blessing, and honour, and glory, and power, be unto him that sitteth upon the throne, and unto the Lamb, for ever and ever*[12].

[1] Heb. ix. 28.        [2] John xi. 51, 52.        [3] 1 Pet. iii. 18.
[4] Matt. xx. 28; Mark x. 45; 1 Tim. ii. 6.
[5] 2 Pet. ii. 1; Rev. xiv. 4; 1 Cor. vi. 20.
[6] 1 Pet. i. 19; Rev. v. 9; Gal. iii. 13.    [7] Heb. vii. 25; 1 John ii. 1, 2.
[8] Heb. ii. 10, v. 9.        [9] 2 Cor. v. 19; Rom. v. 10; Eph. ii. 16.
[10] Heb. ii. 14. See also a remarkable passage in the book of Job, xxxiii. 24.
[11] Phil. ii. 8, 9; John iii. 35, v. 22, 23.        [12] Rev. v. 12, 13.

These passages of Scripture seem to comprehend and express the chief parts of Christ's office as Mediator between God and man, so far, I mean, as the nature of this his office is revealed; and it is usually treated of by divines under three heads.

*First.* He was by way of eminence the Prophet, *that Prophet that should come into the world* [1] to declare the divine will. He published anew the law of nature, which men had corrupted; and the very knowledge of which, to some degree, was lost among them. He taught mankind, taught us authoritatively, to *live soberly, righteously, and godly, in this present world,* in expectation of the future judgment of God.

He confirmed the truth of this moral system of nature, and gave us additional evidence of it, the evidence of testimony [2]. He distinctly revealed the manner in which God would be worshipped, the efficacy of repentance, and the rewards and punishments of a future life. Thus he was a prophet in a sense in which no other ever was. To which is to be added, that he set us a perfect *example, that we should follow his steps.*

*Secondly.* He has a *kingdom which is not of this world.* He founded a church to be to mankind a standing memorial of religion, and invitation to it; which he promised to be with always even to the end. He exercises an invisible government over it himself, and by his Spirit: over that part of it which is militant here on earth, a government of discipline, *for the perfecting of the saints, for the edifying his body : till we all come in the unity of the faith, and of the knowledge of the Son of God, unto a perfect man, unto the measure of the stature of the fulness of Christ* [3]. Of this church, all persons scattered over the world, who live in obedience to his laws, are members. For these he is *gone to prepare a place,* and *will come again to receive them unto himself, that where he is, there they may be also ; and reign with him for ever and ever* [4]: and likewise *to take vengeance on them that know not God, and obey not his Gospel* [5].

Against these parts of Christ's office I find no objections but what are fully obviated in the beginning of this chapter.

*Lastly.* Christ offered himself a propitiatory sacrifice, and

[1] John vi. 14.          [2] P. 196.          [3] Eph. iv. 12, 13.
[4] John xiv. 2, 3; Rev. iii. 21, xi. 15.          [5] 2 Thess. i. 8.

made atonement for the sins of the world; which is mentioned last, in regard to what is objected against it. Sacrifices of expiation were commanded the Jews, and obtained amongst most other nations, from tradition, whose original probably was revelation. And they were continually repeated, both occasionally, and at the returns of stated times; and made up great part of the external religion of mankind. *But now once in the end of the world Christ appeared to put away sin by the sacrifice of himself*[1]. And this sacrifice was, in the highest degree and with the most extensive influence, of that efficacy for obtaining pardon of sin which the heathens may be supposed to have thought their sacrifices to have been, and which the Jewish sacrifices really were in some degree, and with regard to some persons.

How and in what particular way it had this efficacy, there are not wanting persons who have endeavoured to explain; but I do not find that the Scripture has explained it[2]. We seem to be very much in the dark concerning the manner in which the ancients understood atonement to be made, *i. e.*, pardon to be obtained by sacrifices. And if the Scripture has, as surely it has, left this matter of the satisfaction of Christ mysterious, left somewhat in it unrevealed, all conjectures about it must be, if not evidently absurd, yet at least uncertain. Nor has any one reason to complain for want of further information, unless he can show his claim to it.

Some have endeavoured to explain the efficacy of what Christ has done and suffered for us, beyond what the Scripture has authorized: others, probably because they could not explain it, have been for taking it away, and confining his office as Redeemer of the world to his instruction, example, and government of the church. Whereas the doctrine of the Gospel appears to be, not only that he taught the efficacy of repentance, but rendered it of the efficacy of which it is, by what he did and suffered for us: that he obtained for us the benefit of having our repentance accepted unto eternal life: not only that he revealed to

[1] Heb. ix. 26.
[2] All conjectures on a subject which is only partially revealed must be uncertain at the very best; and upon such deep subjects we cannot complain of want of further information to which we can show no claim.—(*W.*)

sinners that they were in a capacity of salvation, and how they might obtain it, but, moreover, that he put them into this capacity of salvation by what he did and suffered for them; put us into a capacity of escaping future punishment, and obtaining future happiness. And it is our wisdom thankfully to accept the benefit, by performing the conditions upon which it is offered, on our part, without disputing how it was procured on his. For,

VII. Since we neither know by what means punishment in a future state would have followed wickedness in this, nor in what manner it would have been inflicted had it not been prevented; nor all the reasons why its infliction would have been needful; nor the particular nature of that state of happiness which Christ is gone to prepare for his disciples: and since we are ignorant how far anything which we could do, would, alone and of itself, have been effectual to prevent that punishment to which we were obnoxious, and recover that happiness which we had forfeited; it is most evident we are not judges, antecedently to revelation, whether a mediator was or was not necessary to obtain those ends; to prevent that future punishment, and bring mankind to the final happiness of their nature [1]. And for the very same reasons, upon supposition of the necessity of a mediator, we are no more judges, antecedently to revelation, of the whole nature of his office, or the several parts of which it consists, of what was fit and requisite to be assigned him, in order to accomplish the ends of divine Providence in the appointment. And from hence it follows, that to object against the expediency or usefulness of particular things, revealed to have been done or suffered by him, because we do not see how they were conducive to those ends, is highly absurd. Yet nothing is more common to be met with than this absurdity. But if it be acknowledged beforehand that we are not judges in the case, it is evident that no objection can, with any shadow of reason, be urged against any particular part of Christ's mediatorial

[1] We next pass on to consider the worthlessness of all objections against the necessity of a mediator and against the mediatorial office of Jesus Christ; for we are incompetent judges, before revelation, of the necessity of a mediator, and, even upon the supposition that a mediator is necessary, we are incompetent judges as to the nature of his mediatorial office, until it is revealed to us.—*Ed.*

office revealed in Scripture, till it can be shown positively
not to be requisite or conducive to the ends proposed to be
accomplished, or that it is in itself unreasonable.

And there is one objection made against the satisfaction
of Christ, which looks to be of this positive kind : that the
doctrine of his being appointed to suffer for the sins of the
world, represents God as being indifferent whether he
punished the innocent or the guilty. Now from the foregoing observations we may see the extreme slightness of
all such objections ; and (though it is most certain all who
make them do not see the consequence) that they conclude
altogether as much against God's whole original constitution of nature, and the whole daily course of divine Providence in the government of the world [1], *i. e.*, against the
whole scheme of Theism and the whole notion of Religion,
as against Christianity. For the world is a constitution or
system, whose parts have a mutual reference to each other :
and there is a scheme of things gradually carrying on,
called the course of nature, to the carrying on of which
God has appointed us in various ways to contribute. And
when, in the daily course of natural providence, it is
appointed that innocent people should suffer for the faults
of the guilty, this is liable to the very same objection as the
instance we are now considering. The infinitely greater
importance of that appointment of Christianity which is
objected against, does not hinder, but it may be, as it
plainly is, an appointment of the very same kind, with
what the world affords us daily examples of. Nay, if there
were any force at all in the objection, it would be stronger,
in one respect, against natural providence than against
Christianity ; because under the former we are in many
cases commanded, and even necessitated, whether we will
or no, to suffer for the faults of others ; whereas the sufferings of Christ were voluntary. The world's being under
the righteous government of God does indeed imply, that
finally and upon the whole, every one shall receive according to his personal deserts ; and the general doctrine of
the whole Scripture is, that this shall be the completion of

---

[1] In other words, the objection, if it proves anything, proves too much :
for it applies equally to nature; nay, it applies to it with even stronger
force, because in the natural world the innocent often suffer for the guilty
involuntarily, whereas Christ suffered for us voluntarily.—*Ed.*

the divine government. But during the progress, and, for aught we know, even in order to the completion of this moral scheme, vicarious punishments may be fit, and absolutely necessary. Men, by their follies, run themselves into extreme distress; into difficulties which would be absolutely fatal to them, were it not for the interposition and assistance of others. God commands by the law of nature, that we afford them this assistance, in many cases where we cannot do it without very great pains, and labour, and sufferings to ourselves. And we see in what variety of ways one person's sufferings contribute to the relief of another; and how, or by what particular means, this comes to pass, or follows, from the constitution and laws of nature which came under our notice; and, being familiarized to it, men are not shocked with it. So that the reason of their insisting upon objections of the foregoing kind against the satisfaction of Christ is, either that they do not consider God's settled and uniform appointments as his appointments at all, or else they forget that vicarious punishment is a providential appointment of every day's experience; and then, from their being unacquainted with the more general laws of nature or divine government over the world, and not seeing how the sufferings of Christ could contribute to the redemption of it, unless by arbitrary and tyrannical will; they conclude his sufferings could not contribute to it any other way. And yet, what has been often alleged in justification of this doctrine, even from the apparent natural tendency of this method of our redemption; its tendency to vindicate the authority of God's laws, and deter his creatures from sin; this has never yet been answered, and is, I think, plainly unanswerable, though I am far from thinking it an account of the whole of the case. But without taking this into consideration, it abundantly appears, from the observations above made, that this objection is not an objection against Christianity, but against the whole general constitution of nature. And if it were to be considered as an objection against Christianity, or considering it as it is, an objection against the constitution of nature, it amounts to no more in conclusion than this, that a divine appointment cannot be necessary or expedient, because the objector does not discern it to be so, though he must own that the nature of the case is such as renders him incapable of judging whether it be so or not, or of seeing it to be necessary, though it were so.

It is indeed a matter of great patience to reasonable men, to find people arguing in this manner; objecting against the credibility of such particular things revealed in Scripture, that they do not see the necessity or expediency of them. For though it is highly right, and the most pious exercise of our understanding, to inquire with due reverence into the ends and reasons of God's dispensation; yet when those reasons are concealed, to argue from our ignorance, that such dispensations cannot be from God, is infinitely absurd. The presumption of this kind of objections seems almost lost in the folly of them. And the folly of them is yet greater, when they are urged, as usually they are, against things in Christianity analogous or like to those natural dispensations of Providence which are matter of experience. Let reason be kept to; and if any part of the Scripture account of the redemption of the world by Christ can be shown to be really contrary to it, let the Scripture, in the name of God, be given up; but let not such poor creatures as we go on objecting against an infinite scheme, that we do not see the necessity or usefulness of all its parts, and call this reasoning; and, which still further heightens the absurdity in the present case, parts which we are not actively concerned in. For it may be worth mentioning,

*Lastly.* That not only the reason of the thing, but the whole analogy of nature, should teach us not to expect to have the like information concerning the divine conduct, as concerning our own duty. God instructs us by experience (for it is not reason, but experience which instructs us) what good or bad consequences will follow from our acting in such and such manners; and by this he directs us how we are to behave ourselves. But though we are sufficiently instructed for the common purposes of life, yet it is but an almost infinitely small part of natural providence which we are at all let into. The case is the same with regard to revelation. The doctrine of a mediator between God and man, against which it is objected that the expediency of some things in it is not understood, relates only to what was done on God's part in the appointment, and on the Mediator's in the execution of it. For what is required of us in consequence of this gracious dispensation is another subject, in which none can complain for want of information. The constitution of the world, and God's natural govern-ment over it, is all mystery, as much as the Christian dispensation. Yet under the first he has given men all things pertaining to life; and under the other all things pertaining unto godliness. And it may be added, that there is nothing hard to be accounted for in any of the common precepts of Christianity; though if there were, surely a divine command is abundantly sufficient to lay us under the strongest obligations to obedience. But the fact is, that the reasons of all the Christian precepts are evident. Positive institutions are manifestly necessary to keep up and propagate religion amongst mankind. And our duty to Christ, the internal and external worship of him; this part of the religion of the Gospel manifestly arises out of what he has done and suffered, his authority and dominion, and the relation which he is revealed to stand in to us[1].

## CHAPTER VI.

OF THE WANT OF UNIVERSALITY IN REVELATION; AND OF
THE SUPPOSED DEFICIENCY IN THE PROOF OF IT[2].

IT has been thought by some persons that if the evidence of revelation appears doubtful, this itself turns into a posi-tive argument against it, because it cannot be supposed that, if it were true, it would be left to subsist upon doubtful evidence. And the objection against revelation from its not being universal is often insisted upon as of great weight.

Now the weakness of these opinions may be shown by observing the suppositions on which they are founded, which are really such as these:—that it cannot be thought God would have bestowed any favour at all upon us, unless

[1] P. 201, &c.
[2] Proceeding with the removal of objections against the Christian scheme, two are considered in this chapter:—(1.) *The supposed deficiency in the evi-dence of revelation ;* for apparent doubtfulness in the evidence of revelation is turned into a positive argument against it, on the supposition that a true revelation would not be left dependent upon doubtful evidence. (2.) *The want of universality in the light of revelation.* These objections may be urged against natural as well as against revealed religion; and the answers here given are almost equally applicable in both cases.—(*W.*)

in the degree which we think he might, and which we imagine would be most to our particular advantage; and also that it cannot be thought he would bestow a favour upon any unless he bestowed the same upon all—suppositions which we find contradicted not by a few instances in God's natural government of the world, but by the general analogy of nature together[1].

Persons who speak of the evidence of religion as doubtful, and of this supposed doubtfulness as a positive argument against it, should be put upon considering what that evidence indeed is, which they act upon with regard to their temporal interests. For it is not only extremely difficult, but in many cases absolutely impossible, to balance pleasure and pain, satisfaction and uneasiness, so as to be able to say on which side the overplus is. There are the like difficulties and impossibilities in making the due allowances for a change of temper and taste, for satiety, disgusts, ill-health; any of which render men incapable of enjoying, after they have obtained what they most eagerly desired. Numberless too are the accidents, besides that one of untimely death, which may even probably disappoint the best concerted schemes: and strong objections are often seen to lie against them, not to be removed or answered, but which seem overbalanced by reasons on the other side; so as that the certain difficulties and dangers of the pursuit are by every one thought justly disregarded, upon account of the appearing greater advantages in case of success, though there be but little probability of it. Lastly, every one observes our liableness, if we be not upon our guard, to be deceived by the falsehood of men and the false appearances of things; and this danger must be greatly increased if there be a strong bias within, suppose from indulged passion, to favour the deceit. Hence arises that great uncertainty and doubtfulness of proof

---

[1] Stated in syllogistic form, the answer to the above objections is this:— All objections resting upon weak suppositions are themselves weak ; these objections rest on weak suppositions; therefore, these objections are weak.

To prove the minor premiss we remark that the above objections rest on no stronger suppositions than the following :—(1.) That it is improbable that God would have bestowed any favour on us except in the degree which seems to us the best. (2.) That it is improbable that God should have bestowed a favour on any which he has not bestowed upon all. Now these suppositions are contradicted by the general analogy of nature altogether. —(W.)

wherein our temporal interest really consists, what are the most probable means of attaining it, and whether those means will eventually be successful. And numberless instances there are, in the daily course of life, in which all men think it reasonable to engage in pursuits, though the probability is greatly against succeeding; and to make such provision for themselves as it is supposable they may have occasion for, though the plain acknowledged probability is that they never shall. Then those who think the objection against revelation, from its light not being universal, to be of weight, should observe, that the Author of Nature, in numberless instances, bestows that upon some which he does not upon others, who seem equally to stand in need of it. Indeed, he appears to bestow all his gifts with the most promiscuous variety among creatures of the same species : health and strength, capacities of prudence and of knowledge, means of improvement, riches, and all external advantages. And as there are not any two men found of exactly like shape and features, so it is probable there are not any two of an exactly like constitution, temper, and situation with regard to the goods and evils of life. Yet, notwithstanding these uncertainties and varieties, God does exercise a natural government over the world, and there is such a thing as a prudent and imprudent institution of life, with regard to our health and our affairs, under that his natural government.

As neither the Jewish nor Christian revelation have been universal, and as they have been afforded to a greater or less part of the world at different times, so likewise at different times both revelations have had different degrees of evidence. The Jews who lived during the succession of prophets, that is, from Moses till after the Captivity, had higher evidence of the truth of their religion, than those had who lived in the interval between the last-mentioned period and the coming of Christ. And the first Christians had higher evidence of the miracles wrought in attestation of Christianity than what we have now[1]. They had also a

---

[1] The evidence for Christianity from miracles, and from the lives of its professors, was stronger to the first Christians than it is to us ; on the other hand, the evidence from the fulfilment of prophecy is stronger to us than it was to the first Christians. See the same argument repeated by Butler in the opening sentences of Sermon i. (pp. 385, 386) on Human Nature.—*Ed.*

strong presumptive proof of the truth of it, perhaps of much
greater force in way of argument than many think, of which
we have very little remaining; I mean the presumptive proof
of its truth from the influence which it had upon the lives
of the generality of its professors.   And we, or future ages,
may possibly have a proof of it, which they could not have,
from the conformity between the prophetic history, and the
state of the world and of Christianity.   And further, if we
were to suppose the evidence which some have of religion
to amount to little more than seeing that it may be true,
but that they remain in great doubts and uncertainties
about both its evidence and its nature, and great perplexities
concerning the rule of life ; others to have a full conviction
of the truth of religion, with a distinct knowledge of their
duty, and others severally to have all the intermediate
degrees of religious light and evidence which lie between
these two—if we put the case, that for the present, it was
intended revelation should be no more than a small light, in
the midst of a world greatly overspread, notwithstanding it,
with ignorance and darkness ; that certain glimmerings of
this light should extend and be directed to remote distances,
in such a manner as that those who really partook of it
should not discern from whence it originally came; that
some in a nearer situation to it should have its light
obscured, and, in different ways and degrees, intercepted :
and that others should be placed within its clearer influence,
and be much more enlivened, cheered, and directed by it;
but yet that even to these it should be no more than *a light
shining in a dark place;* all this would be perfectly uniform,
and of a piece with the conduct of Providence, in the distribution of its other blessings.   If the fact of the case really
were that some have received no light at all from the Scripture, as many ages and countries in the heathen world ; that
others, though they have, by means of it, had essential or
natural religion enforced upon their consciences, yet have
never had the genuine Scripture revelation with its real
evidence proposed to their consideration ; and the ancient
Persians and modern Mahometans may possibly be in
stances of people in a situation somewhat like to this ; that
others, though they have had the Scripture laid before them
as of divine revelation, yet have had it with the system and
evidence of Christianity so interpolated, the system so cor-

rupted, the evidence so blended with false miracles, as to leave the mind in the utmost doubtfulness and uncertainty about the whole, which may be the state of some thoughtful men in most of those nations who call themselves Christian; and lastly, that others have had Christianity offered to them in its genuine simplicity, and with its proper evidence, as persons in countries and churches of civil and of Christian liberty; but however that even these persons are left in great ignorance in many respects, and have by no means light afforded them enough to satisfy their curiosity, but only to regulate their life, to teach them their duty, and encourage them in the careful discharge of it; I say, if we were to suppose this somewhat of a general true account of the degrees of moral and religious light and evidence which were intended to be afforded mankind, and of what has actually been and is their situation in their moral and religious capacity; there would be nothing in all this ignorance, doubtfulness, and uncertainty, in all these varieties and supposed disadvantages of some in comparison of others, respecting religion, but may be paralleled by manifest analogies in the natural dispensations of Providence at present, and considering ourselves merely in our temporal capacity.

Nor is there anything shocking in all this, or which would seem to bear hard upon the moral administration in nature, if we would really keep in mind, that every one shall be dealt equitably with : instead of forgetting this, or explaining it away, after it is acknowledged in words [1]. All shadow of injustice, and indeed all harsh appearances, in this various economy of Providence, would be lost, if we would keep in mind, that every merciful allowance shall be made, and no more be required of any one, than what might have been equitably expected of him, from the circumstances in which he was placed: and not what might have been expected had he been placed in other circumstances : *i. e.*, in Scripture language, that every man shall be *accepted according to what he had, not according to what he had*

[1] We are thus to guard against two possible false inferences from what has been stated above. First, it is not implied that all men's religious condition is equally advantageous. Secondly, the fact that some are in a less advantageous religious condition than others is no reason why they should not endeavour themselves, and others for them, to improve their condition. —(*W.*)

*not* [1]. This, however, doth not by any means imply, that all persons' condition here is equally advantageous with respect to futurity. And Providence's designing to place some in greater darkness with respect to religious knowledge, is no more a reason why they should not endeavour to get out of that darkness, and others to bring them out of it, than why ignorant and slow people, in matters of other knowledge, should not endeavour to learn, or should not be instructed.

It is not unreasonable to suppose, that the same wise and good principle, whatever it was, which disposed the Author of Nature to make different kinds and orders of creatures, disposed him also to place creatures of like kinds in different situations: and that the same principle which disposed him to make creatures of different moral capacities, disposed him also to place creatures of like moral capacities in different religious situations; and even the same creatures in different periods of their being. And the account or reason of this is also most probably the account why the constitution of things is such as that creatures of moral natures or capacities, for a considerable part of that duration in which they are living agents, are not at all subjects of morality and religion, but grow up to be so, and grow up to be so more and more gradually from childhood to mature age.

What, in particular, is the account or reason of these things, we must be greatly in the dark, were it only that we know so very little even of our own case [2]. Our present state may possibly be the consequence of somewhat past, which we are wholly ignorant of, as it has a reference to somewhat to come, of which we know scarce any more than is necessary for practice. A system, or constitution, in its notion, implies variety; and so complicated a one as this world, very great variety. So that were revelation universal, yet, from men's different capacities of understanding, from the different lengths of their lives, their different educations and other external circumstances, and from their difference

---

[1] 2 Cor. viii. 12.

[2] To expect a distinct comprehensive view of the whole subject, clear of difficulties and objections, is to forget our nature and condition, neither of which admit of such knowledge with respect to any science whatever; and to inquire with this expectation is not to inquire as a man, but as one of another order of creatures.—*Butler's Sermon on the Ignorance of Man.* (*Ed.*)

of temper and bodily constitution; their religious situations would be widely different, and the disadvantage of some in comparison of others, perhaps, altogether as much as at present. And the true account, whatever it be, why mankind, or such a part of mankind, are placed in this condition of ignorance, must be supposed also the true account of our further ignorance in not knowing the reasons why, or whence it is, that they are placed in this condition. But the following practical reflections may deserve the serious consideration of those persons who think the circumstances of mankind or their own, in the forementioned respects, a ground of complaint.

*First.* The evidence of religion not appearing obvious, may constitute one particular part of some men's trial in the religious sense; as it gives scope for a virtuous exercise, or vicious neglect of their understanding, in examining or not examining into that evidence. There seems no possible reason to be given, why we may not be in a state of moral probation, with regard to the exercise of our understanding upon the subject of religion, as we are with regard to our behaviour in common affairs. The former is as much a thing within our power and choice as the latter. And I suppose it is to be laid down for certain, that the same character, the same inward principle, which, after a man is convinced of the truth of religion, renders him obedient to the precepts of it, would, were he not thus convinced, set him about an examination of it, upon its system and evidence being offered to his thoughts; and that in the latter state his examination would be with an impartiality, seriousness, and solicitude, proportionable to what his obedience is in the former. And as inattention, negligence, want of all serious concern, about a matter of such a nature and such importance, when offered to men's consideration, is, before a distinct conviction of its truth, as real immoral depravity and dissoluteness, as neglect of religious practice after such conviction; so active solicitude about it, and fair impartial consideration of its evidence, before such conviction, is as really an exercise of a morally right temper, as is religious practice after. Thus, that religion is not intuitively true, but a matter of deduction and inference; that a conviction of its truth is not forced upon every one, but left to be, by some, collected with heedful attention to premises; this as much constitutes religious probation, as much affords sphere, scope, opportunity, for right and wrong behaviour, as anything whatever does. And their manner of treating this subject, when laid before them, shows what is in their heart, and is an exertion of it.

*Secondly.* It appears to be a thing as evident, though it is not so much attended to, that if, upon consideration of religion, the evidence of it should seem to any persons doubtful, in the highest supposable degree, even this doubtful evidence will, however, put them into a *general state of probation* in the moral and religious sense [1]. For, suppose a man to be really in doubt whether such a person had not done him the greatest favour; or, whether his whole temporal interest did not depend upon that person: no one, who had any sense of gratitude and of prudence, could possibly consider himself in the same situation, with regard to such person, as if he had no such doubt. In truth, it is as just to say that certainty and doubt are the same, as to say the situations now mentioned would leave a man as entirely at liberty in point of gratitude or pru- dence, as he would be were he certain he had received no favour from such person, or that he no way depended upon him. And thus, though the evidence of religion which is afforded to some men should be little more than that they are given to see the system of Christianity, or religion in general, to be supposable and credible, this ought in all reason to beget a serious practical apprehension that it may be true. And even this will afford matter of exercise for religious suspense and deliberation, for moral resolution and self-government; because the apprehension that re- ligion may be true does as really lay men under obligations as a full conviction that it is true. It gives occasion and motives to consider further the important subject, to pre- serve attentively upon their minds a general implicit sense that they may be under divine moral government, an awful solicitude about religion, whether natural or revealed. Such apprehension ought to turn men's eyes to every degree of new light which may be had, from whatever side it comes;

[1] The supposed deficiency (even if it lead to the highest degree of doubt) in the evidence of revelation may constitute a *general moral probation*, for even the highest degree of religious doubt concerning the evidence of revela- tion imposes the practical obligations of religious deliberation.—(*W.*)

and induce them to refrain, in the mean time, from all immoralities, and live in the conscientious practice of every common virtue. Especially are they bound to keep at the greatest distance from all dissolute profaneness, for this the very nature of the case forbids, and to treat with highest reverence a matter upon which their own whole interest and being, and the fate of nature, depend. This behaviour, and an active endeavour to maintain within themselves this temper, is the business, the duty, and the wisdom of those persons who complain of the doubtfulness of religion; is what they are under the most proper obligations to [1], and such behaviour is an exertion of, and has a tendency to improve in them that character which the practice of all the several duties of religion, from a full conviction of its truth, is an exertion of, and has a tendency to improve in others: others, I say, to whom God has afforded such conviction. Nay, considering the infinite importance of religion, revealed as well as natural, I think it may be said in general, that whoever will weigh the matter thoroughly, may see there is not near so much difference, as is commonly imagined, between what ought in reason to be the rule of life, to those persons who are fully convinced of its truth, and to those who have only a serious doubting apprehension that it may be true. Their hopes, and fears, and obligations, will be in various degrees; but as the subject-matter of their hopes and fears is the same, so the subject-matter of their obligations, what they are bound to do and to refrain from, is not so very unlike.

It is to be observed further, that, from a character of understanding, or a situation of influence in the world, some persons have it in their power to do infinitely more harm or good, by setting an example of profaneness and avowed disregard to all religion, or, on the contrary, of a serious, though perhaps doubting, apprehension of its truth, and of a reverend regard to it under this doubtfulness, than they can do

[1] For would it not be madness for a man to forsake a safe road, and prefer to it one in which he acknowledges there is an even chance, likewise, of his going safe through it? Yet there are people absurd enough to take the supposed doubtfulness of religion for the same thing as a proof of its falsehood, after they have concluded it doubtful, from having it often called in question. This shows how infinitely unreasonable sceptical men are with regard to religion, and that they really lay aside their reason upon this subject as much as the most *extravagant enthusiasts.—Butler's Charge.* (*Ed.*)

by acting well or ill in all the common intercourses amongst
mankind. And consequently they are most highly accountable for a behaviour, which, they may easily foresee, is of
such importance, and in which there is most plainly a right
and a wrong, even admitting the evidence of religion to be
as doubtful as is pretended.

The ground of these observations, and that which renders
them just and true, is that doubting[1] necessarily implies
some degree of evidence for that of which we doubt. For
no person would be in doubt concerning the truth of a number of facts so and so circumstanced, which should accidentally come into his thoughts, and of which he had no evidence at all. And though in the case of an even chance,
and where consequently we were in doubt, we should in
common language say that we had no evidence at all for
either side; yet that situation of things, which renders it an
even chance and no more, that such an event will happen,
renders this case equivalent to all others, where there is
such evidence on both sides of a question[2], as leaves the
mind in doubt concerning the truth. Indeed in all these
cases, there is no more evidence on one side than on the
other; but there is (what is equivalent to) much more for
either, than for the truth of a number of facts, which come
into one's thoughts at random. And thus, in all these cases,
doubt as much presupposes evidence, lower degrees of evidence, as belief presupposes higher, and certainty higher
still. Any one who will a little attend to the nature of
evidence, will easily carry this observation on, and see that
between no evidence at all, and that degree of it which
affords ground of doubt, there are as many intermediate
degrees, as there are between that degree which is the
ground of doubt and demonstration. And though we have
not faculties to distinguish these degrees of evidence with
any sort of exactness, yet, in proportion as they are discerned, they ought to influence our practice. For it is as
real an imperfection in the moral character, not to be

---

[1] "*Doubting*" is a relative term, and implies only that a *preponderance* of
evidence is against a fact or position. In this is clearly implied that there is
on the other side *some* amount of evidence, greater or smaller; and if so,
this evidence, whatever its weight may be, has a fair claim to be taken into
account.—*Ed.*

[2] Introduction.

influenced in practice by a lower degree of evidence when
discerned, as it is in the understanding not to discern it.
And as, in all subjects which men consider, they discern the
lower as well as higher degrees of evidence, proportionably
to their capacity of understanding : so, in practical subjects,
they are influenced in practice by the lower as well as
higher degrees of it, proportionably to their fairness and
honesty.    And as, in proportion to defects in the under
standing, men are unapt to see lower degrees of evidence,
are in danger of overlooking evidence when it is not glaring,
and are easily imposed upon in such cases ; so, in propor
tion to the corruption of the heart, they seem capable of
satisfying themselves with having no regard in practice to
evidence acknowledged real, if it be not overbearing.  From
these things it must follow, that doubting concerning
religion implies such a degree of evidence for it, as, joined
with the consideration of its importance, unquestionably
lays men under the obligations before mentioned, to have a
dutiful regard to it in all their behaviour.

*Thirdly.*  The difficulties in which the evidence of religion is involved, which some complain of, is no more a
just ground of complaint, than the external circumstances
of temptation which others are placed in, or than difficulties in the practice of it, after a full conviction of its
truth.    Temptations render our state a more improving
state of discipline[1], than it would be otherwise : as they
give occasion for a more attentive exercise of the virtuous principle, which confirms and strengthens it, more
than an easier or less attentive exercise of it could.  Now
speculative difficulties are, in this respect, of the very
same nature with these external temptations.  For the
evidence of religion not appearing obvious is to some
persons a temptation to reject it, without any consideration at all ; and therefore requires such an attentive exercise of the virtuous principle, seriously to consider that
evidence, as there would be no occasion for, but for such
temptation.  And the supposed doubtfulness of its evidence, after it has been in some sort considered, affords
opportunity to an unfair mind of explaining away, and
deceitfully hiding from itself, that evidence which it might
see ; and also for men's encouraging themselves in vice,

[1] Part I. chap. v.

from hopes of impunity, though they do clearly see thus much at least, that these hopes are uncertain: in like manner as the common temptation to many instances of folly, which end in temporal infamy and ruin, is the ground for hope of not being detected, and of escaping with impunity; *i. e.*, the doubtfulness of the proof before-hand, that such foolish behaviour will thus end in infamy and ruin. On the contrary, supposed doubtfulness in the evidence of religion calls for a more careful and attentive exercise of the virtuous principle, in fairly yielding them-selves up to the proper influence of any real evidence, though doubtful; and in practising conscientiously all virtue, though under some uncertainty, whether the government in the universe may not possibly be such, as that vice may escape with impunity. And in general, temptation, meaning by this word the lesser allurements to wrong and difficulties in the discharge of our duty, as well as the greater ones; temptation, I say, as such and of every kind and degree, as it calls forth some virtuous efforts, additional to what would otherwise have been wanting, cannot but be an additional discipline and improvement of virtue, as well as probation of it in the other senses of that word [1]. So that the very same account is to be given, why the evidence of religion should be left in such a manner, as to require, in some, an attentive, solicitous, perhaps painful exercise of their under-standing about it; as why others should be placed in such circumstances, as that the practice of its common duties, after a full conviction of the truth of it, should require at-tention, solicitude, and pains; or, why appearing doubtfulness should be permitted to afford matter of temptation to some; as why external difficulties and allurements should be per-mitted to afford matter of temptation to others [2]. The same account also is to be given, why some should be exercised with temptations of both these kinds; as why others should be exercised with the latter in such very high degrees, as some have been, particularly as the primitive Christians were.

[1] Part I., chap. iv., and p. 160.

[2] Since temptation, of whatever kind (inasmuch as it calls forth virtuous efforts), cannot but conduce to moral discipline and improvement, the same reason is to be given why the deficiency in the *evidence* of religion should be an intellectual temptation to some, as why difficulties in the *practice* of religion should be a practical temptation and consequent virtuous discipline to others.—(*W.*)

Nor does there appear any absurdity in supposing, that the speculative difficulties, in which the evidence of religion is involved, may make even the principal part of some persons' trial. For as the chief temptations of the generality of the world are the ordinary motives to injustice or unrestrained pleasure; or to live in the neglect of religion from that frame of mind, which renders many persons almost without feeling as to anything distant, or which is not the object of their senses: so there are other persons without this shallowness of temper, persons of a deeper sense as to what is invisible and future; who not only see, but have a general practical feeling, that what is to come will be present, and that things are not less real for their not being the objects of sense; and who, from their natural constitution of body and of temper, and from their external condition, may have small temptations to behave ill, small difficulty in behaving well, in the common course of life. Now when these latter persons have a distinct full conviction of the truth of religion, without any possible doubts or difficulties, the practice of it is to them unavoidable, unless they will do a constant violence to their own minds; and religion is scarce any more a discipline to them, than it is to creatures in a state of perfection. Yet these persons may possibly stand in need of moral discipline and exercise in a higher degree, than they would have by such an easy practice of religion. Or it may be requisite, for reasons unknown to us, that they should give some further manifestation[1] what is their moral character, to the creation of God, than such a practice of it would be. Thus in the great variety of religious situations in which men are placed, what constitutes, what chiefly and peculiarly constitutes, the probation, in all senses, of some persons, may be the difficulties in which the evidence of religion is involved; and their principal and distinguished trial may be, how they will behave under and with respect to these difficulties. Circumstances in men's situation in their temporal capacity, analogous in good measure to this respecting religion, are to be observed. We find some persons are placed in such a situation in the world, as that their chief difficulty with regard to conduct, is not the doing what is prudent when it is known; for this, in numberless cases, is, as easy as the contrary; but to some

[1] P. 160.

the principal exercise is recollection and being upon their
guard against deceits, the deceits suppose of those about
them; against false appearances of reason and prudence.
To persons in some situations, the principal exercise with
respect to conduct is, attention in order to inform themselves what is proper, what is really the reasonable and
prudent part to act.

But as I have hitherto gone upon supposition, that men's
dissatisfaction with the evidence of religion is not owing to
their neglects or prejudices; it must be added, on the other
hand, in all common reason, and as what the truth of the
case plainly requires should be added, that such dissatisfaction possibly may be owing to those, possibly may be men's
own fault [1]. For,

If there are any persons who never set themselves
heartily and in earnest to be informed in religion; if there
are any who secretly wish it may not prove true; and are
less attentive to evidence than to difficulties, and more to
objections than to what is said in answer to them: these
persons will scarce be thought in a likely way of seeing the
evidence of religion, though it were most certainly true, and
capable of being ever so fully proved. If any accustom
themselves to consider this subject usually in the way of
mirth and sport; if they attend to forms and representations,
and inadequate manners of expression, instead of the real
things intended by them; (for signs often can be no more
than inadequately expressive of the things signified;) or if
they substitute human errors in the room of divine truth;
why may not all, or any of these things, hinder some men
from seeing that evidence, which really is seen by others;
as a like turn of mind, with respect to matters of common
speculation and practice, does, we find by experience, hinder
them from attaining that knowledge and right understanding, in matters of common speculation and practice, which
more fair and attentive minds attain to [2]? And the effect
will be the same, whether their neglect of seriously con-

---

[1] The preceding arguments have gone on the supposition that men's dissatisfaction with the evidence of revelation does not proceed from their own
vices and prejudices, and is not their own fault. But possibly, after all, the
fault may lie in the objector, not in the thing objected to.—(*W.*) This is
what Butler goes on to consider here.—*Ed.*

[2] The *internal* evidence of religion seems chiefly to have been intended as
a means of moral probation. See St. John vii. 17.—*Ed.*

sidering the evidence of religion, and their indirect behaviour with regard to it, proceed from mere carelessness, or from the grosser vices; or whether it be owing to this, that forms and figurative manners of expression, as well as errors, administer occasions of ridicule, when the things intended, and the truth itself, would not. Men may indulge a ludicrous turn so far as to lose all sense of conduct and prudence in worldly affairs, and even, as it seems, to impair their faculty of reason. And in general, levity, carelessness, passion, and prejudice *do* hinder us from being rightly informed, with respect to common things; and they *may*, in like manner, and perhaps in some further providential manner, with respect to moral and religious subjects; may hinder evidence from being laid before us, and from being seen when it is. The Scripture[1] does declare, that every one *shall not understand*. And it makes no difference, by what providential conduct this comes to pass: whether the evidence of Christianity was, originally and with design, put and left so, as that those who are desirous of evading moral obligations should not see it; and that honest-minded persons should: or whether it comes to pass by any other means.

Further: the general proof of natural religion and of Christianity does, I think, lie level to common men; even those, the greatest part of whose time, from childhood to old age, is taken up with providing for themselves and their families the common conveniences, perhaps necessaries, of life: those, I mean, of this rank who ever think at all of asking after proof, or attending to it. Common men, were they as much in earnest about religion as about their temporal affairs, are capable of being convinced, upon real evidence, that there is a God who governs the world, and they feel themselves to be of a moral nature, and accountable creatures. And as Christianity entirely falls in with this their natural sense of things, so they are capable, not only of

---

[1] Dan. xii. 10. See also Isa. xxix. 13, 14. Matt. vi. 23, and xi. 25, and xiii. 11, 12. John iii. 19, and v. 44. 1 Cor. ii. 14, and 2 Cor. iv. 4. 2 Tim. iii. 13 ; and that affectionate as well as authoritative admonition, so very many times inculcated, *He that hath ears to hear, let him hear.* Grotius saw so strongly the thing intended in these and other passages of Scripture of the like sense, as to say that the proof given us of Christianity was less than it might have been, for this very purpose: *Ut ita sermo Evangelii tanquam lapis esset Lydius ad quem ingenia sanabilia explorarentur.* De Ver. R. C. lib. ii. towards the end.

being persuaded, but of being made to see, that there is evidence of miracles wrought in attestation of it, and many appearing completions of prophecy. But though this proof is real and conclusive, yet it is liable to objections, and may be run up into difficulties, which, however, persons who are capable not only of talking of, but of really seeing, are capable also of seeing through : *i. e.*, not of clearing up and answering them, so as to satisfy their curiosity, for of such knowledge we are not capable with respect to any one thing in nature ; but capable of seeing that the proof is not lost in these difficulties, or destroyed by these objections. But then a thorough examination into religion with regard to these objections, which cannot be the business of every man, is a matter of pretty large compass, and, from the nature of it, requires some knowledge, as well as time and attention ; to see how the evidence comes out, upon balancing one thing with another, and what, upon the whole, is the amount of it. Now, if persons who have picked up these objections from others, and take for granted they are of weight, upon the word of those from whom they received them, or, by often retailing of them, come to see or fancy they see them to be of weight; will not prepare themselves for such an examination, with a competent degree of knowledge ; or will not give that time and attention to the subject which, from the nature of it, is necessary for attaining such information ; in this case they must remain in doubtfulness, ignorance, or error: in the same way as they must, with regard to common sciences and matters of common life, if they neglect the necessary means of being informed in them.

But still perhaps it will be objected, that if a prince or common master were to send directions to a servant, he would take care that they should always bear the certain marks who they came from, and that their sense should be always plain : so as that there should be no possible doubt, if he could help it, concerning the authority or meaning of them. Now, the proper answer to all this kind of objections is, that, wherever the fallacy lies, it is even certain we cannot argue thus with respect to Him who is the governor of the world : and particularly that he does not afford us such information, with respect to our temporal affairs and interests, as experience abundantly shows. However, there is a full answer to this objection[1], from the very nature of religion. For, the reason why a prince would give his directions in this plain manner is, that he absolutely desires such an external action should be done, without concerning himself with the motive or principle upon which it is done: *i. e.*, he regards only the external event, or the thing's being done, and not at all, properly speaking, the doing of it or the action. Whereas, the whole of morality and religion consisting merely in action itself, there is no sort of parallel between the cases. But if the prince be supposed to regard only the action; *i. e.*, only to desire to exercise, or in any sense prove, the understanding or loyalty of a servant; he would not always give his orders in such a plain manner. It may be proper to add, that the will of God, respecting morality and religion, may be considered either as absolute, or as only conditional. If it be absolute, it can only be thus, that we should act virtuously in such given circumstances; not that we should be brought to act so by his changing of our circumstances. And if God's will be thus absolute, then it is in our power, in the highest and strictest sense, to do or to contradict his will; which is a most weighty consideration. Or his will may be considered only as conditional, that if we act so and so, we shall be rewarded; if otherwise, punished: of which conditional will of the Author of Nature, the whole constitution of it affords most certain instances.

Upon the whole : that we are in a state of religion necessarily implies that we are in a state of probation : and the credibility of our being at all in such a state being admitted, there seems no peculiar difficulty in supposing our probation to be, just as it is in those respects which are above objected against. There seems no pretence, from *the reason of the thing*, to say that the trial cannot equitably be anything, but whether persons will act suitably to certain information, or such as admits no room for doubt; so as that there can be no danger of miscarriage, but either from their not attending to what they certainly know, or from overbearing passion hurrying them on to act contrary to it.

[1] This objection may be answered directly and indirectly—(1.) God does not look to mere outward *act*, as an earthly master, but to action and its motive. (2.) The will of God is either absolute or conditional : and whether it be the former or the latter, the objection vanishes.—*Ed.*

For, since ignorance and doubt afford scope for probation in all senses, as really as intuitive conviction or certainty; and since the two former are to be put to the same account as difficulties in practice, men's moral probation may also be, whether they will take due care to inform themselves by impartial consideration, and afterwards whether they will act as the case requires upon the evidence which they have, however doubtful. And this, we find by *experience*, is frequently our probation[1] in our temporal capacity. For the information which we want with regard to our worldly interests is by no means always given us of course, without any care of our own. And we are greatly liable to self-deceit from inward secret prejudices, and also to the deceits of others. So that to be able to judge what is the prudent part often requires much and difficult consideration. Then, after we have judged the very best we can, the evidence upon which we must act, if we will live and act at all, is perpetually doubtful to a very high degree. And the constitution and course of the world in fact is such, as that want of impartial consideration what we have to do, and venturing upon extravagant courses because it is doubtful what will be the consequence, are often naturally, *i. e.*, providentially, altogether as fatal, as misconduct occasioned by heedless inattention to what we certainly know, or disregarding it from overbearing passion.

Several of the observations here made may well seem strange, perhaps unintelligible, to many good men. But if the persons for whose sake they are made think so; persons who object as above, and throw off all regard to religion under pretence of want of evidence; I desire them to consider again, whether their thinking so be owing to any thing unintelligible in these observations, or to their own not having such a sense of religion and serious solicitude about it, as even their state of scepticism does in all reason require? It ought to be forced upon the reflection of these persons, that our nature and condition necessarily require us, in the daily course of life, to act upon evidence much lower than what is commonly called probable; to guard, not only against what we fully believe will, but also against what we think it supposable may, happen; and to engage in pursuits when the probability is greatly against

[1] Pp. 113, 266, &c.

success, if it be credible, that possibly we may succeed in
them.

## CHAPTER VII.

### OF THE PARTICULAR EVIDENCE FOR CHRISTIANITY [1].

THE presumptions against revelation, and objections against
the general scheme of Christianity, and particular things
relating to it, being removed; there remains to be considered what positive evidence we have for the truth of it;
chiefly in order to see what the analogy of nature suggests
with regard to that evidence, and the objections against it:
or to see what is, and is allowed to be, the plain natural
rule of judgment and of action in our temporal concerns,
in cases where we have the same kind of evidence, and the
same kind of objections against it, that we have in the case
before us.

Now in the evidence of Christianity there seem to be
several things of great weight not reducible to the head,
either of miracles, or the completion of prophecy, in the
common acceptation of the words. But these two are
its direct and fundamental proofs; and those other things,
however considerable they are, yet ought never to be urged
apart from its direct proofs, but always to be joined with
them. Thus the evidence of Christianity will be a long
series of things, reaching, as it seems, from the beginning
of the world to the present time, of great variety and
compass, taking in both the direct and also the collateral,
proofs, and making up, all of them together, one argument; the conviction arising from which kind of proof
may be compared to what they call *the effect* in architecture or other works of art; a result from a great
number of things so and so disposed, and taken into
one view. I shall therefore, *first*, make some observations

[1] Having answered objections against a revelation in the abstract, and also
against the Christian revelation, both generally and particularly, Butler proceeds to the consideration of the *positive* evidence in favour of Christianity,
with the objections against that evidence. The subject is divided into—(1.)
The direct evidence for Christianity from miracles and the completion of
prophecy, with objections against that evidence. (2.) The general argument
for the truth of Christianity, consisting both of the direct and collateral evidence, considered as making up one argument.—(*W.*)

relating to miracles, and the appearing completions of prophecy; and consider what analogy suggests in answer to the objections brought against this evidence. And, *secondly*, I shall endeavour to give some account of the general argument now mentioned, consisting both of the direct and collateral evidence, considered as making up one argument; this being the kind of proof upon which we determine most questions of difficulty concerning common facts, alleged to have happened, or seeming likely to happen; especially questions relating to conduct.

*First*. I shall make some observations upon the direct proof of Christianity from miracles and prophecy, and upon the objections alleged against it.

I. Now the following observations relating to the historical evidence of miracles wrought in attestation of Christianity appear to be of great weight.

1. The Old Testament affords us the same historical evidence of the miracles of Moses and of the prophets, as of the common civil history of Moses and the kings of Israel, or as of the affairs of the Jewish nation. And the *Gospels* and *the Acts* afford us the same historical evidence of the miracles of Christ and the Apostles, as of the common matters related in them. This, indeed, could not have been affirmed by any reasonable man, if the authors of these books, like many other historians, had appeared to make an entertaining manner of writing their aim, though they had interspersed miracles in their works, at proper distances and upon proper occasions. These might have animated a dull relation, amused the reader, and engaged his attention. And the same account would naturally have been given of them, as of the speeches and descriptions of such authors: the same account, in a manner, as is to be given, why the poets made use of wonders and prodigies. But the facts, both miraculous and natural, in Scripture, are related in plain unadorned narratives; and both of them appear, in all respects, to stand upon the same foot of historical evidence. Further: some parts of Scripture containing an account of miracles fully sufficient to prove the truth of Christianity, are quoted as genuine, from the age in which they are said to be written, down to the present: and no other parts of them, material in the present question, are omitted to be quoted in such manner as to afford any

sort of proof of their not being genuine.   And, as common history, when called in question in any instance, may often be greatly confirmed by contemporary or subsequent events more known and acknowledged : and as the common Scripture history, like many others, is thus confirmed, so likewise is the miraculous history of it, not only in particular instances, but in general.   For, the establishment of the Jewish and Christian religions, which were events contemporary with the miracles related to be wrought in attestation of both, or subsequent to them, these events are just what we should have expected, upon supposition such miracles were really wrought to attest the truth of those religions.   These miracles are a satisfactory account of those events : of which no other satisfactory account can be given ; nor any account at all but what is imaginary merely, and invented.   It is to be added, that the most obvious, the most easy and direct account of this history, how it came to be written and to be received in the world as a true history, is, that it really is so : nor can any other account of it be easy and direct.   Now, though an account, not at all obvious, but very far-fetched and indirect, may indeed be, and often is, the true account of a matter, yet it cannot be admitted on the authority of its being asserted.   Mere guess, supposition, and possibility, when opposed to historical evidence, prove nothing, but that historical evidence is not demonstrative.

Now the just consequence from all this, I think, is, that the Scripture-history in general is to be admitted as an authentic genuine history, till somewhat positive be alleged sufficient to invalidate it[1].   But no man will deny the consequence to be, that it cannot be rejected, or thrown by as of no authority, till it can be proved to be of none ; even though the evidence now mentioned for its authority were doubtful.   This evidence may be confronted by historical evidence on the other side, if there be any ; or general incredibility in the things related, or inconsistence in the general turn of the history, would prove it to be of no

[1] Upon the principles of moral evidence laid down at the opening of the Preface to the Analogy, this testimony in favour of the miraculous history of Scripture must be admitted until something positive be proved against it. —(*W.*)   In other words, until the balance of evidence be proved to preponderate on the other side.—*Ed.*

authority. But since, upon the face of the matter, upon a
first and general view, the appearance is, that it is an
authentic history; it cannot be determined to be fictitious
without some proof that it is so. And the following observations in support of these, and coincident with them, will
greatly confirm the historical evidence for the truth of
Christianity.

2. The Epistles of St. Paul, from the nature of epistolary
writing, and, moreover, from several of them being written,
not to particular persons, but to churches, carry in them
evidences of their being genuine, beyond what can be in a
mere historical narrative, left to the world at large. This
evidence, joined with that which they have in common with
the rest of the New Testament, seems not to leave so much
as any particular pretence for denying their genuineness,
considered as an ordinary matter of fact, or of criticism : I
say *particular* pretence for *denying* it; because any single
fact, of such a kind and such antiquity, may have *general
doubts* raised concerning it, from the very nature of human
affairs and human testimony. There is also to be mentioned a distinct and particular evidence of the genuineness
of the epistle chiefly referred to here, the first to the
Corinthians; from the manner in which it is quoted by
Clemens Romanus, in an epistle of his own to that church[1].
Now these epistles afford a proof of Christianity, detached
from all others, which is, I think, a thing of weight; and
also a proof of a nature and kind peculiar to itself. For,

In them the author declares, that he received the Gospel
in general, and the institution of the Communion in particular, not from the rest of the Apostles, or jointly together
with them, but alone, from Christ himself; whom he declares likewise, conformably to the history in the Acts, that
he saw after his ascension[2]: so that the testimony of St.
Paul is to be considered as detached from that of the rest
of the Apostles.

And he declares further, that he was endued with a power
of working miracles, as what was publicly known to those
very people, speaks of frequent and great variety of
miraculous gifts as then subsisting in those very churches
to which he was writing; which he was reproving for several

[1] Clem. Rom. Ep. 1, c. 47.
[2] Gal. i.; 1 Cor. xi. 23, &c.; 1 Cor. xv. 8.

irregularities; and where he had personal opposers: he mentions these gifts incidentally, in the most easy manner, and without effort; by way of reproof to those who had them, for their indecent use of them; and by way of depreciating them, in comparison of moral virtues: in short, he speaks of these churches, of these miraculous powers, in the manner any one would speak to another of a thing, which was as familiar, and as much known in common to them both, as anything in the world[1]. And this, as hath been observed by several persons, is surely a very considerable thing.

3. It is an acknowledged historical fact, that Christianity offered itself to the world, and demanded to be received, upon the allegation, *i. e.*, as unbelievers would speak, upon the pretence, of miracles, publicly wrought to attest the truth of it in such an age; and that it was actually received by great numbers in that very age, and upon the professed belief of the reality of these miracles. And Christianity, including the dispensation of the Old Testament, seems distinguished by this from all other religions. I mean, that this does not appear to be the case with regard to any other; for surely it will not be supposed to lie upon any person to prove by positive historical evidence that it was not. It does in no sort appear that Mahometanism was first received in the world upon the foot of supposed miracles[2], *i. e.*, public ones: for, as revelation is itself miraculous, all pretence to it must necessarily imply some pretence of miracles[3]. And it is a known fact, that

---

[1] Rom. xv. 19; 1 Cor. xii. 8, 9, 10–28, &c., and xiii. 1, 2, 8, and the whole xivth chapter; 2 Cor. xii. 12, 13; Gal. iii. 2, 5.

[2] See the Koran, ch. xiii. and ch. xvii.

[3] Mahomet neither claimed nor disclaimed the power of miracles. When pressed to give this proof of his mission, he involves himself in the obscure boast of vision and prophecy, appeals to the internal proofs of his doctrine, and shields himself behind the providence of God, who refuses these signs and wonders, which would depreciate the merit of faith, and aggravate the guilt of infidelity. . . . The passages in the Koran which deny his miracles are clear and positive; and those that seem to assert them are ambiguous and insufficient.—*Gibbon's Decline and Fall*, ch. 50, and note 96.

This was all that Mahomet pretended to—" The Koran itself is a miracle." So far was he from claiming to himself the working of *public* miracles, that he declared he did *not* work them, since those wrought by others, the Prophets, Apostles, and Jesus Christ, failed to bring conviction with them.—(*H*.)

Nának, the founder of the Sikhs, never pretended to work miracles, but de-it was immediately, at the very first, propagated by other means. And as particular institutions, whether in Paganism or Popery, said to be confirmed by miracles after those institutions had obtained, are not to the purpose: so, were there what might be called historical proof, that any of them were introduced by a supposed divine command, believed to be attested by miracles; these would not be in any wise parallel. For single things of this sort are easy to be accounted for, after parties are formed, and have power in their hands; and the leaders of them are in veneration with the multitude; and political interests are blended with religious claims and religious distinctions. But before anything of this kind, for a few persons, and those of the lowest rank, all at once, to bring over such numbers to a new religion, and get it to be received upon the particular evidence of miracles; this is quite another thing. And I think it will be allowed by any fair adversary, that the fact now mentioned, taking in all the circumstances of it, is peculiar to the Christian religion. However, the fact itself is allowed, that Christianity obtained, *i. e.*, was professed to be received in the world, upon the belief of miracles, immediately in the age in which it is said those miracles were wrought: or that this is what its first converts would have alleged, as the reason for their embracing it. Now certainly it is not to be supposed that such numbers of men, in the most distant parts of the world, should forsake the religion of their country, in which they had been educated; separate themselves from their friends, particularly in their festival shows and solemnities, to which the common people are so greatly addicted, and which were of a nature to engage them much more than anything of that sort amongst us; and embrace a religion, which could not but expose them to many inconveniences, and indeed must have been a giving up the world in a great degree, even from the very first, and before the empire engaged in form against them: it cannot be supposed, that such numbers should make so great, and, to say the least, so inconvenient a change in their whole institution of life, unless they were really convinced of the

rided those who did, as deriving power from evil spirits. When urged to give a miraculous proof of his mission, he replied, " I have nothing to exhibit worthy of you to behold. A holy teacher has no defence but the purity of his doctrine; the world may change, but the Creator is unchangeable!"— *Col. Malcolm's Sketch of the Sikhs*, pp. 17, 21. (*Ed.*)

truth of those miracles upon the knowledge or belief of which they professed to make it.   And it will, I suppose, readily be acknowledged, that the generality of the first converts to Christianity must have believed them: that as by becoming Christians they declared to the world, they were satisfied of the truth of those miracles; so this declaration was to be credited.   And this their testimony is the same kind of evidence for those miracles, as if they had put it in writing, and these writings had come down to us.   And it is real evidence, because it is of facts, which they had capacity and full opportunity to inform themselves of.   It is also distinct from the direct or express historical evidence, though it is of the same kind: and it would be allowed to be distinct in all cases.   For were a fact expressly related by one or more ancient historians, and disputed in after ages; that this fact is acknowledged to have been believed by great numbers of the age in which the historian says it was done, would be allowed an additional proof of such fact, quite distinct from the express testimony of the historian.   The credulity of mankind is acknowledged: and the suspicions of mankind ought to be acknowledged too; and their backwardness even to believe, and greater still to practise, what makes against their interest.   And it must particularly be remembered, that education, and prejudice, and authority, were against Christianity, in the age I am speaking of.   So that the immediate conversion of such numbers is a real presumption of somewhat more than human in this matter: I say presumption, for it is not alleged as a proof alone and by itself.   Nor need any one of the things mentioned in this chapter be considered as a proof by itself: and yet all of them together may be one of the strongest[1].

Upon the whole: as there is large historical evidence, both direct and circumstantial, of miracles wrought in attestation of Christianity, collected by those who have writ upon the subject; it lies upon unbelievers to show, why this evidence is not to be credited[2].   This way of

---

[1] P. 306, &c.

[2] Clearly there can be no positive probability against miracles occurring to interrupt the ordinary course of nature, unless we had some parallel world or system from which to argue.   We are therefore, after all, left to weigh the evidence for and against them, and to judge accordingly.   The positive

speaking is, I think, just; and what persons who write in defence of religion naturally fall into.   Yet, in a matter of such unspeakable importance, the proper question is, not whom it lies upon, according to the rules of argument, to maintain or confute objections : but whether there really are any, against this evidence, sufficient, in reason, to destroy the credit of it.   However, unbelievers seem to take upon them the part of showing that there are.

They allege, that numberless enthusiastic people, in different ages and countries, expose themselves to the same difficulties which the primitive Christians did; and are ready to give up their lives for the most idle follies imaginable.   But it is not very clear, to what purpose this objection is brought.   For every one, surely, in every case, must distinguish between opinions and facts.   And though testimony is no proof of enthusiastic opinions, or of any opinions at all; yet it is allowed, in all other cases, to be a proof of facts.   And a person's laying down his life in attestation of facts or of opinions, is the strongest proof of his believing them.   And if the Apostles and their contemporaries did believe the facts, in attestation of which they exposed themselves to sufferings and death; this their belief, or rather knowledge, must be a proof of those facts : for they were such as came under the observation of their senses.   And though it is not of equal weight, yet it is of weight, that the martyrs of the next age, notwithstanding they were not eyewitnesses of those facts, as were the Apostles and their contemporaries, had, however, full opportunity to inform themselves, whether they were true or not, and gave equal proof of their believing them to be true.

But enthusiasm, it is said, greatly weakens the evidence of testimony even for facts, in matters relating to religion :

evidence of *facts* is in their favour.   Where is the positive evidence against them?

"If it be objected that it is rather slender ground on which to stand, merely *that we cannot prove the contrary or the falsehood of the thing,* we may answer that it is not intended to be ground to *rest on*—it is intended to set us in motion, and the evidence will grow in proportion to our earnestness and sincerity to ascertain the point.   Now is there not a moral fitness in this, that evidence should be progressive, and that in proportion to the singleness of eye and the diligence with which it is sought and investigated?"— *Wolfe's Remains.   (Ed.)*

some seem to think it totally and absolutely destroys the
evidence of testimony upon this subject. And indeed the
powers of enthusiasm, and of diseases too, which operate
in a like manner, are very wonderful, in particular instances.
But if great numbers of men, not appearing in any peculiar degree weak, nor under any peculiar suspicion of
negligence, affirm that they saw and heard such things
plainly with their eyes and their ears, and are admitted to
be in earnest; such testimony is evidence of the strongest
kind we can have, for any matter of fact. Yet possibly it
may be overcome, strong as it is, by incredibility in the
things thus attested, or by contrary testimony. And in an
instance where one thought it was so overcome, it might be
just to consider, how far such evidence could be accounted
for, by enthusiasm; for it seems as if no other imaginable
account were to be given of it. But till such incredibility
be shown, or contrary testimony produced, it cannot surely
be expected, that so far fetched, so indirect and wonderful
an account of such testimony, as that of enthusiasm must
be an account so strange, that the generality of mankind
can scarce be made to understand what is meant by it : it
cannot, I say, be expected, that such account will be
admitted of such evidence ; when there is this direct, easy.
and obvious account of it, that people really saw and heard
a thing not incredible, which they affirm sincerely and with
full assurance, they did see and hear. Granting then that
enthusiasm is not (strictly speaking) an absurd, but a
possible account of such testimony ; it is manifest, that the
very mention of it goes upon the previous supposition, that
the things so attested are incredible : and therefore need
not be considered, till they are shown to be so. Much
less need it be considered, after the contrary has been
proved, and I think it has been proved, to full satisfaction,
that there is no incredibility in a revelation, in general ; or
in such a one as the Christian, in particular. However, as
religion is supposed peculiarly liable to enthusiasm, it may
just be observed, that prejudices almost without number,
and without name, romance, affectation, humour, a desire to
engage attention, or to surprise, the party spirit, custom, little
competitions, unaccountable likings and dislikings ; these
influence men strongly in common matters. And as these
prejudices are often scarce known or reflected upon by the

persons themselves who are influenced by them, they are to
be considered as influences of a like kind to enthusiasm.
Yet human testimony in common matters is naturally and
justly believed notwithstanding.

It is intimated further, in a more refined way of observation, that though it should be proved, that the Apostles
and first Christians could not, in some respects, be deceived
themselves, and, in other respects, cannot be thought to
have intended to impose upon the world; yet it will not
follow, that their general testimony is to be believed, though
truly handed down to us: because they might still in part,
*i. e.*, in other respects, be deceived themselves, and in part
also designedly impose upon others; which, it is added, is
a thing very credible, from that mixture of real enthusiasm,
and real knavery, to be met with in the same characters.
And I must confess, I think the matter of fact contained in
this observation upon mankind is not to be denied; and that
somewhat very much akin to it is often supposed in Scripture as a very common case, and most severely reproved.
But it were to have been expected, that persons capable of
applying this observation as applied in the objection, might
also frequently have met with the like mixed character, in
instances where religion was quite out of the case. The
thing plainly is, that mankind are naturally endued with
reason, or a capacity of distinguishing between truth and
falsehood; and as naturally they are endued with veracity, or
a regard to truth in what they say; but from many occasions
they are liable to be prejudiced and biassed and deceived
themselves, and capable of intending to deceive others, in
every different degree: insomuch that, as we are all liable
to be deceived by prejudice, so likewise it seems to be not
an uncommon thing, for persons, who, from their regard to
truth, would not invent a lie entirely without any foundation at all, to propagate it with heightening circumstances,
after it is once invented and set agoing. And others,
though they would not *propagate* a lie, yet, which is a
lower degree of falsehood, will let it pass without contradiction. But, notwithstanding all this, human testimony
remains still a natural ground of assent; and this assent
a natural principle of action.

It is objected further, that however it has happened, the
*fact* is, that mankind have, in different ages, been strangely

deluded with pretences to miracles and wonders[1]. But it is by no means to be admitted, that they have been oftener, or are at all more liable to be deceived by these pretences, than by others.

It is added, that there is a very considerable degree of historical evidence for miracles, which are, on all hands, acknowledged to be fabulous. But suppose there were even[2] *the like* historical evidence for these, to what there is for those alleged in proof of Christianity, which yet is in no wise allowed, but suppose this; the consequence would not be that the evidence of the latter is not to be admitted. Nor is there a man in the world, who, in common cases, would conclude thus. For what would such a conclusion really amount to but this, that evidence confuted by contrary evidence, or any way overbalanced, destroys the credibility of other evidence, neither confuted nor overbalanced? To argue, that because there is, if there were, like evidence from testimony, for miracles acknowledged false, as for those in attestation of Christianity, therefore the evidence in the latter case is not to be credited; this is the same as to argue, that if two men of equally good reputation had given evidence in different cases no way connected, and one of them had been convicted of perjury, this confuted the testimony of the other.

Upon the whole, then, the general observation, that human creatures are so liable to be deceived, from enthusiasm in religion, and principles equivalent to enthusiasm in common matters, and in both from negligence; and that they are so capable of dishonestly endeavouring to deceive others; this does indeed weaken the evidence of testimony in all cases, but does not destroy it in any. And these things will appear, to different men, to weaken the evidence of testimony, in different degrees: in degrees proportionable to the observations they have made, or the notions they have any way taken up, concerning the weak-

---

[1] *Counterfeit coin* supposes that there is such a thing in the world as *good money*, and *no one* would pretend outwardly to be virtuous, unless *some* were really so. In the same manner, false miracles suppose the existence of real ones; and the cheats that have been imposed upon the world, far from furnishing us with reasons to reject all miracles in general, are, on the contrary, a strong proof that *some*, of which they are imitations, have been genuine. —*Douglas on Miracles.* (*Ed.*)

[2] See Paley's Evidences, part ii., where the point is fully discussed.—*Ed.*

ness and negligence and dishonesty of mankind; or concerning the powers of enthusiasm, and prejudices equivalent to it. But it seems to me, that people do not know
what they say, who affirm these things to destroy the evidence from testimony, which we have of the truth of
Christianity. Nothing can destroy the evidence of testimony in any case, but a proof or probability, that persons
are not competent judges of the facts to which they give
testimony; or that they are actually under some indirect
influence in giving it, in such particular case. Till this be
made out, the *natural* laws of human actions require, that
testimony be admitted. It can never be sufficient to overthrow direct historical evidence, indolently to say, that there
are so many principles, from whence men are liable to be
deceived themselves, and disposed to deceive others, especially in matters of religion, that one knows not what to
believe. And it is surprising persons can help reflecting,
that this very manner of speaking supposes they are not
satisfied that there is nothing in the evidence, of which
they speak thus; or that they can avoid observing, if they
do make this reflection, that it is on such a subject, a very
material one[1].

And over against all these objections is to be set the
importance of Christianity, as what must have engaged
the attention of its first converts, so as to have rendered
them less liable to be deceived from carelessness, than
they would in common matters; and likewise the strong
obligations to veracity, which their religion laid them
under; so that the first and most obvious presumption is,
that they could not be deceived themselves nor would deceive
others. And this presumption, in this degree, is peculiar
to the testimony we have been considering.

In argument, assertions are nothing in themselves, and
have an air of positiveness which sometimes is not very
easy; yet they are necessary, and necessary to be repeated;
in order to connect a discourse, and distinctly to lay before
the view of the reader, what is proposed to be proved, and
what is left as proved. Now the conclusion from the foregoing observations is, I think, beyond all doubt, this: that
unbelievers must be forced to admit the external evidence
for Christianity, *i. e.*, the proof of miracles wrought to

[1] See the foregoing chapter.

attest it, to be of real weight and very considerable; though they cannot allow it to be sufficient, to convince them of the reality of those miracles[1]. And as they must, in all reason, admit this; so it seems to me, that upon consideration they would, in fact, admit it; those of them, I mean, who know anything at all of the matter; in like manner as persons, in many cases, own they see strong evidence from testimony, for the truth of things, which yet they cannot be convinced are true: cases, suppose, where there is contrary testimony; or things which they think, whether with or without reason, to be incredible. But there is no testimony contrary to that which we have been considering; and it has been fully proved, that there is no incredibility in Christianity in general, or in any part of it.

II. As to the evidence for Christianity from prophecy, I shall only make some few general observations, which are suggested by the Analogy of Nature; *i. e.*, by the acknowledged natural rules of judging in common matters, concerning evidence of a like kind to this from prophecy.

1. The obscurity or unintelligibleness of one part of a prophecy does not, in any degree, invalidate the proof of foresight, arising from the appearing completion of those other parts, which are understood. For the case is evidently the same, as if those parts, which are not understood, were lost, or not written at all, or written in an unknown tongue. Whether this observation be commonly attended to or not, it is so evident, that one can scarce bring oneself to set down an instance in common matters, to exemplify it. However, suppose a writing, partly in cipher, and partly in plain words at length; and that in the part one understood, there appeared mention of several known facts; it would never come into any man's thoughts to imagine, that if he understood the whole, perhaps he might find, that those facts were not in reality known by the writer. Indeed, both in this example and the thing intended to be exemplified by it, our not understanding the

---

[1] The proof of miracles must be admitted by an unbeliever to be considerable, if not sufficient; and indeed it would be so admitted, in like manner as the evidence of testimony is often admitted to be strong in support of cases which in themselves are incredible, or where there is contrary testimony. But in the case of Christianity, there is neither the one nor the other difficulty.—(*W.*)

whole (the whole, suppose, of a sentence or a paragraph)
might sometimes occasion a doubt, whether one understood
the literal meaning of such a part: but this comes under
another consideration.

For the same reason, though a man should be incapable,
for want of learning, or opportunities of inquiry, or from not
having turned his studies this way, even so much as to
judge whether particular prophecies have been throughout
completely fulfilled[1]; yet he may see, in general, that they
have been fulfilled to such a degree as, upon very good
ground, to be convinced of foresight more than human in
such prophecies, and of such events being intended by
them. For the same reason also, though, by means of the
deficiencies in civil history and the different accounts of
historians, the most learned should not be able to make
out to satisfaction, that such parts of the prophetic history
have been minutely and throughout fulfilled; yet a very
strong proof of foresight may arise from that general completion of them which is made out: as much proof of foresight, perhaps, as the giver of prophecy intended should ever
be afforded by such parts of prophecy.

2. A long series of prophecy being applicable to such
and such events, is itself a proof that it was intended of
them: as the rules by which we naturally judge and determine, in common cases parallel to this, will show. This
observation I make in answer to the common objection
against the application of the prophecies, that, considering
each of them distinctly by itself, it does not at all appear
that they were intended of those particular events, to which
they are applied by Christians; and therefore it is to be
supposed, that, if they meant anything, they were intended
of other events unknown to us, and not of these at all.

Now there are two kinds of writing, which bear a great
resemblance to prophecy, with respect to the matter before
us: the mythological and the satirical, where the satire is,
to a certain degree, concealed. And a man might be assured, that he understood what an author intended by a
fable or parable, related without any application or moral,
merely from seeing it to be easily capable of such application, and that such a moral might naturally be deduced

---

[1] Our ignorance of the *whole* completion of prophecy does not weaken the
proof of foresight arising from the *general* completion of it.—*Ed.*

from it.    And he might be fully assured, that such persons
and events were intended in a satirical writing, merely from
its being applicable to them.    And, agreeable to the last
observation, he might be in a good measure satisfied of it,
though he were not enough informed in affairs or in the
story of such persons to understand half the satire.    For
his satisfaction, that he understood the meaning, the intended meaning of these writings, would be greater or less
in proportion as he saw the general turn of them to be capable of such application; and in proportion to the number
of particular things capable of it.    And thus, if a long
series of prophecy is applicable to the present state of the
church, and to the political situations of the kingdoms of
the world, some thousand years after these prophecies were
delivered, and a long series of prophecy delivered before
the coming of Christ is applicable to him; these things are
in themselves a proof, that the prophetic history was intended of him, and of those events: in proportion as the
general turn of it is capable of such application, and to the
number and variety of particular prophecies capable of it.
And though, in all just way of consideration, the appearing
completion of prophecies is to be allowed to be thus explanatory of, and to determine, their meaning; yet it is to
be remembered further, that the ancient Jews applied the
prophecies to a Messiah before his coming, in much the
same manner as Christians do now: and that the primitive
Christians interpreted the prophecies respecting the state
of the church and of the world in the last ages, in the sense
which the event seems to confirm and verify.    And from
these things it may be made appear:

3. That the showing even to a high probability, if that
could be, that the prophets thought of some other events,
in such and such predictions, and not those at all which
Christians allege to be completions of those predictions;
or that such and such prophecies are capable of being
applied to other events than those to which Christians apply them—that this would not confute or destroy the force
of the argument from prophecy, even with regard to those
very instances.    For observe how this matter really is.    If
one knew such a person to be the sole author of such a
book, and was certainly assured, or satisfied to any degree,
that one knew the whole of what he intended in it; one

should be assured or satisfied to such a degree, that one
knew the whole meaning of that book: for the meaning of
a book is nothing but the meaning of the author. But if
one knew a person to have compiled a book out of memoirs, which he received from another, of vastly superior
knowledge in the subject of it, especially if it were a book
full of great intricacies and difficulties; it would in no wise
follow, that one knew the whole meaning of the book, from
knowing the whole meaning of the compiler: for the original memoirs, *i. e.*, the author of them, might have, and
there would be no degree of presumption, in many cases,
against supposing him to have, some further meaning than
the compiler saw. To say, then, that the Scriptures, and
the things contained in them, can have no other or further
meaning than those persons thought or had who first
recited or wrote them, is evidently saying, that those persons
were the original, proper, and sole authors of those books,
*i. e.*, that they are not inspired: which is absurd, whilst
the authority of these books is under examination; *i. e.*, till
you have determined they are of no divine authority at all.
Till this be determined, it must in all reason be supposed,
not indeed that they have, for this is taking for granted that
they are inspired; but that they may have, some further
meaning than what the compilers saw or understood. And,
upon this supposition, it is supposable also, that this further
meaning may be fulfilled. Now events corresponding to
prophecies, interpreted in a different meaning from that, in
which the prophets are supposed to have understood them;
this affords, in a manner, the same proof, that this different
sense was originally intended, as it would have afforded, if
the prophets had not understood their predictions in the
sense it is supposed they did: because there is no presumption of their sense of them being the whole sense
of them. And it has been already shown, that the apparent
completions of prophecy must be allowed to be explanatory
of its meaning. So that the question is, whether a series
of prophecy has been fulfilled in a natural or proper, *i. e.*,
in any real sense of the words of it. For such completion
is equally a proof of foresight more than human, whether
the prophets are, or are not, supposed to have understood
it in a different sense. I say, supposed: for though I think
it clear, that the prophets did not understand the full mean·

ing of their predictions; it is another question how far they thought they did, and in what sense they understood them.

Hence may be seen, to how little purpose those persons busy themselves, who endeavour to prove, that the prophetic history is applicable to events of the age in which it was written, or of ages before it.   Indeed, to have proved this, before there was any appearance of a further completion of it, might have answered some purpose; for it might have prevented the expectation of any such further completion. Thus could Porphyry have shown, that some principal parts of the book of Daniel, for instance, the seventh verse of the seventh chapter, which the Christians interpreted of the latter ages, was applicable to events which happened before or about the age of Antiochus Epiphanes; this might have prevented them from expecting any further completion of it. And, unless there was then, as I think there must have been, external evidence concerning that book, more than is come down to us, such a discovery might have been a stumbling-block in the way of Christianity itself; considering the authority which our Saviour has given to the book of Daniel, and how much the general scheme of Christianity presupposes the truth of it.   But even this discovery, had there been any such[1], would be of very little weight with reasonable men now; if this passage, thus applicable to events before the age of Porphyry, appears to be applicable also to events which succeeded the dissolution of the Roman empire.   I mention this, not at all as intending to insinuate, that the division of this empire into ten parts, for it plainly was divided into about that number, is, alone and by itself, of any moment in verifying the prophetic history, but only as an example of the thing I am speaking of.   And thus upon the whole, the matter of inquiry evidently must be, as above put, Whether the prophecies are applicable to Christ, and to the present state of the world, and of the church; applicable in such a degree, as to imply foresight: not whether they are capable

[1] It appears that Porphyry did nothing worth mentioning in this way. For Jerome on the place says, *Duas posteriores bestias—in uno Macedonum regno ponit.*   And as to the ten kings; *Decem reges enumerat, qui fuerunt sævissimi: ipsosque reges non unius ponit regni, verbi gratia, Macedoniæ, Syriæ, Asiæ, et Ægypti; sed de diversis regnis unum efficit regum ordinem.* And in this way of interpretation, anything may be made of anything.—See Newton on the Prophecies, and Chandler's Vindication of Christianity.

of any other application; though I know no pretence for saying the general turn of them is capable of any other.

These observations are, I think, just; and the evidence referred to in them, real; though there may be people who will not accept of such imperfect information from Scripture. Some too have not integrity and regard enough to truth to attend to evidence, which keeps the mind in doubt, perhaps perplexity, and which is much of a different sort from what they expected. And it plainly requires a degree of modesty and fairness, beyond what every one has, for a man to say, not to the world, but to himself, that there is a real appearance of somewhat of great weight in this matter, though he is not able thoroughly to satisfy himself about it; but it shall have its influence upon him, in proportion to its appearing reality and weight. It is much more easy, and more falls in with the negligence, presumption, and wilfulness of the generality, to determine at once, with a decisive air, There is nothing in it. The prejudices arising from that absolute contempt and scorn, with which this evidence is treated in the world, I do not mention. For what indeed can be said to persons, who are weak enough in their understandings to think this any presumption against it; or, if they do not, are yet weak enough in their temper to be influenced by such prejudices, upon such a subject?

I shall now, *Secondly,* endeavour to give some account of the general argument for the truth of Christianity, consisting both of the direct and circumstantial evidence, considered as making up one argument[1]. Indeed to state and examine this argument fully, would be a work much beyond the compass of this whole treatise; nor is so much as a proper abridgment of it to be expected here. Yet the present subject requires to have some brief account of it

[1] The reasons for considering this general argument are—(1) that collateral evidence arising from various coincidences which confirm each other is the evidence on which most practical difficulties are determined ; (2) because it is not duly attended to that the proof of revelation consists partly of direct evidence, such as miracles and prophecy; partly of circumstantial evidence, that is, particulars not reducible to either of these heads ; (3) because, in order to ascertain the full force of this evidence, the particular points must be viewed not separately but collectively ; (4) because an attentive consideration of the particulars of this circumstantial evidence, first separately and then collectively, must have great weight with unbelievers who acknowledge the facts alleged.

given. For it is the kind of evidence upon which most questions of difficulty, in common practice, are determined: evidence arising from various coincidences, which support and confirm each other, and in this manner prove, with more or less certainty, the point under consideration. And I choose to do it also: First, because it seems to be of the greatest importance, and not duly attended to by every one, that the proof of revelation is, not some direct and express things only, but a great variety of circumstantial things also; and that though each of these direct and circumstantial things is indeed to be considered separately, yet they are afterwards to be joined together; for that the proper force of the evidence consists in the result of those several things, considered in their respects to each other, and united into one view: and in the next place, because it seems to me, that the matters of fact here set down, which are acknowledged by unbelievers, must be acknowledged by them also to contain together a degree of evidence of great weight, if they could be brought to lay these several things before themselves distinctly, and then with attention consider them together, instead of that cursory thought of them to which we are familiarized. For being familiarized to the cursory thought of things, as really hinders the weight of them from being seen, as from having its due influence upon practice.

The thing asserted, and the truth of which is to be inquired into, is this: That over and above our reason and affections, which God has given us for the information of our judgment and the conduct of our lives, he has also, by external revelation, given us an account of himself and his moral government over the world, implying a future state of rewards and punishments, *i. e.*, hath revealed the system of natural religion: for natural religion may be externally[1] revealed by God, as the ignorant may be taught it by mankind, their fellow-creatures—that God, I say, has given us the evidence of revelation, as well as the evidence of reason, to ascertain this moral system, together with an account of a particular dispensation of Providence, which reason could no way have discovered, and a particular institution of religion founded on it, for the recovery of mankind out of their present wretched condition, and

[1] P. 195.

raising them to the perfection and final happiness of their nature.

This revelation, whether real or supposed, may be considered as wholly historical. For prophecy is nothing but the history of events before they come to pass; doctrines also are matters of fact; and precepts come under the same notion. And the general design of Scripture, which contains in it this revelation, thus considered as historical, may be said to be, to give us an account of the world, in this one single view, as God's world: by which it appears essentially distinguished from all other books, so far as I have found, except such as are copied from it. It begins with an account of God's creation of the world, in order to ascertain, and distinguish from all others, who is the object of our worship, by what he has done: in order to ascertain who he is, concerning whose providence, commands, promises, and threatenings, this sacred book, all along, treats; the Maker and Proprietor of the world, he whose creatures we are, the God of Nature: in order likewise to distinguish him from the idols of the nations, which are either imaginary beings, *i. e.*, no beings at all; or else part of that creation, the historical relation of which is here given. And St. John, not improbably with an eye to this Mosaic account of the creation, begins his Gospel with an account of our Saviour's pre-existence, and that *all things were made by him; and without him was not anything made that was made*[1]; agreeably to the doctrine of St. Paul, that *God created all things by Jesus Christ*[2]. This being premised, the Scripture, taken together, seems to profess to contain a kind of an abridgment of the history of the world in the view just now mentioned; that is, a general account of the condition of religion and its professors, during the continuance of that apostasy from God, and state of wickedness, which it everywhere supposes the world to lie in. And this account of the state of religion carries with it some brief account of the political state of things, as religion is affected by it. Revelation indeed considers the common affairs of this world, and what is going on in it, as a mere scene of distraction; and cannot be supposed to concern itself with foretelling at what time Rome, or Babylon, or Greece, or any particular place, should be the most conspicuous seat of that tyranny

[1] John i. 3.                    [2] Eph. iii. 9.

and dissoluteness, which all places equally aspire to be; cannot, I say, be supposed to give any account of this wild scene for its own sake. But it seems to contain some very general account of the chief governments of the world, as the general state of religion has been, is, or shall be, affected by them, from the first transgression, and during the whole interval of the world's continuing in its present state, to a certain future period, spoken of both in the Old and New Testament, very distinctly, and in great variety of expression: *The times of the restitution of all things* [1]: when *the mystery of God shall be finished, as he hath declared to his servants the prophets* [2]: when *the God of heaven shall set up a kingdom, which shall never be destroyed: and the kingdom shall not be left to other people* [3], as it is represented to be during this apostasy, but *judgment shall be given to the saints* [4], *and they shall reign* [5]: *and the kingdom and dominion, and the greatness of the kingdom under the whole heaven, shall be given to the people of the saints of the Most High* [6].

Upon this general view of the Scripture, I would remark, how great a length of time the whole relation takes up, near six thousand years of which are past; and how great a variety of things it treats of; the natural and moral system or history of the world, including the time when it was formed, all contained in the very first book, and evidently written in a rude and unlearned age; and in subsequent books, the various common and prophetic history, and the particular dispensation of Christianity. Now all this together gives the largest scope for criticism; and for confutation of what is capable of being confuted, either from reason, or from common history, or from any inconsistence in its several parts. And it is a thing which deserves, I think, to be mentioned, that whereas some imagine the supposed doubtfulness of the evidence for revelation implies a positive argument that it is not true; it appears, on the contrary, to imply a positive argument that it is true. For, could any common relation of such antiquity, extent, and variety (for in these things the stress of what I am now observing lies), be proposed to the examination of the world: that it could not, in an age of knowledge and liberty, be confuted, or shown to have nothing in it, to the satisfaction

[1] Acts iii. 21.    [2] Rev. x. 7.    [3] Dan. ii. 44.
[4] Dan. vii. 22.    [5] Rev. xx. 6.    [6] Dan. vii. 27.

of reasonable men; this would be thought a strong presumptive proof of its truth.   And indeed it must be a proof
of it, just in proportion to the probability, that if it were
false, it might be shown to be so: and this, I think, is
scarce pretended to be shown, but upon principles and in
ways of arguing, which have been clearly obviated[1].   Nor
does it at all appear, that any set of men, who believe natural
religion, are of the opinion, that Christianity has been thus
confuted.   But to proceed:

Together with the moral system of the world, the Old
Testament contains a chronological account of the beginning of it, and from thence, an unbroken genealogy of
mankind for many ages, before common history begins; and
carried on as much farther as to make up a continued thread
of history of the length of between three and four thousand years.   It contains an account of God's making a
covenant with a particular nation, that they should be his
people, and he would be their God, in a peculiar sense; of
his often interposing miraculously in their affairs; giving
them the promise, and, long after, the possession of a particular country; assuring them of the greatest national
prosperity in it, if they would worship him, in opposition
to the idols which the rest of the world worshipped, and
obey his commands; and threatening them with un-
exampled punishments if they disobeyed him, and fell into
the general idolatry: insomuch that this one nation should
continue to be the observation and the wonder of all the
world.   It declares particularly, that *God would scatter them
among all people, from one end of the earth unto the other;* but
that *when they should return unto the Lord their God, he would
have compassion upon them, and gather them from all the
nations, whither he had scattered them:* that *Israel should be
saved in the Lord, with an everlasting salvation; and not be
ashamed or confounded world without end.*   And as some of
these promises are conditional, others are as absolute, as
anything can be expressed: that the time should come,
when *the people should be all righteous, and inherit the land
for ever:* that *though God would make a full end of all nations
whither he had scattered them, yet would he not make a full end
of them:* that *he would bring again the captivity of his people
Israel, and plant them upon their land, and they should be no*

[1] Ch. ii. iii., &c.

*more pulled up out of their land: that the seed of Israel should not cease from being a nation for ever* [1]. It foretells, that God would raise them up a particular person, in whom all his promises should finally be fulfilled; the Messiah, who should be, in a high and eminent sense, their anointed Prince and Saviour. This was foretold in such a manner, as raised a general expectation of such a person in the nation, as appears from the New Testament, and is an acknowledged fact; an expectation of his coming at such a particular time, before any one appeared claiming to be that person, and when there was no ground for such an expectation, but from the prophecies: which expectation, therefore, must in all reason be presumed to be explanatory of those prophecies, if there were any doubt about their meaning. It seems moreover to foretell, that this person should be rejected by that nation, to whom he had been so long promised, and though he was so much desired by them [2]. And it expressly foretells, that he should be the Saviour of the Gentiles; and even that the completion of the scheme contained in this book, and then begun, and in its progress, should be somewhat so great, that in comparison with it, the restoration of the Jews alone would be but of small account. *It is a light thing that thou shouldest be my servant to raise up the tribes of Jacob, and to restore the preserved of Israel: I will also give thee for a light to the Gentiles, that thou mayest be my salvation unto the end of the earth.* And, *In the last days, the mountain of the Lord's house shall be established in the top of the mountains, and shall be exalted above the hills; and all nations shall flow into it— for out of Zion shall go forth the law, and the word of the Lord from Jerusalem. And he shall judge among the nations —and the Lord alone shall be exalted in that day, and the idols he shall utterly abolish* [3]. The Scripture further contains an account, that at the time the Messiah was expected, a person rose up in this nation, claiming to be that Messiah, to be the person whom all the prophecies referred to, and

[1] Deut. xxviii. 64, xxx. 2, 3; Isa. xlv. 17, lx. 21; Jer. xxx. 11, xlvi. 28; Amos ix. 14, 15; Jer. xxxi. 36.

[2] Isa. viii. 14, 15, xlix. 5, ch. liii.; Mal. i. 10, 11, and ch. iii.

[3] Isa. xlix. 6, ch. ii., ch. xi., ch. lvi. 7; Mal. i. 11. To which must be added the other prophecies of the like kind, several in the New Testament, and very many in the Old, which describe what shall be the completion of the revealed plan of Providence.

in whom they should centre: that he spent some years in
a continued course of miraculous works; and endued his
immediate disciples and followers with a power of doing
the same, as a proof of the truth of that religion, which
he commissioned them to publish: that, invested with this
authority and power, they made numerous converts in the
remotest countries, and settled and established his religion
in the world; to the end of which the Scripture professes
to give a prophetic account of the state of this religion
amongst mankind.

Let us now suppose a person utterly ignorant of history,
to have all this related to him out of the Scripture.   Or
suppose such a one, having the Scripture put into his hands,
to remark these things in it, not knowing but that the whole,
even its civil history, as well as the other parts of it, might
be from beginning to end an entire invention; and to ask,
What truth was in it, and whether the revelation here related
was real, or a fiction? And instead of a direct answer, suppose him, all at once, to be told the following confessed
facts; and then to unite them into one view.

Let him first be told, in how great a degree the profession
and establishment of natural religion, the belief that there
is one God to be worshipped, that virtue is his law, and that
mankind shall be rewarded and punished hereafter, as they
obey and disobey it here; in how very great a degree, I
say, the profession and establishment of this moral system
in the world is owing to the revelation, whether real or supposed, contained in this book: the establishment of this
moral system, even in those countries which do not acknowledge the proper authority of the Scripture [1].   Let him be
told also, what number of nations do acknowledge its proper
authority.   Let him then take in the consideration of what
importance religion is to mankind.   And upon these things
he might, I think, truly observe, that this supposed revelation's obtaining and being received in the world with all
the circumstances and effects of it, considered together as
one event, is the most conspicuous and important event in
the history of mankind: that a book of this nature, and
thus promulged and recommended to our consideration,
demands, as if by a voice from heaven, to have its claims
most seriously examined into: and that, before such exami-

[1] P. 260.

nation, to treat it with any kind of scoffing and ridicule, is an offence against natural piety. But it is to be remembered, that how much soever the establishment of natural religion in the world is owing to the Scripture revelation, this does not destroy the proof of religion from reason, any more than the proof of Euclid's Elements is destroyed, by a man's knowing or thinking that he should never have seen the truth of the several propositions contained in it, nor had those propositions come into his thoughts, but for that mathematician.

Let such a person as we are speaking of be, in the next place, informed of the acknowledged antiquity of the first parts of this book; and that its chronology, its account of the time when the earth, and the several parts of it, were first peopled with human creatures, is no way contradicted, but is really confirmed, by the natural and civil history of the world, collected from common historians, from the state of the earth, and from the late invention of arts and sciences. And as the Scripture contains an unbroken thread of common and civil history, from the creation to the captivity, for between three and four thousand years; let the person we are speaking of be told in the next place, that this general history, as it is not contradicted, but is confirmed by profane history as much as there would be reason to expect, upon supposition of its truth; so there is nothing in the whole history *itself*, to give any reasonable ground of suspicion of its not being, in the general, a faithful and literally true genealogy of men, and series of things. I speak here only of the common Scripture history, or of the course of ordinary events related in it, as distinguished from miracles, and from the prophetic history. In all the Scripture narrations of this kind, following events arise out of foregoing ones, as in all other histories [1]. There appears nothing related as done in any age, not conformable to the manners of that age: nothing in the account of a succeeding age, which one would say could not be true, or was improbable, from the

---

[1] There are several objections to passages of Scripture, occasioned by not considering them in reference to the manners of the times. Thus it appears that the things objected to, like many others that are censured in Christianity and in Scripture, are, in a greater or less degree, actual *proofs* of their truth and authenticity.—(*H.*)

account of things in the preceding one.  There is nothing
in the characters which would raise a thought of their being
feigned; but all the internal marks imaginable of their being
real.  It is to be added also, that mere genealogies, bare
narratives of the number of years, which persons called by
such and such names lived, do not carry the face of fiction;
perhaps do carry some presumption of veracity; and all
unadorned narratives, which have nothing to surprise, may
be thought to carry somewhat of the like presumption too.
And the domestic and the political history is plainly credible.  There may be incidents in Scripture which, taken
alone in the naked way they are told, may appear strange,
especially to persons of other manners, temper, education;
but there are also incidents of undoubted truth in many
or most persons' lives, which, in the same circumstances,
would appear to the full as strange.  There may be mistakes of transcribers, there may be other real or seeming
mistakes, not easy to be particularly accounted for; but
there are certainly no more things of this kind in the
Scripture than what were to have been expected in books
of such antiquity; and nothing in any wise sufficient to
discredit the general narrative.  Now that a history claiming to commence from the creation, and extending in one
continued series, through so great a length of time and
variety of events, should have such appearances of reality
and truth in its whole contexture, is surely a very remarkable circumstance in its favour.  And as all this is applicable to the common history of the New Testament, so
there is a further credibility, and a very high one, given to
it by profane authors: many of these writing of the same
times, and confirming the truth of customs and events,
which are incidentally as well as more purposely mentioned
in it.  And this credibility of the common Scripture history
gives some credibility to its miraculous history, especially
as this is interwoven with the common, so as that they
imply each other, and both together make up one relation [1].
Let it then be more particularly observed to this person,

[1] The credibility of the common history of Scripture gives a strong incidental confirmation of the credibility of the miraculous part of the narrative;
on the principle that what is true of one part of any great whole or system
is in some degree probably true of the other.—*Ed.*

that it is an acknowledged matter of fact, which is indeed implied in the foregoing observation, that there was such a nation as the Jews, of the greatest antiquity, whose government and general polity was founded on the law, here related to be given them by Moses as from heaven : that natural religion, though with rites additional yet no way contrary to it, was their established religion, which cannot be said of the Gentile world ; and that their very being as a nation, depended upon their acknowledgment of one God, the God of the universe.  For, suppose in their captivity in Babylon they had gone over to the religion of their conquerors, there would have remained no bond of union to keep them a distinct people.  And whilst they were under their own kings, in their own country, a total apostasy from God would have been the dissolution of their whole government.   They in such a sense nationally acknowledged and worshipped the Maker of heaven and earth, when the rest of the world were sunk in idolatry, as rendered them, in fact, the peculiar people of God.  And this so remarkable an establishment and preservation of natural religion amongst them, seems to add some peculiar credibility to the historical evidence for the miracles of Moses and the Prophets; because these miracles are a full satisfactory account of this event, which plainly wants to be accounted for, and cannot otherwise.

Let this person, supposed wholly ignorant of history, be acquainted further, that one claiming to be the Messiah of Jewish extraction, rose up at the time when this nation, from the prophecies above mentioned, expected the Messiah [1]: that he was rejected, as it seemed to have been foretold he should, by the body of the people, under the direction of their rulers: that in the course of a very few years he was

[1] See Bishop Chandler's " Vindication of Christianity," where it is fully proved that this expectation was general among the Jews and Samaritans. The effects of it may be judged by its extension among the Gentiles.  To say nothing of the Arabians, and of the appearing of the Star to the Eastern Magi ; and to omit all reference to Virgil's celebrated Eclogue, in which he celebrates the expected birth of a son to Pollio in terms almost identical with the prophecy of Isaiah ; Suetonius (Vespas. cap. iv. 8) thus writes : " Percrebuerat oriente toto vetus et constans opinio, esse in fatis ut eo tempore Judæâ profecti rerum potirentur."  And so also Tacitus (Hist. v. 9) testifies, " Pluribus persuasio inerat, antiquis sacerdotum literis contineri, eo ipso tempore fore ut valesceret oriens, profectique Judæâ rerum potirentur."—Ed.

believed on and acknowledged as the promised Messiah by
great numbers among the Gentiles, agreeably to the prophecies of Scripture, yet not upon the evidence of prophecy,
but of miracles [1], of which miracles we have also strong
historical evidence, (by which I mean here no more than
must be acknowledged by unbelievers; for let pious frauds
and follies be admitted to weaken, it is absurd to say they
destroy, our evidence of miracles wrought in proof of Christianity [2] :) that this religion approving itself to the reason of
mankind, and carrying its own evidence with it, so far as
reason is a judge of its system, and being no way contrary
to reason in those parts of it which require to be believed
upon the mere authority of its Author; that this religion, I
say, gradually spread and supported itself for some hundred
years, not only without any assistance from temporal power,
but under constant discouragements, and often the bitterest
persecutions from it, and then became the religion of the
world; that in the mean time the Jewish nation and government were destroyed in a very remarkable manner, and the
people carried away captive and dispersed through the most
distant countries, in which state of dispersion they have remained fifteen hundred years; and that they remain a
numerous people united amongst themselves, and distinguished from the rest of the world, as they were in the
days of Moses, by the profession of his law; and everywhere looked upon in a manner, which one scarce knows
how distinctly to express, but in the words of the prophetic
account of it, given so many ages before it came to pass :
*Thou shalt become an astonishment, a proverb, and a by-word,
among all nations whither the Lord shall lead thee* [3].

The appearance of a standing miracle, in the Jews remaining a distinct people in their dispersion, and the confirmation which this event appears to give to the truth of
revelation, may be thought to be answered by their religion's forbidding them intermarriages with those of any
other, and prescribing them a great many peculiarities in
their food, by which they are debarred from the means of
incorporating with the people in whose countries they live.
This is not, I think, a satisfactory account of that which it
pretends to account for. But what does it pretend to

[1] P. 279.          [2] P. 285.          [3] Deut. xxviii. 37.

account for? The correspondence between this event and the prophecies, or the coincidence of both, with a long dispensation of Providence, of a peculiar nature, towards that people formerly? No. It is only the event itself which is offered to be thus accounted for; which single event, taken alone, abstracted from all such correspondence and coincidence, perhaps would not have appeared miraculous; but that correspondence and coincidence may be so, though the event itself be supposed not. Thus the concurrence of our Saviour's being born at Bethlehem, with a long foregoing series of prophecy and other coincidences, is doubtless miraculous; the series of prophecy, and other coincidences, and the event, being admitted: though the event itself, his birth at that place, appears to have been brought about in a natural way; of which, however, no one can be certain.

And as several of these events seem, in some degree expressly, to have verified the prophetic history already, so likewise they may be considered further as having a peculiar aspect towards the full completion of it, as affording some presumption that the whole of it shall, one time or other, be fulfilled. Thus, that the Jews have been so wonderfully preserved in their long and wide dispersion, which is indeed the direct fulfilling of some prophecies, but is now mentioned only as looking forward to somewhat yet to come; that natural religion came forth from Judea, and spread, in the degree it has done over the world, before lost in idolatry; which, together with some other things, have distinguished that very place, in like manner as the people of it are distinguished; that this great change of religion over the earth was brought about under the profession and acknowledgment, that Jesus was the promised Messiah: things of this kind naturally turn the thoughts of serious men towards the full completion of the prophetic history, concerning the final restoration of that people; concerning the establishment of the everlasting kingdom among them, the kingdom of the Messiah; and the future state of the world, under this sacred government. Such circumstances and events, compared with these prophecies, though no completions of them, yet would not, I think, be spoken of as nothing in the argument, by a person upon his first being informed of them. They fall in with the prophetic history of things still future, give it some additional credibility, have the appearance of being somewhat in order to the full completion of it.

Indeed it requires a good degree of knowledge, and great calmness and consideration, to be able to judge thoroughly of the evidence for the truth of Christianity, from that part of the prophetic history which relates to the situation of the kingdoms of the world, and to the state of the church, from the establishment of Christianity to the present time. But it appears from a general view of it, to be very material. And those persons who have thoroughly examined it, and some of them were men of the coolest tempers, greatest capacities, and least liable to imputations of prejudice, insist upon it as determinately conclusive.

Suppose now a person quite ignorant of history, first to recollect the passages above mentioned out of Scripture, without knowing but that the whole was a late fiction, then to be informed of the correspondent facts now mentioned, and to unite them all into one view: that the profession and establishment of natural religion in the world is greatly owing in different ways, to this book, and the supposed revelation which it contains; that it is acknowledged to be of the earliest antiquity; that its chronology and common history are entirely credible; that this ancient nation, the Jews, of whom it chiefly treats, appear to have been, in fact, the people of God, in a distinguished sense; that, as there was a national expectation amongst them, raised from the prophecies, of a Messiah to appear at such a time, so one at this time appeared claiming to be that Messiah; that he was rejected by this nation, but received by the Gentiles, not upon the evidence of prophecy, but of miracles; that the religion he taught supported itself under the greatest difficulties, gained ground, and at length became the religion of the world; that in the mean time the Jewish polity was utterly destroyed, and the nation dispersed over the face of the earth; that notwithstanding this, they have remained a distinct numerous people for so many centuries, even to this day; which not only appears to be the express completion of several prophecies concerning them, but also renders it, as one may speak, a visible and easy possibility that the promises made to them as a nation, may yet be fulfilled. And to these acknowledged truths, let the person we have been supposing add, as I think he ought, whether every one will allow it or no, the obvious appearances which there are, of the state of the world, in other respects besides what relates to the Jews, and of the Christian church, having so long answered, and still answering, to the prophetic history. Suppose, I say, these facts set over against the things before mentioned out of the Scripture, and seriously compared with them; the joint view of both together must, I think, appear of very great weight to a considerate reasonable person: of much greater indeed, upon having them first laid before him, than is easy for us, who are so familiarized to them, to conceive, without some particular attention for that purpose.

All these things, and the several particulars contained under them, require to be distinctly and most thoroughly examined into; that the weight of each may be judged of, upon such examination, and such conclusion drawn as results from their united force [1]. But this has not been attempted here. I have gone no further than to show, that the general imperfect view of them now given, the confessed historical evidence for miracles, and the many obvious appearing completions of prophecy, together with the collateral things [2] here mentioned, and there are several others of the like sort; that all this together, which, being

[1] We may thus sum up the concluding observations on this view of the direct and collateral evidence for Christianity, taken together as one argument.

1. Each particular should be weighed separately, and the conclusion drawn from their united force.

2. The whole evidence, viewed collectively, must be acknowledged by unbelievers to prove something more than human.

3. The high degree of proof resulting from a joint review of the several particulars should be noticed, for they not only increase it, but multiply it.

4. A mistake on the side of rejecting Christianity is much more dangerous than a mistake on the other side; and it is right to choose the safer course.

5. The truth of Christianity depends on all the evidence taken together. In other words, Christianity is true, unless the whole series of facts, and each particular fact, can be reasonably supposed accidental.—*Ed.*

[2] All the particular things mentioned in this chapter, not reducible to the head of certain miracles, or determinate completions of prophecy. See p. 275.

fact, must be acknowledged by unbelievers, amounts to real
evidence of somewhat more than human in this matter:
evidence much more important than careless men, who
have been accustomed only to transient and partial views of
it, can imagine; 'and indeed abundantly sufficient to act
upon.   And these things, I apprehend, must be acknowledged by unbelievers.   For though they may say, that the
historical evidence of miracles wrought in attestation of
Christianity, is not sufficient to convince them that such
miracles were really wrought: they cannot deny, that there
is such historical evidence, it being a known matter of fact
that there is.   They may say, the conformity between the
prophecies and events is by accident: but there are many
instances in which such conformity itself cannot be denied.
They may say, with regard to such kind of collateral things
as those above mentioned, that any odd accidental events,
without meaning, will have a meaning found in them by
fanciful people: and that such as are fanciful in any one
certain way, will make out a thousand coincidences, which
seem to favour their peculiar follies.   Men, I say, may talk
thus: but no one who is serious, can possibly think these
things to be nothing, if he considers the importance of
collateral things, and even of lesser circumstances, in the
evidence of probability, as distinguished in nature, from the
evidence of demonstration.   In many cases indeed it seems
to require the truest judgment, to determine with exactness
the weight of circumstantial evidence: but it is very often
altogether as convincing as that which is the most express
and direct.

This general view of the evidence for Christianity, considered as making one argument, may also serve to recommend to serious persons, to set down everything which they
think may be of any real weight at all in proof of it, and
particularly the many seeming completions of prophecy:
and they will find, that, judging by the natural rules, by
which we judge of probable evidence in common matters,
they amount to a much higher degree of proof, upon such a
joint review, than could be supposed upon considering them
separately, at different times; how strong soever the proof
might before appear to them, upon such separate views of
it.   For probable proofs, by being added, not only increase
the evidence, but multiply it.   Nor should I dissuade any

one from setting down, what he thought made for the contrary side. But then it is to be remembered, not in order to influence his judgment[1], but his practice, that a mistake on one side may be, in its consequences, much more dangerous than a mistake on the other. And what course is most safe, and what most dangerous, is a consideration thought very material, when we deliberate, not concerning events, but concerning conduct in our temporal affairs. To be influenced by this consideration in our judgment, to believe or disbelieve upon it, is indeed as much prejudice as anything whatever. And, like other prejudices, it operates contrary ways in different men; for some are inclined to believe what they hope, and others what they fear. And it is manifest unreasonableness to apply to men's passions in order to gain their assent. But in deliberations concerning conduct, there is nothing which reason more requires to be taken into the account, than the importance of it. For, suppose it doubtful, what would be the consequence of acting in this, or in a contrary manner: still, that taking one side could be attended with little or no bad consequence, and taking the other might be attended with the greatest, must appear, to unprejudiced reason, of the highest moment towards determining how we are to act. But the truth of our religion, like the truth of common matters, is to be judged of by all the evidence taken together. And unless the whole series of things which may be alleged in this argument, and every particular thing in it, can reasonably be supposed to have been by accident (for here the stress of the argument for Christianity lies); then is the truth of it proved; in like manner, as if in any common case, numerous events acknowledged, were to be alleged in proof of any other event disputed; the truth of the disputed event would be proved, not only if any one of the acknowledged ones did of itself clearly imply it, but, though no one of

[1] Thus, though it is absurd to talk of the greater merit of assent upon little or no evidence, than upon demonstration, yet the strict discharge of our duty with less sensible evidence does imply in it a better character than the same diligence in the discharge of it upon more sensible evidence. This fully accounts for and explains that assertion of our Saviour,—" *Blessed are they that have not seen and yet have believed*"—have become Christians, and believed the gospel, upon less sensible evidence than that which Thomas, to whom he is speaking, insisted upon.—*Butler's Sermon on the Ignorance of Man.* (*Ed.*)

them singly did so, if the whole of the acknowledged events taken together could not in reason be supposed to have happened, unless the disputed one were true [1].

It is obvious, how much advantage the nature of this evidence gives to those persons who attack Christianity, especially in conversation. For it is easy to show, in a short and lively manner, that such and such things are liable to objection, that this and another thing is of little weight in itself; but impossible to show, in like manner, the united force of the whole argument in one view.

However, lastly, as it has been made appear, that there is no presumption against a revelation as miraculous; that the general scheme of Christianity, and the principal parts of it, are conformable to the experienced constitution of things, and the whole perfectly credible: so the account now given of the positive evidence for it shows, that this evidence is such, as, from the nature of it, cannot be destroyed, though it should be lessened.

## CHAPTER VIII.

### OF THE OBJECTIONS WHICH MAY BE MADE AGAINST ARGUING FROM THE ANALOGY OF NATURE, TO RELIGION.

IF every one would consider, with such attention as they are bound, even in point of morality, to consider, what they

---

[1] The evidences of religion being so exceedingly dissimilar are highly characteristic of its truth. If man's contrivance or if the favour of accidents *could* have given to Christianity any of its apparent testimonies—either its miracles or its prophecy, its morals or its propagation, or, if I may so speak, its Founder—there could be no room to believe, nor even to imagine, that all these appearances of great credibility would be united together by any such causes. If a successful craft could have contrived its public miracles, or so much as the pretence of them, it required another reach of craft and new resources to provide and adapt its prophecies to the same object. Further, it demanded, not only a different art, but a totally opposite character, to conceive and promulgate its admirable morals. Again, the achievement of its propagation in defiance of the powers and terrors of the world—but the hypothesis sinks under its incredibility. For *each* of these suppositions of contrivance being arbitrary, as it certainly is, and unsupported, the *climax* of them is an extravagance; and if the imbecility of *art* is foiled in the hypothesis, then combinations of *accident* are too vain to be thought of.—*Davison on Prophecy.* (*Ed.*)

judge and give characters of; the occasion of this chapter would be, in some good measure at least, superseded. But since this is not to be expected; for some we find do not concern themselves to understand even what they write against: since this treatise, in common with most others, lies open to objections, which may appear very material to thoughtful men at first sight; and, besides that, seems peculiarly liable to the objections of such as can judge without thinking, and of such as can censure without judging; it may not be amiss to set down the chief of these objections which occur to me, and consider them to their hands. And they are such as these:

" That it is a poor thing to solve difficulties in revelation by saying, that there are the same in natural religion; when what is wanting is to clear both of them of these their common, as well as other their respective, difficulties: but that it is a strange way indeed of convincing men of the obligations of religion, to show them, that they have as little reason for their worldly pursuits: and a strange way of vindicating the justice and goodness of the Author of Nature, and of removing the objections against both, to which the system of religion lies open, to show, that the like objections lie against natural providence; a way of answering objections against religion, without so much as pretending to make out, that the system of it, or the particular things in it objected against, are reasonable—especially, perhaps some may be inattentive enough to add, Must this be thought strange, when it is confessed that analogy is no answer to such objections: that when this sort of reasoning is carried to the utmost length it can be imagined capable of, it will yet leave the mind in a very unsatisfied state; and that it must be unaccountable ignorance of mankind, to imagine they will be prevailed with to forego their present interests and pleasures, from regard to religion, upon doubtful evidence."

Now, as plausible as this way of talking may appear, that appearance will be found in a great measure owing to half views, which show but part of an object, yet show that indistinctly, and to undeterminate language. By these means weak men are often deceived by others, and ludicrous men, by themselves. And even those, who are serious and considerate, cannot always readily disentangle, and at once clearly see through the perplexities, in which subjects themselves are involved; and which are heightened by the deficiencies and the abuse of words. To this latter sort of persons, the following reply to each part of this objection severally, may be of some assistance; as it may also tend a little to stop and silence others.

*First.* The thing wanted, *i. e.*, what men require, is to have all difficulties cleared[1]. And this is, or, at least for anything we know to the contrary, it may be, the same, as requiring to comprehend the divine nature, and the whole plan of Providence from everlasting to everlasting. But it hath always been allowed to argue from what is acknowledged, to what is disputed. And it is in no other sense a poor thing to argue from natural religion to revealed, in the manner found fault with, than it is to argue in numberless other ways of probable deduction and inference, in matters of conduct, which we are continually reduced to the necessity of doing. Indeed the epithet *poor* may be applied, I fear as properly, to great part or the whole of human life, as it is to the things mentioned in the objection. Is it not a poor thing, for a physician to have so little knowledge in the cure of diseases, as even the most eminent have? To act upon conjecture and guess, where the life of man is concerned? Undoubtedly it is: but not in comparison of having no skill at all in that useful art, and being obliged to act wholly in the dark.

Further: since it is as unreasonable, as it is common, to urge objections against revelation, which are of equal weight against natural religion; and those who do this, if they are not confused themselves, deal unfairly with others, in making it seem, that they are arguing only against revelation, or particular doctrines of it, when in reality they are

[1] This is a natural desire, but it partakes of the character of pride, and is the direct opposite to the spirit of faith. It is of the very essence of faith that it is concerned with the unseen; and if everything which concerns the scheme of God's revelations were reduced to the level of our reason, there could be no such a virtue as faith. This infidel spirit it is the design of God to check and control by giving man just so much insight into his counsels as may serve to awaken his interest in them, and not too much to supersede the necessity of exercising faith. It was this desire of being wise about what is given which led to the fall of the angels, and constituted a part of the sin of Adam. Butler, it will be observed, here speaks of this spirit of infidelity in terms not only of censure, but of contempt.—*Ed.*

arguing against moral providence; it is a thing of consequence to show, that such objections are as much levelled against natural religion, as against revealed. And objections, which are equally applicable to both, are properly speaking answered, by its being shown that they are so, provided the former be admitted to be true [1]. And without taking in the consideration how distinctly this is admitted, it is plainly very material to observe, that as the things objected against in natural religion are of the same kind with what is certain matter of experience in the course of providence, and in the information which God affords us concerning our temporal interest under his government; so the objections against the system of Christianity, and the evidence of it, are of the very same kind with those which are made against the system and evidence of natural religion. However, the reader upon review may see, that most of the analogies insisted upon, even in the latter part of this treatise, do not necessarily require to have more taken for granted than is in the former; that there is an Author of Nature, or natural Governor of the world; and Christianity is vindicated, not from its analogy to natural religion, but chiefly from its analogy to the experienced constitution of nature.

*Secondly.* Religion is a practical thing, and consists in such a determinate course of life, as being what, there is reason to think, is commanded by the Author of Nature, and will, upon the whole, be our happiness under his government. Now if men can be convinced that they have the like reason to believe this, as to believe that taking care of their temporal affairs will be to their advantage; such conviction cannot but be an argument to them for the practice of religion. And if there be really any reason for believing one of these, and endeavouring to preserve life, and secure ourselves the necessaries and conveniences of it, then there is reason also for believing the other, and endeavouring to secure the interest it proposes to us. And if the interest, which religion proposes to us, be infinitely greater than our whole temporal interest; then there must be proportionably

---

[1] It *is* of consequence to show that objections which lie against revealed religion lie equally against natural religion, provided that the truth of the natural religion be admitted. For in that case any plain person may see that revealed religion is not affected by any such objections.—*Ed.*

greater reason for endeavouring to secure one, than the other; since, by the supposition, the probability of our securing one is equal to the probability of our securing the other. This seems plainly unanswerable; and has a tendency to influence fair minds, who consider what our condition really is, or upon what evidence we are naturally appointed to act; and who are disposed to acquiesce in the terms upon which we live, and attend to and follow that practical instruction, whatever it be, which is afforded us.

But the chief and proper force of the argument referred to in the objection, lies in another place. For, it is said that the proof of religion is involved in such inextricable difficulties, as to render it doubtful; and that it cannot be supposed, that, if it were true, it would be left upon doubtful evidence. Here then, over and above the force of each particular difficulty or objection, these difficulties and objections taken together are turned into a positive argument against the truth of religion, which argument would stand thus. If religion were true, it would not be left doubtful, and open to objections to the degree in which it is [1]: therefore that it is thus left, not only renders the evidence of it weak, and lessens its force, in proportion to the weight of such objections; but also shows it to be false, or is a general presumption of its being so. Now the observation, that, from the natural constitution and course of things, we must in our temporal concerns, almost continually, and in matters of great consequence, act upon evidence of a like kind and degree to the evidence of religion, is an answer to this argument; because it shows, that it is according to the conduct and character of the Author of Nature to appoint we should act upon evidence like to that, which this argument presumes he cannot be supposed to appoint we should act upon: it is an instance, a general one, made up of numerous particular ones, of somewhat in his dealing with us, similar to what is said to be incredible. And as the force of this answer lies merely in the parallel, which there is between the evidence for religion and for our temporal conduct; the answer is equally just and con-

---

[1] The objection, stated briefly, is this:—It is incredible that God should have given us only doubtful evidence for religion. Our answer is, that he has given us only doubtful evidence for our worldly pursuits. And if so, it is not incredible that he should do the same in regard to religion.—*Ed.*

clusive, whether the parallel be made out, by showing the evidence of the former to be higher, or the evidence of the latter to be lower.

*Thirdly.* The design of this treatise is not to vindicate the character of God, but to show the obligations of men : it is not to justify his providence, but to show what belongs to us to do [1]. These are two subjects, and ought not to be confounded. And though they may at length run up into each other, yet observations may immediately tend to make out the latter, which do not appear, by any immediate connection, to the purpose of the former; which is less our concern, than many seem to think. For, first, it is not necessary we should justify the dispensations of Providence against objections, any farther than to show, that the things objected against may, for aught we know, be consistent with justice and goodness. Suppose then, that there are things in the system of this world, and plan of Providence relating to it, which taken alone would be unjust : yet it has been shown unanswerably, that if we could take in the reference, which these things may have to other things present, past, and to come; to the whole scheme, which the things objected against are parts of; these very things might, for aught we know, be found to be, not only consistent with justice, but instances of it. Indeed it has been shown, by the analogy of what we see, not only possible that this may be the case, but credible that it is. And thus objections, drawn from such things, are answered, and Providence is vindicated, as far as religion makes its vindication necessary. Hence it appears, secondly, that objections against the divine justice and goodness are not endeavoured to be removed, by showing that the like objections, allowed to be really conclusive, lie against natural providence : but those objections being supposed and shown not to be conclusive, the things objected against, considered as matters of fact, are farther shown to be credible, from their conformity to the constitution of nature ; for instance, that God will reward and punish men for their

---

[1] Analogical evidence is generally more successful in silencing objections than in evincing truth. Though it rarely refutes, it frequently repels refutation ; like those weapons, which, though they cannot kill the enemy, ward off his blows.—*Dr. Campbell's Philosophy of Rhetoric.* We may observe that Butler never intended to do more than to "silence objections" in his *Analogy.—Ed.*

actions hereafter, from the observation, that he does reward and punish them for their actions here. And this, I apprehend, is of weight. And I add, thirdly, it would be of weight, even though those objections were not answered. For, there being the proof of religion above set down; and religion implying several facts; for instance again, the fact last mentioned, that God will reward and punish men for their actions hereafter; the observation, that his present method of government is by rewards and punishments, shows that future fact not to be incredible: whatever objections men may think they have against it, as unjust or unmerciful, according to their notions of justice and mercy; or as improbable from their belief of necessity. I say, *as improbable:* for it is evident no objection against it, *as unjust,* can be urged from necessity; since this notion as much destroys injustice, as it does justice. Then, fourthly, though objections against the reasonableness of the system of religion cannot indeed be answered without entering into consideration of its reasonableness; yet objections against the credibility or truth of it may. Because the system of it is reducible into what is properly matter of fact: and the truth, the probable truth, of facts, may be shown without consideration of their reasonableness. Nor is it necessary, though, in some cases and respects, it is highly useful and proper, yet it is not necessary, to give a proof of the reasonableness of every precept enjoined us, and of every particular dispensation of Providence, which comes into the system of religion. Indeed the more thoroughly a person of a right disposition is convinced of the perfection of the divine nature and conduct, the farther he will advance towards that perfection of religion, which St. John[1] speaks of. But the general obligations of religion are fully made out, by proving the reasonableness of the practice of it. And that the practice of religion *is* reasonable, may be shown, though no more could be proved, than that the system of it *may be* so, for aught we know to the contrary: and even without entering into the distinct consideration of this. And from hence, fifthly, it is easy to see, that though the analogy of nature is not an immediate answer to objections against the wisdom, the justice, or goodness, of any doctrine or precept of religion; yet it may

[1] 1 John iv. 18.

be, as it is, an immediate and direct answer to what is really intended by such objections; which is, to show that the things objected against are incredible.

*Fourthly.* It is most readily acknowledged, that the foregoing treatise is by no means satisfactory[1]; very far indeed from it: but so would any natural institution of life appear, if reduced into a system, together with its evidence. Leaving religion out of the case, men are divided in their opinions, whether our pleasures overbalance our pains: and whether it be, or be not, eligible to live in this world. And were all such controversies settled, which perhaps, in speculation, would be found involved in great difficulties; and were it determined upon the evidence of reason, as nature has determined it to our hands, that life is to be preserved, yet still, the rules which God has been pleased to afford us, for escaping the miseries of it, and obtaining its satisfactions, the rules, for instance, of preserving health, and recovering it when lost, are not only fallible and precarious, but very far from being exact. Nor are we informed by nature, in future contingencies and accidents, so as to render it at all certain, what is the best method of managing our affairs. What will be the success of our temporal pursuits, in the common sense of the word Success, is highly doubtful. And what will be the success of them in the proper sense of the word, *i. e.*, what happiness or enjoyment we shall obtain by them, is doubtful in a much higher degree. Indeed the unsatisfactory nature of the evidence, with which we are obliged to take up, in the daily course of life, is scarce to be expressed. Yet men do not throw away life, or disregard the interests of it, upon account of this doubtfulness. The evidence of religion, then, being admitted real, those who object against it as not satisfactory, *i. e.*, as not being what they wish it, plainly forget the very condition of our being: for satisfaction, in this sense, does not belong to such a creature as man. And, which is more material, they forget also the very nature of religion. For, religion presupposes, in all those who will embrace it, a certain degree of integrity and

---

[1] Objections against the *credibility* of a system may be answered without considering its *reasonableness;* for the system of religion consists of matters of fact; and credibility depends on these facts, not on our preconceived notions of what is reasonable.—*Ed.*

honesty; which it was intended to try whether men have
or not, and to exercise in such as have it, in order to its
improvement. Religion presupposes this as much, and in
the same sense, as speaking to a man presupposes he
understands the language in which you speak; or as warning a man of any danger presupposes that he hath
such a regard to himself as that he will endeavour to
avoid it. And therefore the question is not at all, Whether
the evidence of religion be satisfactory; but Whether it be,
in reason, sufficient to prove and discipline that virtue,
which it presupposes. Now the evidence of it is fully
sufficient for all those purposes of probation, how far soever
it is from being satisfactory, as to the purposes of curiosity,
or any other: and, indeed, it answers the purposes of the
former in several respects, which it would not do, if it were
as overbearing as is required. One might add further;
that whether the motives or the evidence for any course of
action be satisfactory, meaning here, by that word, what
satisfies a man, that such a course of action will in event
be for his good; this need never be, and I think, strictly
speaking, never is, the practical question in common matters.
But the practical question in all cases is, Whether the evidence for a course of action be such as, taking in all circumstances, makes the faculty within us, which is the guide and
judge of conduct[1], determine that course of action to be
prudent. Indeed, satisfaction that it will be for our interest
or happiness, abundantly determines an action to be
prudent: but evidence almost infinitely lower than this,
determines actions to be so too; even in the conduct of
every day.

*Fifthly.* As to the objection concerning the influence
which this argument, or any part of it, may, or may not
be expected to have upon men; I observe, as above, that
religion being intended for a trial and exercise of the
morality of every person's character, who is a subject of
it; and there being, as I have shown, such evidence for it,
as is sufficient, in reason, to influence men to embrace it:
to object, that it is not to be imagined mankind will be
influenced by such evidence, is nothing to the purpose of
the foregoing treatise. For the purpose of it is not to
inquire, what sort of creatures mankind are; but what the

[1] See Dissert. II.

light and knowledge, which is afforded them, requires they should be: to show how, in reason, they ought to behave; not how, in fact, they will behave. This depends upon themselves, and is their own concern; the personal concern of each man in particular. And how little regard the generality have to it, experience indeed does too fully show. But religion, considered . as a probation, has had its end upon all persons, to whom it has been proposed with evidence sufficient in reason to influence their practice: for by this means they have been put into a state of probation; let them behave as they will in it. And thus, not only revelation, but reason also, teaches us, that by the evidence of religion being laid before men, the designs of Providence are carrying on, not only with regard to those who will, but likewise with regard to those who will not, be influenced by it. However, lastly, the objection here referred to, allows the things insisted upon in this treatise to be of some weight; and if so, it may be hoped it will have some influence. And if there be a probability that it will have any at all, there is the same reason in kind, though not in degree, to lay it before men, as there would be, if it were likely to have a greater influence.

And further, I desire it may be considered, with respect to the whole of the foregoing objections [1], that in this treatise I have argued upon the principles of others [2], not my own; and have omitted what I think true, and of the utmost importance, because by others thought unintelligible, or not true. Thus I have argued upon the principles of the Fatalists, which I do not believe; and have omitted a thing of the utmost importance which I do believe [3],

[1] With reference to the whole of these objections, Butler observes, concerning the argument of the treatise, (1) that the argument proceeds not upon his own principles, but upon those of others, *i. e.*, that he allows those principles for the sake of argument to be true; and (2) that, the two abstract principles of liberty and moral fitness being omitted, religion can only be considered as a matter of fact, as is here done.—(*W.*)

[2] By *arguing upon the principles of others,* the reader will observe is meant, not proving anything *from* those principles, but *notwithstanding* them. Thus religion is proved, not *from* the opinion of necessity, which is absurd, but *notwithstanding* or *even though* that opinion were admitted to be true.

[3] Bishop Butler throughout the present work has only considered the *moral* difference by which virtue and vice, as such, are approved and disapproved. Dr. Samuel Clarke has demonstrated (*vide* his Sermons at

the moral fitness and unfitness of actions, prior to all will whatever; which I apprehend as certainly to determine the Divine conduct, as speculative truth and falsehood necessarily determine the Divine judgment. Indeed, the principle of liberty, and that of moral fitness, so force themselves upon the mind, that moralists, the ancients as well as moderns, have formed their language upon it. And probably it may appear in mine: though I have endeavoured to avoid it; and, in order to avoid it, have sometimes been obliged to express myself in a manner, which will appear strange to such as do not observe the reason for it: but the general argument here pursued does not at all suppose, or proceed upon these principles. Now, these two abstract principles of liberty and moral fitness being omitted, religion can be considered in no other view than merely as a question of fact: and in this view it is here considered. It is obvious, that Christianity, and the proof of it, are both historical. And even natural religion is, properly, a matter of fact. For, that there is a righteous Governor of the world, is so: and this proposition contains the general system of natural religion. But then, several abstract truths, and in particular those two principles, are usually taken into consideration in the proof of it: whereas it is here treated of only as a matter of fact. To explain this: that the three angles of a triangle are equal to two right ones, is an abstract truth: but that they appear so to our mind, is only a matter of fact. And this last must have been admitted, if anything was, by those ancient sceptics, who would not have admitted the former: but pretended to doubt, Whether there were any such thing as truth, or Whether we could certainly depend upon our faculties of understanding for the knowledge of it any case. So likewise, that there is, in the nature of things, an original standard of right and wrong in actions, independent upon all will, but which unalterably determines the will of God, to exercise that moral government over the world, which religion teaches, *i. e.*, finally and upon the

Boyle's Lectures) that there are essential differences in the qualities of human actions established in nature, and this *natural* difference of things prior to, and independent of all will, creates a natural FITNESS in the agent to act agreeably to it. It is obvious that the introduction of this principle would materially confirm Bishop Butler's arguments.—*Ed.*

whole to reward and punish men respectively as they act right or wrong; this assertion contains an abstract truth, as well as matter of fact. But suppose, in the present state, every man, without exception, was rewarded and punished, in exact proportion as he followed or transgressed that sense of right and wrong, which God has implanted in the nature of every man: this would not be at all an abstract truth, but only a matter of fact. And though this fact were acknowledged by every one; yet the very same difficulties might be raised as are now, concerning the abstract questions of liberty and moral fitness: and we should have a proof, even the certain one of experience, that the government of the world was perfectly moral, without taking in the consideration of those questions: and this proof would remain, in what way soever they were determined. And thus, God having given mankind a moral faculty, the object of which is actions, and which naturally approves some actions as right, and of good desert, and condemns others as wrong, and of ill desert; that he will, finally and upon the whole, reward the former and punish the latter, is not an assertion of an abstract truth, but of what is as mere a fact, as his doing so at present would be. This future fact I have not, indeed, proved with the force with which it might be proved, from the principles of liberty and moral fitness; but without them have given a really conclusive practical proof of it, which is greatly strengthened by the general analogy of nature: a proof easily cavilled at, easily shown not to be demonstrative, for it is not offered as such; but impossible, I think, to be evaded, or answered. And thus the obligations of religion are made out, exclusively of the questions concerning liberty and moral fitness; which have been perplexed with difficulties and abstruse reasonings, as everything may.

Hence, therefore, may be observed distinctly, what is the force of this treatise. It will be, to such as are convinced of religion upon the proof arising out of the two last-mentioned principles, an additional proof and a confirmation of it: to such as do not admit those principles, an original proof of it[1], and a confirmation of that proof. Those who believe will here find the scheme of Chris-

[1] P. 169.

tianity cleared of objections, and the evidence of it in a
peculiar manner strengthened : those who do not believe,
will at least be shown the absurdity of all attempts to
prove Christianity false, the plain undoubted credibility of
it; and, I hope, a good deal more.

And thus, though some perhaps may seriously think,
that analogy, as here urged, has too great stress laid upon
it; and ridicule, unanswerable ridicule, may be applied, to
show the argument from it in a disadvantageous light; yet
there can be no question, but that it is a real one.  For
religion, both natural and revealed, implying in it numerous
facts; analogy, being a confirmation of all facts to which
it can be applied, as it is the only proof of most, cannot
but be admitted by every one to be a material thing, and
truly of weight on the side of religion, both natural and
revealed : and it ought to be particularly regarded by such
as profess to follow nature, and to be less satisfied with
abstract reasonings.


## CONCLUSION.

WHATEVER account may be given of the strange inattention
and disregard, in some ages and countries, to a matter of
such importance as Religion; it would, before experience,
be incredible, that there should be the like disregard in those,
who have had the moral system of the world laid before
them, as it is by Christianity, and often inculcated upon
them : because this moral system carries in it a good degree
of evidence for its truth, upon its being barely proposed to
our thoughts.  There is no need of abstruse reasonings
and distinctions, to convince an unprejudiced understanding,
that there is a God who made and governs the world, and
will judge it in righteousness; though they may be necessary to answer abstruse difficulties, when once such are
raised : when the very meaning of those words, which
express most intelligibly the general doctrine of religion,
is pretended to be uncertain; and the clear truth of the
thing itself is obscured by the intricacies of speculation.
But to an unprejudiced mind, ten thousand thousand instances of design cannot but prove a designer.  And it is
intuitively manifest, that creatures ought to live under a

dutiful sense of their Maker; and that justice and charity must be his laws, to creatures whom he has made social, and placed in society. Indeed the truth of revealed religion, peculiarly so called, is not self-evident, but requires external proof, in order to its being received. Yet inattention, among us, to revealed religion, will be found to imply the same dissolute immoral temper of mind, as inattention to natural religion; because, when both are laid before us, in the manner they are in Christian countries of liberty, our obligations to inquire into both, and to embrace both upon supposition of their truth, are obligations of the same nature. For revelation claims to be the voice of God : and our obligation to attend to his voice is surely moral in all cases. And as it is insisted, that its evidence is conclusive, upon thorough consideration of it; so it offers itself to us with manifest obvious appearances of having something more than human in it, and therefore in all reason requires to have its claims most seriously examined into. It is to be added, that though light and knowledge, in what manner soever afforded us, is equally from God; yet a miraculous revelation has a peculiar tendency, from the first principles of our nature, to awaken mankind, and inspire them with reverence and awe : and this is a peculiar obligation to attend to what claims to be so with such appearances of truth. It is therefore most certain, that our obligations to inquire seriously into the evidence of Christianity, and, upon supposition of its truth, to embrace it, are of the utmost importance, and moral in the·highest and most proper sense. Let us then suppose, that the evidence of religion in general, and of Christianity, has been seriously inquired into, by all reasonable men among us. Yet we find many professedly to reject both, upon speculative principles of infidelity. And all of them do not content themselves with a bare neglect of religion, and enjoying their imaginary freedom from its restraints. Some go much beyond this. They deride God's moral government over the world. They renounce his protection, and defy his justice. They ridicule and vilify Christianity, and blaspheme the author of it; and take all occasions to manifest a scorn and contempt of revelation. This amounts to an active setting themselves against religion; to what may be considered as a positive principle of irreligion; which they cultivate within themselves, and, whether they intend this effect or not, render habitual, as a good man does the contrary principle. And others who are not chargeable with all this profligateness, yet are in avowed opposition to religion, as if discovered to be groundless. Now admitting, which is the supposition we go upon, that these persons act upon what they think principles of reason, and otherwise they are not to be argued with ; it is really inconceivable, that they should imagine they clearly see the whole evidence of it, considered in itself, to be nothing at all : nor do they pretend this. They are far indeed from having a just notion of its evidence : but they would not say its evidence was nothing, if they thought the system of it, with all its circumstances, were credible, like other matters of science or history. So that their manner of treating it must proceed, either from such kind of objections against all religion, as have been answered or obviated in the former part of this treatise ; or else from objections and difficulties, supposed more peculiar to Christianity. Thus, they entertain prejudices against the whole notion of a revelation, and miraculous interpositions. They find things in Scripture, whether in incidental passages, or in the general scheme of it, which appear to them unreasonable. They take for granted, that if Christianity were true, the light of it must have been more general, and the evidence of it more satisfactory, or rather overbearing : that it must and would have been, in some way, otherwise put and left, than it is. Now this is not imagining they see the evidence itself to be nothing, or inconsiderable ; but quite another thing. It is being fortified against the evidence, in some degree acknowledged, by thinking they see the system of Christianity, or somewhat which appears to them necessarily connected with it, to be incredible or false ; fortified against that evidence, which, might otherwise, make great impression upon them. Or lastly, if any of these persons are, upon the whole, in doubt concerning the truth of Christianity ; their behaviour seems owing to their taking for granted, through strange inattention, that such doubting is, in a manner, the same thing as being certain against it.

To these persons, and to this state of opinion concerning religion, the foregoing treatise is adapted. For, all the general objections against the moral system of nature hav-

ing been obviated, it is shown, that there is not any peculiar
presumption at all against Christianity, either considered
as not discoverable by reason, or as unlike to what is so
discovered; nor any worth mentioning against it as miraculous, if any at all; none, certainly, which can render
it in the least incredible. It is shown, that, upon supposition of a divine revelation, the analogy of nature renders
it beforehand highly credible, I think probable, that many
things in it must appear liable to great objections; and
that we must be incompetent judges of it, to a great degree. This observation is, I think, unquestionably true,
and of the very utmost importance: but it is urged, as I
hope it will be understood, with great caution of not vili-
fying the faculty of reason, which is *the candle of the Lord
within us*[1]; though it can afford no light, where it does not
shine; nor judge, where it has no principles to judge
upon. The objections here spoken of, being first answered in the view of objections against Christianity as
a matter of fact, are in the next place considered as urged
more immediately against the wisdom, justice, and goodness of the Christian dispensation. And it is fully made
out, that they admit of exactly the like answer, in every
respect, to what the like objections against the constitution
of nature admit of: that, as partial views give the appearance of wrong to things, which, upon further consideration
and knowledge of their relations to other things, are found
just and good; so it is perfectly credible, that the things
objected against the wisdom and goodness of the Christian dispensation, may be rendered instances of wisdom
and goodness, by their reference to other things beyond
our view: because Christianity is a scheme as much above
our comprehension, as that of nature; and like that, a
scheme in which means are made use of to accomplish
ends, and which, as is most credible, may be carried on
by general laws. And it ought to be attended to, that this
is not an answer taken merely or chiefly from our ignorance; but from somewhat positive, which our observation
shows us. For, to like objections, the like answer is experienced to be just, in numberless parallel cases. The
objections against the Christian dispensation, and the
method by which it is carried on, having been thus ob-

[1] Prov. xx. 27.

viated, in general and together; the chief of them are
considered distinctly, and the particular things objected
to are shown credible, by their perfect analogy, each apart,
to the constitution of nature. Thus, if man be fallen from
his primitive state, and to be restored, and infinite wisdom
and power engages in accomplishing our recovery: it were
to have been expected, it is said, that this should have
been effected at once; and not by such a long series of
means, and such a various economy of persons and things;
one dispensation preparatory to another, this to a further
one, and so on through an indefinite number of ages, before the end of the scheme proposed can be completely
accomplished; a scheme conducted by infinite wisdom,
and executed by almighty power. But now, on the contrary, our finding that everything in the constitution and
course of nature is thus carried on, shows such expectations concerning revelation to be highly unreasonable;
and is a satisfactory answer to them, when urged as objections against the credibility, that the great scheme of
Providence in the redemption of the world may be of this
kind, and to be accomplished in this manner. As to the
particular method of our redemption, the appointment of
a Mediator between God and man: this has been shown
to be most obviously analogous to the general conduct of
nature, *i. e.*, the God of nature, in appointing others to be
the instruments of his mercy, as we experience in the
daily course of providence. The condition of this world,
which the doctrine of our redemption by Christ presup
poses, so much falls in with natural appearances, that
heathen moralists inferred it from those appearances : inferred, that human nature was fallen from its original
rectitude, and in consequence of this, degraded from its
primitive happiness. Or, however this opinion came into
the world, these appearances must have kept up the tradition, and confirmed the belief of it. And as it was the
general opinion under the light of nature, that repentance
and reformation, alone and by itself, was not sufficient to
do away sin, and procure a full remission of the penalties
annexed to it; and as the reason of the thing does not at
all lead to any such conclusion; so every day's experience
shows us, that reformation is not, in any sort, sufficient to
prevent the present disadvantages and miseries, which, in

the natural course of things, God has annexed to folly and extravagance. Yet there may be ground to think, that the punishments, which, by the general laws of divine government, are annexed to vice, may be prevented: that provision may have been, even originally, made, that they should be prevented by some means or other, though they could not by reformation alone. For we have daily instances of *such mercy*, in the general conduct of nature: compassion provided for misery[1], medicines for diseases, friends against enemies. There is provision made, in the original constitution of the world, that much of the natural bad consequences of our follies, which persons themselves alone cannot prevent, may be prevented by the assistance of others; assistance, which nature enables, and disposes, and appoints them to afford. By a method of goodness analogous to this, when the world lay in wickedness, and consequently in ruin, *God so loved the world, that he gave his only begotten Son*, to save it: and *he being made perfect by suffering, became the author of eternal salvation to all them that obey him*[2]. Indeed, neither reason nor analogy would lead us to think, in particular, that the interposition of Christ, in the manner in which he did interpose, would be of that efficacy for recovery of the world, which the Scripture teaches us it was : but neither would reason nor analogy lead us to think, that other particular means would be of the efficacy, which experience shows they are, in numberless instances. And therefore, as the case before us does not admit of experience ; so, that neither reason nor analogy can show how, or in what particular way, the interposition of Christ, as revealed in Scripture, is of that efficacy, which it is there represented to be; this is no kind nor degree of presumption against its being really of that efficacy. Further, the objections against Christianity, from the light of it not being universal, nor its evidence so strong as might possibly be given us, have been answered by the general analogy of nature. That God has made such variety of creatures, is indeed an answer to the former : but that he dispenses his gifts in such variety, both of degrees and kinds, amongst creatures of the same species, and even to the same individuals at different times ; is a more obvious and full answer to it. And it is so far

[1] Serm. at the Rolls, p. 106.          [2] John iii. 16 ; Heb. v. 9.

from being the method of Providence in other cases, to afford us such overbearing evidence, as some require in proof of Christianity; that, on the contrary, the evidence upon which we are naturally appointed to act in common matters, throughout a very great part of life, is doubtful in a high degree. And admitting the fact, that God has afforded to some no more than doubtful evidence of religion; the same account may be given of it, as of difficulties and temptations with regard to practice. But as it is not impossible[1], surely, that this alleged doubtfulness may be men's own fault; it deserves their most serious consideration, whether it be not so. However, it is certain, that doubting implies a degree of evidence for that of which we doubt : and that this degree of evidence as really lays us under obligations as demonstrative evidence.

The whole, then, of religion is throughout credible : nor is there, I think, anything relating to the revealed dispensation of things, more different from the experienced constitution and course of nature, than some parts of the constitution of nature are from other parts of it. And if so, the only question which remains is, what positive evidence can be alleged for the truth of Christianity? This too, in general, has been considered, and the objections against it estimated. Deduct, therefore, what is to be deducted from that evidence, upon account of any weight which may be thought to remain in these objections, after what the analogy of nature has suggested in answer to them : and then consider, what are the practical consequences from all this, upon the most sceptical principles one can argue upon (for I am writing to persons who entertain these principles): and upon such consideration it will be obvious, that immorality, as little excuse as it admits of in itself, is greatly aggravated, in persons who have been made acquainted with Christianity, whether they believe it or not : because the moral system of nature, or natural religion, which Christianity lays before us, approves itself, almost intuitively, to a reasonable mind, upon seeing it proposed. In the next place, with regard to Christianity, it will be observed; that there is a middle between a full satisfaction of the truth of it, and a satisfaction of the contrary. The middle state of mind between these two, consists in a serious apprehension, that it may

[1] P. 270.

be true, joined with doubt whether it be so. And this, upon the best judgment I am able to make, is as far towards speculative infidelity, as any sceptic can at all be supposed to go, who has had true Christianity, with the proper evidence of it, laid before him, and has in any tolerable measure considered them. For I would not be mistaken to comprehend all who have ever heard of it: because it seems evident, that in many countries called Christian, neither Christianity, nor its evidence, are fairly laid before men. And in places where both are, there appear to be some, who have very little attended to either, and who reject Christianity with a scorn proportionate to their inattention; and yet are by no means without understanding in other matters. Now it has been shown, that a serious apprehension that Christianity may be true, lays persons under the strictest obligations of a serious regard to it, throughout the whole of their life: a regard, not the same exactly, but in many respects nearly the same, with what a full conviction of its truth would lay them under. Lastly, it will appear, that blasphemy and profaneness, I mean with regard to Christianity, are absolutely without excuse. For there is no temptation to it, but from the wantonness of vanity or mirth: and these, considering the infinite importance of the subject, are no such temptations as to afford any excuse for it. If this be a just account of things, and yet men can go on to vilify or disregard Christianity, which is to talk and act as if they had a demonstration of its falsehood; there is no reason to think they would alter their behaviour to any purpose, though there were a demonstration of its truth.